# 'Insubordinate Irish'

MANCHESTER
1824

Manchester University Press

# 'Insubordinate Irish'

## Travellers in the text

Mícheál Ó hAodha

Manchester University Press
Manchester and New York

distributed in the United States exclusively
by Palgrave Macmillan

Published by Manchester University Press
Oxford Road, Manchester M13 9NR, UK
and Room 400, 175 Fifth Avenue, New York, NY 10010, USA
www.manchesteruniversitypress.co.uk

Distributed in the United States exclusively by
Palgrave Macmillan, 175 Fifth Avenue, New York,
NY 10010, USA

Distributed in Canada exclusively by
UBC Press, University of British Columbia, 2029 West Mall,
Vancouver, BC, Canada V6T 1Z2

British Library Cataloguing-in-Publication Data
A catalogue record for this book is available from the British Library

Library of Congress Cataloging-in-Publication Data applied for

ISBN    978 0 7190 8304 4    hardback

ISBN    978 0 7190 8305 1    paperback

First published 2011

Typeset
by 4word Ltd, Bristol
Printed in Great Britain
by TJ International Ltd, Padstow

# Dedication

This book is dedicated to Dr Brian Coates and his wife Eileen, without whose guidance and support generations of scholars in the Munster region would never have prospered.

I would also like to thank the staff of UCD and (especially) NUIG, Galway who were always very helpful and welcoming when I visited their centres to read the various Irish Folklore Commission archives over the span of about six years and who encouraged me in the project as a worthwhile endeavour. I would also like to thank my wife Caroline and my five children – Mícheál, Laoise, Seán, Cian, Alannah.

A particular note of thanks to the staff of the Library, NUIG, Galway whose patience and help in accessing the reels of the IFC archive held there was immeasurable.

*Ba mhaith liom buíochas ó chroí a ghabháil leo siúd óna bhfuaireas cúnamh nach beag agus mé i mbun na hoibre seo le sé bliana anuas.*

# Contents

# Introduction

This book is an introduction to Traveller Studies and its corollaries, Romani Studies and Diaspora and Migration Studies. This book traces a number of common themes relating to the representation of Irish Travellers in Irish popular tradition and how these themes have impacted on Ireland's collective imaginary. A particular focus is the development of the 'settled' (i.e. non-Traveller) community's perception of Travellers as an outsider group in Irish society and the representation of Travellers as an Other who are perceived as both inside and outside Ireland's collective ideation.

The initial chapters of the book examine historical attempts to locate and define Irish Travellers and categorise them amongst a pantheon of Travelling groups in the Europe of the nineteenth century. Paradoxically, as with many other traditionally nomadic groups, the first studies of Irish Travellers were intimately linked with foundational myths relating to the development of the modern nation-state and the obsession with origins, authenticity and primal ancestry that characterised many intellectual movements of the late Victorian era. This volume explores the traditional approach of the quasi-scholarly Victorian and primitivist movement known as Gypsiology and the discourses of philological and 'racial' classification that attempted to locate Irish Travellers amongst a hierarchy of diverse travelling groups.

The book proceeds with a brief analysis of how these debates with respect to the cultural definition of this small minority progressed into the modern era, where academic definitions have focused on the theorisation of Travellers in terms of such concepts as sedentarism, racism and ethnicity. A particular focus of this book is on the discussion of the concept of the Otherness or difference as analysed in the European and Irish contexts and as relating to the Traveller minority. The definition of Irishness which accompanied independence was a monologic one and of a history which was unitary or homogeneous and was useful in a postcolonial nation where history itself was both an adaptive mechanism and a form of cultural legitimation. However, this teleological version of Ireland's history had a negative impact for minorities whose histories were elided or left outside the collective. This book explores some of the consequences which accompanied the exclusion of the marginal Other, including Irish Travellers, from this homogeneous and constructed definition of Irishness, an exclusion which has only been exacerbated in the modern State-oriented era. This volume argues that the essentialist versions of Irish history and identity promulgated upon independence meant that reductionist views of the Irish people under colonialism were frequently transferred to the principal visible 'Other within' i.e. Irish Travellers subsequent to Irish independence. That an intimate link exists between the category definitions or representations of a particular group and societal attitudes and behaviours with respect to that group is widely acknowledged. So too is the fact that for well over a century the Irish Travellers have been framed within a regime of degradation and inferiority as encompassing attributions of primitivism and the anti-social (Acton, 1974, 1997; Clark, 2006; Mayall, 1987).

The second half of this book analyses unequal power relations as pervading literary discourse and practice. The Irish tradition is explored as a site of struggle on the part of Irish Travellers. While the colonial enterprise brought dislocation in its wake and separated the colonised from their histories, languages and social relations, the discourses from the Irish oral tradition examined here demonstrate important sites of representational resistance and oppositional agency. Memory as interpretive struggle is analysed within a dissenting tradition where Travellers are seen to represent a counter-hegemonic undercurrent in Irish society, a site of resistance which remains symbolically central despite attempts at its suppression. This counter-hegemonic tradition challenges those frames of representation which became reified and fixed within the Irish imaginary over time, coalescing in a 'regime of truth'. This oppositional agency usurps the hegemonic process at the interstices between the Self and the Other and elucidates the 'constructed' nature that constitutes many representations of Travellers. This counter-tradition is also linked to a discussion concerning the philosophical possibilities for a movement beyond the politics of difference that has, as yet, been constitutive of Traveller alterity and the potential for a postmodernist theorisation of Self/Other relations.

# List of abbreviations

BS    Bailiúchán na Scoil (Schools Collection – Irish Folklore Commission)

GLS   Gypsy Lore Society

IFC   Irish Folklore Commission

Iml.  Volume (Refers to Volume number in the Irish Folklore Commission archive). For example (Iml. 97: 51) refers to Volume 97, page 51.

JGLS  Journal of the Gypsy Lore Society

# 1 Irish Travellers and the nineteenth century 'Others'

Irish Travellers are a minority who have lived on the margins of main-stream Irish society for many centuries. Many contemporary sources refer to the Irish Travellers as an ethnic group, and they are recognised as such in Britain, although not in Ireland. It is estimated that there are at least 36,000 Travellers living in the Republic of Ireland with a further 6,000 in Northern Ireland. There are also significant communities of Travellers who claim Irish descent living in Britain and the United States. They are distinct from the surrounding population due to a range of differing cultural attributes. These include family structure, language, employment patterns and a traditional preference for nomadism or mobility as is inherent in the very ascription they attach to their community. For the past few centuries, these attributes have ensured the renewal of the Traveller community and their way of life from one generation to the next. It has also aided the cohesiveness and survival of this marginal community and its culture in the face of what in recent decades, at least, has frequently been a hostile majority or settled community.

While it is sometimes claimed that Travellers have remained invisible within the official historical record in Ireland, this is not entirely the case. References in the Irish language, as recorded in the oral history tradition in particular, refer to *fir siúil* (travelling men, wanderers, lit: 'walking men') and *mná siúil* (travelling women). It is clear that the people alluded to in these references form a large amalgam of groups and individuals, all of whom are most likely descendants of a range of peripatetic and occupational groups. That some of these people were musicians, travelling poets, entertainers and healers is clear as is the fact that many others were tradespeople of different types including travel-ling tinsmiths, metalworkers, horse dealers, fairground entertainers and farm workers of different types. As with many in the settled population many Traveller families supplemented one trade with another and combined their occupation with hawking or occasional begging. The preference for travelling alone or as part of larger and kin-related family groups varied depending on the travel routes these people used. Until recent decades, many of these Travellers were referred to as 'tinkers', but today they are more commonly referred to as Travellers.

History tells us that a large and diverse number of often peripatetic occupational groups and cultures existed in Ireland prior to the Tudor re-conquest of the sixteenth century and that some of these cultural minorities survived for centuries after the death of the Gaelic order.[1] The antecedents of the group are an amalgam of a range of differing cultural groups, the history of which has been lost for the most part. The history of these peripatetic cultures in both the pre-Gaelic and post-Gaelic eras is still the object of some conjecture and requires future additional research. One element which united each of these diverse travelling peoples and cultures was the fact that they were nomadic for all or part of the year. This preference for nomadism or a peripatetic life has always functioned as a distinctive trait of the Irish Travellers and set them apart from the settled community.

This study is an attempt to understand the contradictory and complex images of the Irish Travellers as constructed within both hegemonic and counter-hegemonic cultural impulses and as viewed by both the settled and travelling populations. Essential to this study, therefore, are the descriptions of Travellers provided in oral and (later) written form during the early 1950s as part of the Irish Folklore Commission's cultural reclamation project. While the bulk of these descriptions were provided to the archive by respondents from the settled community they reflect Irish constructions of Irish people vis-à-vis the self and Other and as relating to the paradigm that was an 'outsider' group at this critical juncture of Irish cultural development and historical self-definition – i.e. the decades immediately subsequent to Irish independence (1922).

The primary source material for this study is the archives of the Irish Folklore Commission, a body of material which includes a Questionnaire on Tinkers that was circulated to members of the settled community in 1950. Central to the discussion in this volume is the idea that the representation of Travellers, i.e. their perceived identity as incorporated in the general attitudes expressed by the Irish people in the Irish Folklore Commission archives, translated Travellers into a dramatic spectacle of cultural Otherness, one which was assimilated into the originary development of the Nationalist imaginary in Ireland, and the very project of Irish identity itself. Travellers are described using a series of popular stereotypes as implicated in discourse. These discursive strategies inculcated an array of suspicions and superstitions. That this array of often reductionist stereotypes have been constantly re-articulated in Ireland over the course of many centuries is acknowledged by most thinkers and writers on this subject. More worrying still is the fact that such labelling and stereotype has in an increasingly globalised and media-saturated modern era frequently assumed the status of some form of objective 'truth' regarding who Travellers are, where they originated and what the essential tenets of their culture comprise. That the reductionist aspects of this discourse sometimes functioned to justify Travellers' exclusion from 'regular' or 'mainstream' society is the most serious aspect of this 'regime of truth'.

It has also been the case in recent decades that any time the Traveller 'question' has been discussed publicly, the discussion has almost inevitably been premised on or peppered with the repetition of long-established and outmoded half-truths and fallacies, many of which have been used to support the 'majority' view that the Traveller issue has only one 'solution' – i.e. that Travellers and their nomadic and 'separate' culture are an apparent anachronism in the modern nation-state and it should therefore be outlawed. Following on from this is the attendant view that it is necessary for Travellers to be assimilated as has happened with so many other cultural minorities before them in this post-Enlightenment era. Currently, this minority versus majority/nation-state 'conflict' or struggle takes place in the domains of discourse and ideology.

One of the most powerful forces the modern nation-state has had in the course of its 'debates' with the Traveller community is the power of definition, the power of the written word in particular. This arena is one which has held particular significance in recent years given the claims for ethnic status that have been pursued by some Traveller activists in Ireland. Until very recent decades, Traveller culture was frequently a non-literate one, a post-colonial reality which meant that the manner whereby their culture was defined was more often than not beyond the control of Travellers themselves. This sees Travellers and other similar (and numerically small) minorities at an enormous disadvantage when attempting to negotiate their struggle for identity and recognition in a society which – in the case of Ireland – is increasingly state-oriented and where media perception and the presentation/manipulation of 'image' is deemed paramount.

The bitter reality is that Irish Travellers have scarcely been able to exercise any influence on the way in which their identity has been constructed over the past century or so, whether in Ireland or amongst the significant populations of Irish Travellers who have formed large Irish diasporas in countries such as Britain and the US. Indeed it is no exaggeration to say that the Traveller image or 'truth', as defined by non-Travellers, has become institutionalised in Ireland and other countries in much the same way that the image of the Roma (Gypsy) people, part-negative and part-exoticist, also became institutionalised within Western tradition. It can be argued that the institutionalisation of representation, image or stereotype in relation to marginalised and 'outsider' minorities such as Travellers and Roma has become so engrained within the Western cultural heritage that it has become reified and irrefutably 'fixed' within the public imaginary. Debates about cultural legitimacy aside, this ossification of 'knowledge' or 'truth' presages that the survival of the Irish Traveller minority and their culture is heavily dependent not only on the ability of the Travelling community to resist the forces of assimilation and acculturation to the majority society, but is also largely dependent on the attitudes and beliefs of the majority towards that community and culture. Hence the imperative to examine the attitudes (both official and non-official) of the non-Traveller majority towards the minority culture in their midst, the evolution of these attitudes over time and the counter-hegemonic views and approaches of the Traveller minority who move between both the 'settled' and 'non-Traveller' cultures and inhabit an area of knowledge or discourse that was often located somewhere in between.

Recent decades have seen debates in Ireland, and indeed Europe, concerning Traveller (and Roma) cultural legitimacy coalesce around one primary theme, i.e. the question of origins. With respect to Irish Travellers' origins, this debate is more often than not a 'red herring'; it is often a diversion from the real issues or sources of contention at hand given that Irish historical sources, particularly those recorded in the English language, exhibit a paucity of evidence concerning the role and nature of peripatetic groups or peoples in Ireland. With Ireland nominally a colonial outpost of Britain for eight centuries, English made little distinction between occupational Traveller groups and other 'wandering Irish'. Irish Travellers do not claim any one standard theory as to their historical origins. Opinions on this issue vary amongst Travellers just as they do amongst the 'settled' community. The modern nation-state has driven a process whereby cultural legitimacy has now often been predicated on historical origins, however, and the question of Traveller origins and cultural development thereafter have assumed a more prominent role in debates about Traveller rights and debates relating to Traveller/settled relations over recent decades. Commentators in both the Travelling and settled communities ascribe Traveller origins to a number of possibilities, some of which may have operated either individually or in tandem with one another. On the overall level, these theories of origin can be divided into three primary schools of thought. One strand of opinion considers Traveller emergence along the following lines. The possibility has been put forward that the Irish Travellers are the descendants of:

1   Peasants evicted from the land by changed economic conditions, socio-economic discord or famine.
2   Peasants who were driven into a nomadic existence because of a sort of social disgrace or ignominy.
3   Native chiefs stripped of their lands and dispossessed by English colonial policies during various centuries (e.g. the 'to Hell or to Connaught' maxim which accompanied Cromwell's clearance policies, to cite but one possible example) (See Binchy, 1993)

Whether taken individually or together, these three possibilities can be seen to form a school of thought or a 'theory' that reflects many contemporary constructions of Travellers in Ireland. This is the view that Travellers have somehow 'fallen away' from a previously sedentary or 'settled' existence, one where they were neither 'outsiders' nor marginalised within Irish society. The likelihood implied here is that the hand of history has deemed them victims of their own human inadequacy or victims of colonial oppression.

The fact that such a derogatory theory reflects the commonplace view in modern Ireland undoubtedly has very serious implications from both the historical and sociological points of view. It is a theory which has also had serious consequences for both the Travelling and settled communities and their interactions with one another. Theorists such as Helleiner (2000) have pointed out that such a hypothesis can serve as a justification for anti-Traveller prejudice or racism in addition to functioning as a catalyst for assimilationist policies as implemented on the part of the Irish State (see McDonagh, 1994). A second proposition places Traveller ethnogenesis at an earlier juncture than the aforementioned 'drop-out from a previously "settled" existence' and hypothesises that Travellers are the descendants of pre-historic or pre-Celtic populations, cultural groups who were displaced by successive invasions in Ireland. This position has been posited by a number of historians and writers including McCormick (1907), MacNeill (1919), Puxon (1967) and O'Toole (1972).

More recently again, a combination of the two main 'schools of thought' has been put forward in the literature. Binchy (1993) who researched Travellers in both Britain and Ireland during the 1980s, has cited Michael Flynn, a medical doctor who traced the genealogies of several large extended Traveller families in the Irish midlands. His research argues that Traveller origins may be located somewhere between the two main prevailing theses:

> I liken the situation to a conveyor belt stretching back into ancient times carrying the traveller population. There would have been a steady trickle of families dropping off and settling in houses while other persons or families would 'hop onto the conveyor belt', or drop out from society, or take on some of the former crafts or occupations of the travellers... . (Flynn in Binchy, 1993: 13)

It is noteworthy that this latter hypothesis has gained support amongst Travellers themselves, as recounted in the expanding canon of life histories and autobiographical literature produced by Travellers themselves in recent years. Traveller musician Pecker Dunne sees the Travelling community as a diverse community which is always an amalgam of an already long-extant travelling peoples and smaller numbers of non-Travellers who frequently joined their community through marriage or because they pursued similar economic interests or work patterns.

> Where did we come from? I've often asked myself that question ... Some say that the Travellers left their houses and started travelling. They left old shacks at the side of the road because they couldn't make a living anymore. People say that it was the landlords and the evictions that were the cause of this. That is only one part of the story though. Some people have always preferred to live their lives on the road. If you go back and read the old stories you will find Travelling people mentioned all the time. When the Gaelic culture was stronger in Ireland travelling was a normal part of the life then and no-one passed any heed to it. Some people travelled for a living and some people preferred to stay in the one place and make their living there. Many poets and healers have always travelled. So too have many musicians like myself. There have always been Travellers in Ireland because some people have always preferred to travel so as to make a living. It's the same in a lot of other countries too. You go to any country and you'll find a group of people who preferred to

travel to make a living. Look at the Aborigines in Australia, the Red Indians in America, the Romany Gypsies in England. There is no way that all the Travellers in Ireland were the product of eviction and famine. Some of us were but not all of us. The Travellers are in Ireland a long, long time. We have been here for centuries – we sure have! (Dunne and Ó hAodha, 2004: 32)

This latter strand of belief, implying an ethnogenesis as a consequence of a range of historical factors, may be the most likely hypothesis. It is also a view which is increasingly apparent in the growing canon of literature emerging from within the Irish Traveller community itself:

This long-held myth that the Irish Travellers were just 'potato people', drop-outs from the Famine. That we were not 'real' Travellers at all and that it was right and proper, and necessary even, to force us to 'settle' down again. With this in mind I decided to trace the stories of five families, all of whom were closely related to me ... The research threw up many interesting facts, some of which would irritate the 'purists' whether in the Traveller or settled communities (Warde, 2009: 81)

Whatever the historical reality, it is unlikely that any definitive answer to the question of Traveller origins and the ethnogenesis of this long-established minority will be arrived at in the near future. That significant numbers of Irish peoples and occupational groups lived a nomadic or semi-nomadic life at various junctures of Irish history is now widely accepted. That many of these individuals or kin-related groups 'took to the road' at different times and for varying reasons is without question. Whether the latter became part of an already extant Traveller community cannot easily be ascertained.

What is a known fact, however, is that the question of Traveller 'origins' played a role in the formation of the Irish imaginary, particularly in the post-colonial period. Exploring the British cultural realm, Nord (2006) has highlighted a similar cultural dynamic whereby traditionally migratory peoples, in this case the British Gypsies, were frequently employed as essentialised literary tropes which encompassed the search for authenticity and the Victorian and colonial obsession with origins. It is also the case that the conventional wisdom in Ireland today tends strongly towards some version of the colonial 'expulsion' theory i.e. that Travellers somehow abandoned a previously settled existence and are the remnants of Ireland's tragedy, the vestiges and relics of our colonial past. Given that group origins, cultural legitimacy and the attendant questions which circumvent such debates have been given so much weight in this, the post-Enlightenment era, the various historical 'versions', 'truths' and myths of Irish Traveller history still play an important role in determining the nexus of Traveller/settled relations in the present day. The past has consequences; it has consequences for the attitudes and approaches adopted with respect to cultural minorities; it also has consequences for the position which the cultural minorities themselves – in this case the Travellers – occupy within modern Irish society.

The 'drop-out' version of Irish Traveller history and origins may hold sway today but this was not always the case. Even in the early 1900s other versions of Irish Traveller history had their place within the Irish collective imaginary and the 'drop-out' version of history did not construe the dominant account; there were other more diverse accounts. Alternative renderings of the historical process existed whereby Travellers were not necessarily constructed as the Irish 'them' or essentialised out of any 'real' historical existence; they were not dislocated from the Irish 'self' or 'othered' from the outside in. It is on the uncovering of these competing and alternative historical discourses that I focus in this volume.

## NOTES

1    The Flight of the Earls in 1607 is often marked as the date which heralded the end of the Gaelic order in Ireland.

# 2  The Traveller colonised

The question of group origins as a marker for cultural legitimacy is today often considered a very recent development, a development that can be attributed entirely to modernity. The issues of ethnogenesis, group origins, kin-related heredity and apparent 'legitimacy' in both cultural and historic terms were all issues which fascinated intellectuals and scholarly communities in the nineteenth century and earlier, however. In fact such subjects or 'objects of enquiry' would actually serve as the backdrop to the very first 'institutionally-inspired' studies of Travellers and Gypsies in Western Europe.

A secondary or marginal interest for much of the nineteenth (and indeed, twentieth) century, the study of Traveller and Gypsy communities and their cultures was a very minor concern. In Western Europe the main source of interest for Gypsies and Travellers (the latter to a much lesser extent) in the late 1900s was the Gypsy Lore Society based in Liverpool, England. This Society was a 'pseudo-scholarly' amalgam of linguists, artists, folklorists, cultural enthusiasts and hobbyists which had originally been founded in 1888. In their day, they were considered Europe's leading authorities on Romany Gypsies and other traditionally nomadic groups with a similar social and cultural history.

Amongst the early members of this Society were some of the leading political and cultural figures of that era including Middle Eastern explorer Sir Richard F. Burton, the highly regarded linguist and Celtic scholar Kuno Meyer, Archduke Joseph of Austria-Hungary and the artist Augustus John, to name but a few. Irish poet William Butler Yeats was also a member of the Society for a short period, a society whose members sought to record folk tales, songs, examples of dialect and genealogical information from Romany Gypsy families in Britain and other parts of Europe. Outside of Britain, their primary European focus was on Gypsies in Central and Eastern Europe, partly because a number of their more prolific contributors/correspondents spent periods of time working and living in the Balkans and in countries such as Bulgaria.[1] It is no coincidence that many aspects of the Gypsy Lore Society's intellectual outlook and scholarly intent held much in common with its closest Irish counterpart, the Irish Folklore Commission[2], albeit the latter organisation was founded in Dublin a few decades later. As with certain elements of the folklore movement which developed in 1920s and 1930s Ireland, the British Gypsiology movement was very much a product of its time and included strong elements of primitivism, romanticism and exoticism in its approach to the study of Gypsies or 'Gypsydom', the latter being the term which the *Journal of the Gypsy Lore Society* used.

Gypsy and Traveller cultures were a particular fascination to the Society's members (sometimes known as Gypsilorists) since they were considered to live a life that was in many ways external to capitalism, state control and the encroaching individualism associated with modernity. The Society's members saw it as their cultural duty or mission to collect all information, cultural or linguistic, relating to the customs, mores and practices of Gypsies before what they considered was the almost inevitable disappearance of such peoples and cultural groups, groups who were perceived to inhabit the 'primitive' or 'exotic' socio-cultural spheres. Modern-day scholars including Delaney (2000) have highlighted the particular nature of this primitivism, a primitivism whereby difference was more often than not encapsulated in the character of the 'doomed primitive' or 'native', a figure who was also often used as a synonym for a more ancient and apparently under-developed society.

Such thinking could be linked with a conception of human development which was then very fashionable, a hierarchical model of human development which ranked societies and cultures into those which were either advanced or primitive. Such a hierarchisation of humanity provided strong cultural and social (i.e. class-related) reference points and functioned to categorise people along more definitive lines in an era when the divisions between peoples were becoming less apparent than in the rural society of previous generations. One obvious short-coming of such a philosophical approach to humanity and society was the fact that such often essentialist demarcations only served to over-ride and obscure the historical specificities of those societal elements and groups which had always been culturally heterogeneous.

Interestingly, the trope of the 'doomed primitive' is still a vibrant designation as attributed to many minorities today, certain traditionally nomadic groups as the Roma Gypsies and the 'indigenous' Traveller groups included. The designation that is the 'ancient' or primitive struggling bravely to cling to whatever shards of cultural individuality are left in today's 'smaller' and increasingly globalised world is in many respects as vibrant a trope today as it was at the end of the nineteenth century. A quick glance at the number of documentary and media channels which regularly explore such subjects attests to the resilience of 'primitivist' phenomena into the modern era.

Increasingly, perhaps, it is through visual media including film and photography that the modern utilisation of this mode of categorisation takes place. Examples of this discourse within the visual culture sphere and as specific to photography would include such photographic projects relating to the Roma Gypsies of the former Eastern bloc, as undertaken by photographers and artists including Ljalja Kuznetsova (Kazakhstan) and Josef Koudelka (in Slovakia). Cultural scholars such as Delaney (2000) have pointed out that such contemporary reflections of the Roma people, while powerful in aesthetic terms, also serve to rejuvenate the trope of 'doomed primitive' as applied to traditionally nomadic Traveller and Gypsy peoples. As today, it was the encroachment of modernity and the inevitable march of 'progress' (Mayall, 1988: 5) which the Gypsilorists deemed the death knell for Gypsies and Travellers. The raison-d'être of the Gypsy Lore Society, i.e. the necessity to record another 'decaying language and culture', was deemed a very appropriate and timely project and this attitude would underlie the intellectual projects and energies of those intellectuals who shaped the folkloristic discourse that was the Gypsy Lore Society (hereinafter GLS).

As with other similar groups of scholars and intellectuals working during the latter decades of the Victorian era, most members of the GLS were members of the British upper middle class, intellectuals, artists and cultural enthusiasts who adopted a strong position against the perceived materialism and atomisation which attended the arrival of the modern, urban and industrial world. The Gypsilorist fascination with Gypsies emerged in part, therefore, from a search for a more 'pure' community of people, a cultural group who had remained 'outside time' and unblemished by the sweeping change and corruption of the modern era. This emphasis on a purity of community cannot be divorced from the context of 'race' and the Gypsilorist discourse was not immune to the ideas and notions relating to nationality and race then prevalent in Britain and throughout the rest of Europe. A product of its time, the GLS absorbed the ideological notions of race then current throughout Europe at this period and such theories and assumptions were frequently invoked in a British context in discussions of minorities such as Gypsies, Travellers, Jews, black people and the Irish (in Britain). That these notions of race had already been employed as ideological bulwarks and 'part justifications' for the colonisation of a number of European countries, Ireland included, is no coincidence. That such hypotheses and presumptions also served to explain evident economic, religious or cultural differences then existing between different countries is also increasingly acknowledged within the scholarly literature today (Miles, 1989).

An offshoot of such debates as undertaken between the members of the GLS and through the pages of their journal, the *Journal of the Gypsy Lore Society*, has since proved one of the most controversial or pernicious issues in relation to early attempts at categorising a range of travelling groups, including the Irish Travellers. In a series of articles published in the *Journal*'s early years, the Gypsilorists attempted to both 'classify' and distinguish between the nomadic groups then travelling throughout Britain and Ireland.

The object of their investigations here related to who could be considered 'true Gypsies' or who could be considered as belonging to other 'indigenous' and 'mixed' (less pure) travelling peoples or communities. This preoccupation with racial classification led the leading intellectuals of the GLS to construct racial classifications of their own, 'ad-hoc' delineations between those Travellers/Gypsies they deemed worthy of cultural study. This hierarchy was based primarily on alleged exotic origins with a (dark) skin colour, a 'traceable' genealogical tree encompassing well-known Gypsy forebears, and the use of *puro jib* or a more unadulterated and allegedly 'purer' form of Romany considered indicators of Romany cultural 'purity' and genealogical legitimacy.

At the head of this bizarre racial hierarchy were the 'true-blooded' (Romany: *tatcho*) Gypsies, while groups about whom little information was known or compiled (such as the Scottish Travellers and the Irish Travellers[3], Tinkers and Irish Tinkers) were placed at a much lower-ranked position in the cultural purity/relevance stakes. The allegedly 'pure-blooded' Romany Gypsies who had originally migrated from India were regarded by the Gypsilorists as the most 'real' of all the Gypsies then travelling throughout Britain. Being classified as the most 'true-blooded' or real also brought with it a range of essentialisations including the apparent 'truth' that such Gypsies were likely the most noble, peaceable and culturally interesting of all the nomadic or semi-nomadic groups then travelling Britain. The Scottish Tinkers, on the other hand, were viewed as lesser-regarded or 'indigenous' Travellers who in some cases had some intermixture of Romany blood. The Irish Tinkers were more suspect again due to their indigenous origins, the fact that many were immigrants to Britain who tended to associate only within their own extended family networks and who appeared to remain aloof from many of the social and cultural concerns of British society in that era. The Irish Travellers were therefore considered one of the 'lowest' groups on the exotic and cultural purity scales created by the Gypsilorists.

This preoccupation with racial classification characteristic of certain elements within late nineteenth century British scholarship – and such fixations or concerns were by no means confined to the Gypsilorists alone – meant that the members of the GLS used the information they collected on Gypsy linguistics and cultural practices to search for what was deemed the overriding question or 'object of enquiry' within Gypsiology at this time, i.e. attempts to 'locate' and find proofs for the racial origin of the 'true' Gypsies then resident in Britain. The Gypsy Lore Society was lucky in that a high proportion of their more active members were linguists. Indeed, it is no exaggeration to say that their members included a number of the English-speaking world's leading philologists and linguists, figures such as John Sampson, Kuno Meyer, Bernard Gilliat-Smith and Dora Yates.

Dora Yates, a British Jewess, was a very accomplished linguist in her own right and would prove one of the last leading figures within the British Gypsiology movement. Taken together, these intellectuals saw themselves as well-positioned to the theories and philological enquiries of old and with respect to Gypsies they based much of their early hypotheses on the work of the eighteenth century German linguist Grellman (1783). By tracking various Romany vocabularies as collected throughout the different parts of Europe through which the Gypsies had migrated, the GLS membership were in general agreement, as are many scholars today, that the Romany Gypsies had originated in India before later migrating across Europe.

The Gypsies then resident in Britain were thus 'racialised' as non-Europeans. GLS members echoed the racialist discourse of colonialism and the 'exotic' discourse of Orientalism, both of which were fashionable at this period, by researching the 'exotic' cultural attributes inherent in Gypsy culture, which were perceived to resemble those of various populations within India. Particular emphasis was placed on those cultural attributes, including purity rituals and linguistic similarities that were common to certain Gypsy groups and which seemed to hark back to their homeland in India. It was assumed that the Gypsy presence in Europe was the consequence of a movement from India. The Gypsilorists also assumed that this 'original' and separate culture, complete with a pure Indian language and a unique racial character, was now under threat of dilution as a consequence of the Gypsy migration from East to West; hence the necessity to record its most salient cultural characteristics. The exact location in India from which this exodus occurred and the timing of this selfsame exodus were major sources of debate within the ranks of Gypsiology. It was as part of this debate that the Irish Travellers, referred to in the GLS literature as 'tinkers', made a brief appearance. The 1888 preface to the first issue of the *Journal of the GLS* outlined the three central hypotheses regarding when the Gypsy migration westwards took place. These included:

- That the Gypsies had entered Europe in 1417 shortly after they left India;
- That the Gypsies had left Persia in approximately 430 AD and had entered Western Europe at a later period; or
- That the Gypsies had been in Europe for two thousand years as metal workers.

The latter theory, which situated the Gypsy presence in Europe in a much older timeframe, negated the first British written reference to Gypsies, referred to as 'Egyptians', which dated to the year 1505. The word 'Gypsy' was itself a derivation from 'Egyptian'. Clébert (1967) claimed that 'all mountebanks and travelling showmen found themselves dubbed "Egyptians" well before Gypsies or "Tsiganes" were publicly recorded in Western Europe in the fourteenth century' (1967: 27). Many of these Gypsies when first arriving in Europe presented themselves as pilgrims from 'Little Egypt' (presumed to be the Middle East) who were fleeing persecution (de Vaux de Foletier, 1961: 20–21). By the mid-1400s these early 'Egyptians', as recorded in Britain, were associated with exotic occupations including fortune-telling, which they exercised 'with crafte and subtyltie' according to a statute of Henry VIII proclaimed in 1530 (cited in Okely, 1984: 53).

Both the persecution and Egyptian angles of the story were further elaborated by an association with religious personages. It was said that the Gypsies had been forced to flee along with Joseph and the Virgin Mary. 'Egyptians' were also associated with 'exotic' occupations including fortune-telling which it was assumed they brought with them from the East. These myths ensured an initial welcome for the migrant Gypsies on their first arrival into Europe, a welcome that was short-lived, however, as Gypsies and other Travellers have been the objects of persecution or prejudice in most European countries from the sixteenth century onwards (Acton, 1974: 61).

The theory that the Gypsies had been working as metal workers in Britain as long ago as the year 1505 could be demonstrated by the earlier references in official records to 'tinkers'. It is worth noting that the term 'tynker' was a trade name in England as far back as the year 1175. The extent to which this term referred to a distinct cultural category of people, however, is still unclear. So too is the possible connection between 'tinkers' and those referred to as Gypsies, Egyptians and the Irish, all of whom were travelling throughout Britain in kin-based groups during the period when British vagrancy came under particular state scrutiny and repression. Beier's (1985) work on the phenomenon of 'masterless men' in sixteenth century Britain indicates that whatever cultural or social differences may have existed between these different Travelling groups, they were of no interest to the British authorities, who applied increasingly repressive legislation to them. For example, all of these Travellers were declared rogues according to a Poor Law enacted in 1596 which targeted 'tynkers wandering abroad' as well as 'all such persons, not being Felons, wandering and p'tending themselves to be Egipcyans or wandering in the Habite Forme or Attyre of counterfayte Egipcians' (Mayall, 1988: 189). Okely (1984) has questioned the evidence regarding the cultural demarcation of the different Travelling people of this era and suggested that there is a great deal of ambiguity regarding the categories of people defined as 'vagabonds', 'tynkers', 'Egyptians', etc. Okely is sceptical as to the foreign origin of many 'Egyptians'. She suggests that the term 'Egyptian' may have been a term of self-ascription utilised by 'indigenous' wanderers who wished to appear exotic or an ascription or 'label imposed by persecuting outsiders' (1984: 54). Irrespective of these various possibilities it was the fact of a possible historical link between these 'Egyptians' (Gypsies) of the sixteenth century and the tinkers of the Middle Ages which stimulated an interest amongst the Gypsilorists in the possible links between contemporary 'Gypsies' and 'tinkers'. Thus the brief upsurge of interest in 'tinkers'/Irish Travellers exhibited by the GLS was in reality only an offshoot of a larger debate regarding the origins and migration of the Gypsies to Western Europe and to Britain in particular. While the GLS had created an artificial 'racial' hierarchy in terms of which nomadic groups were deemed the most 'pure', 'authentic' or worthy of investigation, the Society's publications at this period nevertheless indicated some confusion about the exact status or 'categorisation' of the Irish Travellers ('tinkers'), and whether these tinkers were in fact Scottish or Irish. For the Gypsilorists there was frequently confusion as to whether the Scottish or Irish tinkers should be regarded as Gypsies, or as some type of indigenous or 'mixed' nomadic group. In this aspect the GLS echoed the popular discourse of the late nineteenth century when terms such as 'tinker' and 'Gypsy' were often used interchangeably and in an often confused fashion. Despite the fact that 'tinker' origins were shrouded in doubt, the British Gypsiologists did not hesitate to postulate theories to explain any differences that they perceived existed between the different groups. In any case, they were still inferior from a cultural interest point of view in the eyes of the Gypsilorists and consequently were ranked lower on the racial/purity hierarchy as devised by them.

Philological analysis had been the primary tool of GLS members in their situating of Gypsy genesis in India and GLS members asserted that proof of Irish Traveller/tinker origins could also be established through philological enquiry. This could be done, they believed, by a careful examination of those few wordlists of the tinkers' language, known in academic parlance as Shelta, which had been recorded by the Society's members. The Society considered itself well-positioned to undertake such linguistic enquiry, as it included in its ranks two leading Celtic scholars, the renowned Celticist Kuno Meyer and Welshman John Sampson. While Shelta had been adopted as the academic name for the Travellers' language from an early date, Travellers themselves refer to the language as spoken today as Gammon or Cant. The name Shelta originated with an early member of the Gypsy Lore Society named Charles Leland (1882), who 'discovered' Shelta when speaking to an Irish Traveller in Wales and who stated that his informant called the language 'Shelta' or 'Sheldru'.

The justification for the philological analysis of Shelta as undertaken by the Gypsilorists has two aspects. On the one hand the Gypsilorists felt the need to justify their interest in the language of a Travelling group who were lower on the rungs of the racial/cultural purity scales, as they themselves defined them, than were the Romany Gypsies. The racial hierarchy aside, Gypsilorist attitudes to Irish Travellers differed little from the contemporary racism of the English upper class towards the Irish in general. The justification for investigative work into Shelta was primarily that it served as an adjunct into the primary purpose of the Gypsy Lore Society, i.e. recording the evidence that the Romany Gypsies were culturally and racially superior to other groups. The differentiation of the 'gentle Romany' from the 'swinish Saxon' (Borrow in Binchy, 1993: 107) or 'Celtic vagrant' (Sampson, 1891: 204) was considered a legitimate process within the Victorian obsession with a hierarchical structuring of the various Travelling groups. The second justification for this philological enquiry concerned the 'exoticist' and Orientalist attitudes that were prevalent among the Victorian Gypsilorists. It was necessary to 'exoticise' the Irish Travellers to furnish them with some semblance of cultural legitimacy thereby justifying scholarly enquiry into them. This was achieved by hypothesising on their antiquity as a group with reference to possible Pictish and bardic origins. The possibility that the Irish Travellers had Pictish antecedents was the first theory to be mooted as part of this philological project. As noted, the Travellers'/tinkers' language Shelta was first discovered in 1876 by amateur folklorist and one-time President of the Gypsy Lore Society, Charles Leland. He tells of coming across an itinerant knife grinder in Bath, England, a man selling ferns in Aberystwyth, Wales and an Irish tramp in his home state of Pennsylvania in the US, each of whom mentioned the use of Shelta. These people had also suggested that this 'secret' language was far older than Romani and was habitually spoken by Irish tinkers. Writing in his book *The Gypsies*, published in 1882, Leland described his excitement on discovering a fifth Celtic language and suggested that it might even be the lost language of the Picts, a suggestion that was later mooted by Gypsilorists such as MacRitchie and Sampson: 'It is one of the awfully mysterious arcana of human stupidity that there should have existed for a thousand years in Great Britain a cryptic language … that I should have discovered it … the most curious linguistic discovery of the century, the fifth British Celtic tongue!' (Leland in Macalister, 1937: 153).

Leland's theory was given some support by the Welsh Gypsilorist John Sampson (1891) who also posited a possible Pictish origin for the Travellers. He claimed that one of the old names for the Irish tinkers was the Creenies, which he claimed was a corruption of *na Cruithne*, the Irish for 'the Picts' (1891: 220–221). A note appended to Sampson's article by his editor David MacRitchie mentioned a 'peculiar caste' in Wigtonshire, also known as the Creenies, who it was said were the descendants of 'some savages that came over from Ireland' (1891: 221). The Gypsilorists' claims for a Pictish origin for the Travellers had anecdotal evidence only to support it. Modern linguistic research on the structure and etymology of Shelta indicates the unlikely nature of this theory of origin. Anthony Grant (1994), who has analysed the structure of Shelta, has pointed out for instance that 'our knowledge of Pictish is exiguous and our understanding essentially nil, so that any claims of Pictish influence cannot be substantiated for want of incontrovertible evidence' (1994: 184). Since the grammar and syntax of Shelta has an English structure, most scholars who have examined Shelta are now of the opinion that Shelta was formed in the modern period, possibly at that juncture when the language shift from Irish to English was taking place (see Grant, 1994; Ó Baoill, 1994; Ó hAodha, 2001, 2002a, 2002c). Indeed, Dónall Ó Baoill (1994), who is the only bilingual (i.e. native Irish and English speaker) Irish scholar to have examined Shelta in detail to date, hypothesises that Shelta must have been created at a time when its original speakers were bilingual, having a knowledge of both Irish and English, i.e. some time within the last 350 years or so. The fact that the English language was spoken by high-ranking Irish at the close of the sixteenth century and by the rest of the Irish population at an even later date gives credence to this view.

The temptation to explain Traveller origins with reference to the Picts fitted into the 'racial purity' and exoticist hierarchy of the Gypsilorists. Tinkers, whether classed as Irish or Scottish, were suspect due to their indigenous origins and consequently they were amongst the lower groups on the 'exotic' and 'cultural purity' scales created by the Gypsilorists. For this reason it is possible that the references to Pictish origins were a solution to a Gypsilorist dilemma, i.e. how to accept a nomadic group possibly generated from within the sedentary society. If the presence of the group could not be explained by its migration from a distant exotic location, then some indigenous exoticism might be emphasised in order that the Travellers might be viewed positively. The essays of the various Gypsilorists writing for the *Journal of the Gypsy Lore Society* at this juncture also hint at the existence of a certain element of competition between the different Gypsilorists as to who was better acquainted with the most exotic Gypsies or Travellers.

That Gypsy and Traveller groups sometimes internalised exoticist views of themselves, including the myth of the true or full-blooded/pure Gypsy, and then fed these myths back again to Gypsilorists and others involved in Gypsy Studies is quite likely, as pointed out by Acton (1974) and Ó hAodha (2002b). There is evidence that this happened in the case of the 'Pictish' theory of Traveller origin, in particular in the case of the Scottish tinkers. The Scottish Gypsilorist McCormick (1907) gave an example of how this exoticising worked when he wrote of a famous Scottish tinker named Billy Marshall, who allegedly claimed descent from some 'Pictish kings' rather than any Indian ancestry. The allegedly more favourable genetic inheritance conferred by Romany/Indian ancestry is implied by McCormick's patronising statement that 'many of Billy's worst "peculiarities" are not Romani characteristics, and must be attributed to his Pictish blood' (1907: 19). For a short period after Leland's 'discovery', occasional sightings of Irish tinker groups were reported in the pages of the *Journal of the Gypsy Lore Society*.

It was not until John Sampson commenced his researches into tinker origins and linguistics in 1890, in part as a by-product of the Gypsy origins debate, that attention to the tinkers' language known in academic parlance as Shelta and the collecting of this language became more focused. Sampson was also the first scholar to raise the possibility of bardic influence on the formation of Shelta, a possibility that would permit the Gypsilorists to exoticise the tinkers in much the same way as Leland had exoticised them using the 'Pictish connection'. Sampson collected Shelta from an Irish tinker living in Liverpool and concluded that Shelta was Celtic in origin. He suggested that Shelta was originally derived from a 'prehistoric Celtic' – this despite his admission that much of the vocabulary appeared of more recent origin and included many modern Irish words, which had been transformed so as to be rendered unintelligible to non-speakers by the use of various methods of word disguise (Sampson, 1891: 207–208).

In Sampson's view, this linguistic research provided proof of the independent origins of the two separate groups known as Irish tinkers and English Gypsies, thereby acting as a justification for the Traveller purity hierarchy which the Gypsilorists had created. Sampson's analysis subsequently became the Gypsilorist orthodoxy regarding the ethnogenesis of the tinkers, negating in the process the earlier conclusions of another leading Gypsilorist and expert on the Scottish tinkers named David MacRitchie (1889), who had claimed that the Irish tinkers were a more diverse group of people and included a Romany intermixture. Sampson, whose knowledge of Irish was limited, was helped to develop this view by the leading Celtic scholar of his era, the German Kuno Meyer, to whom he passed on the Shelta material which he had collected for analysis.

Meyer (1891) concluded that Shelta was indeed of Irish origin. He suggested that Shelta was a language of great antiquity and traced its genesis to some time before the eleventh century. He suggested that Shelta had not necessarily originated with the tinkers, although they were now its only speakers: 'though now confined to tinkers, its knowledge was once possessed by Irish poets and scholars, who probably were its original framers' (1891: 258).

Meyer demonstrated the linear relationship that existed between substantial elements of the Shelta vocabulary and the Irish language. Irish words had been 'disguised' by a number of linguistic 'transforming' devices including metathesis, apocope, the reversal of syllables and the use of prefixes. Since it was necessary to fit the tinkers into this 'exoticist' Gypsilorist hierarchy neither Sampson nor Meyer evinced much interest in those elements of Shelta vocabulary which did not emanate from the Irish language but had been incorporated instead from other 'secret' languages with which Shelta was in contact including Anglo-Romani, Scottish Travellers' Cant or English Cant. The principal interest of the Gypsilorist linguists in Irish Travellers and their language was in the light they could throw on the Gypsies and their enthnogenesis. Therefore Sampson and Meyer did not overly concern themselves with the question of Tinker origins and culture. The dismissive attitude evinced towards tinker culture in general accorded with the rather lowly rung they inhabited on the racial purity scale invented by the Gypsilorists. Sampson justified his interest in tinkers, in part, by appealing to philanthropy:

> The Tinker has already been introduced to us by Mr MacRitchie [the Society's president] and he is undoubtedly a good fellow, and worth knowing, there can be no impropriety in further cultivating his acquaintance. Although his less reputable connections may perhaps cause him to be somewhat coldly received by the more exclusive of our members ... yet he still comes of a good old stock, rich, if in nought else, in hereditary and developed characteristics ... an inviting field for the labours of the missionary and social reformer.
>
> (Sampson, 1891: 204–221)

Sampson even extended the 'racial purity' hierarchy by creating further 'racial' classifications of his own within the Shelta-speaking population based on their knowledge of the language and whether they were 'full-blooded tinkers'. To his mind the tinker who spoke a language derived from 'prehistoric Celtic' was undoubtedly a cut above the many English nomads, including hawkers and knife grinders, who also spoke Shelta. The Shelta spoken by the 'knife grinder, street hawker, and other shady characters' was a lesser form of language, however. It was 'corrupt' and 'scarcely a tithe of the words in daily use by the Irish "tinker" are intelligible to his English half-breed cousin' (Sampson 1891: 208). While their studies of Shelta allowed the Gypsilorists to racialise tinkers as 'Celts' in much the same way as they had racialised Gypsies as Indian, it did not happen that the tinkers were allocated a higher rung on the cultural purity scales. The 'racial' hierarchy created by the GLS placed the tinkers only slightly above the 'half-bloods' (i.e. those who were half Gypsy and half English) or other English Travellers, often referred to as 'vagrants'. Despite their belief that some aspects of Shelta indicated its possible antiquity as a language, the tinkers and their culture were still regarded in an ambiguous light by the Gypsilorists. Sampson linked the tinkers' language with their perceived social status: '[the Tinker's] moral and social code, like his language, is certainly of the backslang order' (1891: 220).

This was also clear from comments of Kuno Meyer, who felt the need to explain his interest in Shelta as follows: 'I would scarcely have taken much interest in Shelta, if it were nothing but tinkers' cant, fabricated from Irish in modern times, of a kind not superior to the backslang of costers and cabmen. It was the fact of there being evidence to the great antiquity of Shelta that made me want to know more about it' (Meyer, 1891: 261).

The ambiguous status of the tinkers in the eyes of the Gypsilorists manifested itself not only in relation to linguistic factors but also in relation to other cultural attributes, including nomadism. The literature of Gypsiology at this period exoticised the group of people referred to as the 'true' Romany Gypsies not only in terms of genealogy and linguistic inheritance. Their nomadism was also seen to be 'true' because it was a nomadism that was racially determined. This was in contrast to other travelling groups including tinkers and tramps whose nomadism was generally perceived to be a consequence of degeneracy and opprobrium.

Subsequent to this initial burst of enthusiasm, as a consequence of the debate on Gypsy origins, little further interest was evinced by the Gypsilorists in the possible origins and genesis of the tinkers themselves. Since the tinkers were for the most part non-literate, it was assumed that their use of Shelta was a remnant of the Gaelic past from whence they had emanated. It was thought that they were just the inheritors of a linguistic link with an older culture, one which included the use of perhaps many secret languages by those occupational groups (including druids and stonemasons), aspects of whose lifestyle may have been suppressed by the dominant society.

The only other known 'secret' language or 'cant' to have survived in Ireland into the twentieth century in addition to Shelta was Béarlagair na Saor (the Language of the Stonemasons). Although the name given to this language indicated that it was the cant used by stonemasons, it seems to have been spoken by a much wider range of people including pedlars, beggars, knife grinders, horse trainers, etc. From the evidence that has been recorded it seems to have consisted largely of innovated words or modified Irish words used in an Irish grammatical framework. The question of 'monastic' influence on these 'secret' languages was mooted by scholars like Meyer and Macalister. In fact Macalister (1937: 257) would maintain that the language of today's Irish Travellers (formerly known as Tinkers), Shelta, is just one of a number of 'secret' languages apparently devised or inspired by medieval Irish monks and comprising vocabularies formed from the engineered interaction of Irish Gaelic with other languages including Latin, Greek, Hebrew and English. Charles Leland, the original 'discoverer' of Shelta, summarised the Gypsilorist orthodoxy in an article written in 1891: '[Shelta] appears to have been an artificial, secret, or Ogam tongue, used by the bards and transferred by them, in all probability, to the bronze workers and jewellers – a learned and important body – from whom it descended to the tinkers' (Leland, 1891: 195).

The 'racial purity' classifications of the Gypsilorists could be dismissed as the fashionable obscurantism of a group of late Victorian gentlemen if it were not for the very real and dangerous effects their theorising had on public policy towards Gypsies and Travellers in Britain as the twentieth century progressed. Unlike the folklorists of the Irish Folklore Commission, some of the Gypsilorists held positions of influence in British social life and also had a role as advisers to the government on policy issues concerning Gypsies and Travellers in Britain. Sampson, Leland and others were the first lorists to put forward the concept of 'racial' and 'exoticist' classifications relating to Gypsies and Travellers. After the Second World War, however, there emerged a second generation of Gypsilorists who accepted these classifications with apparent ease.

In his work *Gypsy Politics and Social Change* (1974) Acton has described the practical effects of these exoticist classifications on the Gypsy and Traveller communities in Britain in the second half of the twentieth century at a period when the British state imposed increased controls on nomadism and the Gypsy/Traveller way of life. Many county councils and local government officials in Britain accepted the thesis of 'racial purity' as promulgated by members of the Gypsy Lore Society, including Brian Vesey-Fitzgerald, Rupert Croft-Cooke and Edward Harvey, from just before the Second World War and for some time afterwards. This categorisation of Gypsies into sub-groups as undertaken by the Gypsilorists of the British Gypsy Lore Society allowed local authorities to build up their own inventories of how many 'true' Romany Gypsies as opposed to 'mumpers, half-breeds, didakais and tinkers' there were in a particular area of the UK. These bizarre classifications would have been amusing except for the devastating results they had for Gypsies and Travellers still living on the road, particularly in the period immediately after the Second World War.

The belief that the 'true-blooded Gypsy' was a dying breed lived on in the literature of Gypsiology and officialdom alike and the romantic idealised Gypsy of literary and Gypsy-lore fame became a millstone around the necks of those Gypsies and Travellers agitating for their rights. So-called Gypsy experts such as Edward Harvey and Brian Vesey-Fitzgerald continually warned in their writings of the demise of the 'real' Gypsy and the upsurge of those whose claims to a Gypsy lifestyle were at best spurious. Writing in the *Journal of the Gypsy Lore Society* in the late 1940s both Harvey and Vesey-Fitzgerald continued to propagate the romantic and primitivist myth of the 'true' Gypsy and warned of the demise of this 'true' Gypsy type in Hampshire's New Forest, an area inhabited by Gypsies for centuries. Their thinking was to influence those various bodies responsible for local affairs. A 1960 report of the Hampshire Association of Parish Councils, for example stated:

> The old Romany stock is diluted and there has been an infiltration of 'poor white'. The majority of these people have wandered all their lives. Though, in the past, they had their proud traditions, they, and we too, as thinking people, are faced with the problem that besets a decadent stock. They belong to neither past nor present.
>
> (Cited in Acton, 1974: 191)

The continuing strength of the racial stereotype allowed local authorities to either avoid their responsibilities towards Gypsies and Travellers on the pretext that they would help 'real' Romanies but not the crowd of 'pretenders' and 'mixed-breeds' who were then on the road. In many instances the reports of the true Gypsy's demise aided county councils and local authorities in their efforts either to totally assimilate Gypsies and Travellers or to practise so-called 'rehabilitation' on them, at the same time absolving themselves from any charges of racial oppression. Some local councils such as Kent conducted surveys in the 1950s and attempted to distinguish between the number of so-called 'true'

Romanies and others – a process with uncomfortable echoes of the categorisation of Gypsies into sub-groups and their subsequent 'ethnic cleansing' by the Nazis in the concentration camps only a few years before. To marvel at the longevity of the Gypsilorist stereotype tradition, and the frighteningly precise nature in which the cult of the 'true Gypsy' persists from one generation of public policy makers to another, all we have to do is read the comments made by then British Home Secretary Jack Straw in 1999:

> Now the first thing we have to say is that people have got to stop being sentimental about so-called travellers. There are relatively few Romany Gypsies left, who seem to be able to mind their own business and don't cause trouble to other people, and then there are a lot more people who masquerade as travellers or Gypsies, who trade on the sentiment of people, but who seem to think because they label themselves as travellers that therefore they've got a licence to commit crimes and act in an unlawful way that other people don't have … In the past there has been rather too much toleration of travellers.
>
> (Jack Straw, British Home Secretary in a BBC radio interview, 22 July 1999)

Unsurprisingly, groups campaigning for social rights and cultural autonomy for Gypsies and Travellers are increasingly reassessing the role which the Gypsilorist tradition played in the perpetuation of erroneous stereotypes and myths, many of which are still in common currency and many of which have justified economic and cultural discrimination against Gypsies and Travellers.

## NOTES

1   Bernard Gilliat-Smith is a good example of such a Society member. For many years, he was a regular letter-writer and contributor to the *Journal of the Gypsy Lore Society*. An excellent linguist, he worked in the British Consular service in postings as varied as Constantinople, Beirut, Bulgaria, Denmark, Tabriz, Sarajevo, Leningrad, Bucharest, New Orleans and Turkey.

2   The Irish Folklore Movement, originally titled The Folklore of Ireland Society, was founded in Dublin in 1927. It was the culmination of a growing interest in Irish folklore on the part of antiquarians, creative writers

and members of the Anglo-Irish Literary Revival and the movement that was termed Athbheochan na Gaeilge (The movement to revive the Irish language).

3   Both the Scottish Travellers and the Irish Travellers were more often than not referred to as 'Tinkers' at this juncture. It was in later decades that the term 'tinker' assumed a more derogatory referent.

# 3    Irish Travellers and the bardic tradition

The initial Gypsilorist interest in Irish Travellers/tinkers was a short-lived phenomenon and it faded away after a few years. More than three decades passed before the subject was revived again as a source of interest. Once again, philology and its relation with cultural categorisation would prove the catalyst. It was not until the late 1930s that an interest in Traveller culture resurfaced once more and on this occasion it was the Traveller language known as Cant/Gammon and Shelta which acted as a catalyst for this renewed interest.

In 1937 the Scottish Celtic scholar R. A. S. Macalister gathered together much of the previous research (vocabularies and wordlists) of Meyer and Sampson on Shelta into book form and produced *The Secret Languages of Ireland*, a work that remains to this day the only comprehensive study of Shelta and the other Irish 'secret' languages written to date. He agreed with the theories of both Meyer and Sampson that the genesis and formation of Shelta could not have occurred solely within the occupational group known as tinkers. He surmised that the linguistic inventiveness inherent in Shelta might have been the product of either travelling monks expelled from their monasteries or lay masters of the verbal arts who joined the myriad other itinerants on the Irish roads, including the tinkers.

Macalister disagreed however with aspects of the linguistic analysis undertaken by the earlier Gypsilorists. While Meyer and Sampson had surmised that Shelta was a language that might have dated as far back as the eleventh century or earlier, Macalister demurred. Since Shelta's structure and syntax was based primarily on the English language and since the English language was first spoken only by a few high-ranking Irish nobles at the end of the sixteenth century (and by most other Irish at a later date), Macalister concluded that Shelta probably originated in the modern era, a view that has been reinforced by more recent studies of the language (see Cauley and Ó hAodha, 2004;

Ó Baoill, 1994; Ó hAodha, 2002a, 2002c). Macalister also posited a mixed ethnogenesis for Irish Travellers. He devoted an entire chapter of his 1937 book to examining the way in which the caste-like under-world in ancient Ireland operated. This caste system was a hierarchical one and included kings, nobles, non-noble freemen, etc. At the bottom of this hierarchy was a group comprising those who were unfree, slaves or homeless vagabonds. This latter group had no civil rights under the Gaelic system, were nomadic and wandered between classes in an effort to forge a living wherever they could. Some of them were entertainers 'who specialised in acrobatic and clownish performances' (1937: 124). Macalister believed that modern Travellers were the descendants of people from this group. However, modern Travellers were also in his view descended from another group of people. These were the scholars and druids, some of whom became redundant with the arrival of Christianity in Ireland. Some of these scholars had also formed guilds of poets who wandered from house to house, paying for their board with poetry and harp playing, some of them attaching themselves to the nobles of the great houses. Macalister echoed Meyer (1891; 1909) in proposing these poets in conjunction with travelling monks as the antecedents of many of the literary 'disguise' techniques found in the Travellers' language Shelta.

The likely cross-fertilisation between 'literary' Travellers and travel-ling craftsmen was highlighted by the first Irish-born scholars to take an interest in Travellers and their culture. Pádraig MacGréine or 'Master Greene' as he was known to the Travellers in his home county of Longford worked as a folklore collector on behalf of the Irish Folklore Commission during the 1930s. He discovered Shelta while collecting folktales from a well-known Traveller woman storyteller from the Midlands named Owney Power and wrote a number of articles during the 1930s on this topic for *Béaloideas*, the journal of the Irish Folklore Commission (MacGréine, 1931, 1932a, 1934). He called for further research into the 'traveller-folk' because of their importance as reposi-tories of Irish tradition (MacGréine, 1931: 186). He noted that: 'these "travellers", the bacaigh [Irish: literally 'lame person', beggar, wanderer, etc.] of an earlier time, the poor scholars – the Irish scolares vagantes – had been the medium for the spread of folk tales and all manner of traditions' (1931: 186).

MacGréine's plea for further research into the Travellers was taken on by the Irish Folklore Commission in 1937 when 'Travelling People' was included as one of the many topics about which Irish children wrote short paragraphs for the Bailiúchán na Scoil (Irish Schools

Collection). This Collection was carried out by the Irish National Schools at the request of the Irish Folklore Commission between the years 1937 and 1938, where schoolchildren were given the task of making a collection of folklore as recounted by their family and neighbours. MacGréine's views were taken into account in an even more comprehensive way in 1952 when the Irish Folklore Commission issued the Tinker Questionnaire (under study in this book) to its folklore collectors in an effort to document aspects of the tinker way of life, 'before it is too late' (IFC Tinker Questionnaire, 1952: 5).

The Questionnaire included questions about tinkers under a list of topics including: 'Generic Names', 'Local Tinker Groups', 'Areas Within Which Tinker Groups Operate', 'Customs and Superstitions', 'Religious and Social Practice', 'Visits and Local Encampments', 'Crafts and Means of Livelihood', 'Behaviour', 'Physical and Other Characteristics', 'Tinker Personalities', 'Tinker Society', 'Languages', 'Origins and History', 'Sayings, Proverbs or Songs about Tinkers'. There was a good response to this Questionnaire, with over 800 pages of material forwarded to the Commission by its various respondents.

The primary socio-historical value of the Questionnaire is the insight it gives us into the relationship between the Irish settled and Travelling communities midway through the twentieth century. The Questionnaire is a particularly useful insight into the perceptions that the settled community held of Travellers. It demonstrates the negative stereotypes and false images of Travellers held by those in the settled community who were prejudiced against them. The Questionnaire is one-sided in nature since it was only the views of the settled community which were looked for by its compilers. However, it is still a very useful source of information on Traveller trades, Traveller families, their travelling patterns and the range of societal attitudes and prejudices prevalent among the settled community at this period.

Almost contemporaneous with the issuance of the IFC's Tinker Questionnaire was the work of another IFC folklorist, Seán McGrath. He collected specimens of the Traveller language Shelta and information on other aspects of Traveller culture, including folklore, in County Clare throughout the early 1950s. McGrath's views were an important forerunner of the new orthodoxy of colonial dispossession and the drop-out theory, which were adopted in official Irish discourse as the explanation of Travellers' origins from the 1960s onwards. The fact that he formed his researches into a number of talks which he gave on the national radio station Raidió Éireann also in the early 1950s meant that his views had a much wider audience than those folklorists like Pádraig MacGréine who had come before him and who simply published their material in Béaloideas. McGrath (1955) was of the opinion that a large proportion of the Travellers were the descendants of those evicted during the Famine or those small landowners who were evicted during Cromwell's reign of terror in 1649. In his view only 'genuine' tinkers were of interest because they were 'symbolic of an older Ireland' (1955: 19).

However, he was in doubt about how many genuine tinkers were still living on the Irish roads. By a remarkable coincidence McGrath echoed the racial classifications of Britain's Gypsilorists, the 'second genera-tion' of whom were contemporaneously still engaged in a 'racial' classification of Gypsies and Travellers in Britain. Because of their roles as advisers to the government on policy issues concerning all British Gypsies and Travellers, the 'racial' and 'exoticist' classifications of British Gypsilorists were to have a profound effect on British local government policy towards Gypsies and Travellers until well after the Second World War. While Irish folklorists like McGrath were not to have any public policy role like some of the British Gypsilorists, it is almost uncanny how the style of McGrath's writing echoes the nostalgic and primitivist tone that suffused much of the writings of the Gypsilorists who idealised Britain's Gypsies. Take the following quote, for example: 'Despite the apparent increase in the tinker population, the older type steadily seems to disappear … there are vagrants on the Irish road today, and they are a shame and a disgrace to the genuine tinkers of the country' (1955: 8).

While MacGréine had promulgated the value of all Travellers as a repository of an older Irish traditional culture, McGrath saw only a few of the Travellers as worthy of investigation, since, in his view, only a few of them were actually 'old-style Travellers' and therefore heirs to an 'older Ireland'. While folklorists like McGrath did not have any influ-ence on government policy vis-à-vis the objects of their study, as did his counterparts in the British Gypsy Lore Society, it is likely that his views were common enough among certain strands of the Irish intelli-gentsia in the 1950s. His views on the worth of the Travelling population still on the Irish roads and his view of Traveller origins were soon to become the dominant ones in Irish public discourse. The Irish Folklore Commission deserves a certain credit for its issuance of the 1952 Tinker Questionnaire and the zeal of its local investigators like Pádraig MacGréine, who highlighted the importance of Traveller culture to the project of national reclamation. There is no doubt, however, that the fact that the Commission undertook no systematic survey of the lives or folklore of any group of Travellers, as elucidated by Travellers themselves, can now be seen as an oversight on their part. While one can allow for the grave lack of resources by which the IFC was hampered, and the particular difficulties that might have been inherent in recording nomadic Travellers, it is difficult not to suspect that the fact that no attempt was ever made to record Travellers themselves might also have been in part a political decision – a decision that may have been influenced to some extent by the anti-Traveller prejudices prevalent at the time.

Twentieth century Irish studies of Travellers all seem to circle back to the one seminal report, the 1963 government Report of the Commission on Itinerancy. This report was the first major Irish policy document of any consequence regarding Irish Travellers. While it formed the first ever official enquiry by the state into the Traveller 'issue' it yet proved to have very far-reaching consequences by virtue of its subsequent influence on public policy. This was particularly the case in relation to the question of the settlement and/or assimilation of Travellers. The Report included the first systematic collection of information regarding the living conditions of Irish Travellers. This information was itself of minimal importance to the conclusions of the Report, a fact which is evident even in some of the Report's first pages. In fact, the inaugural meeting of the Commission included a reminder from Charles Haughey, the then parliamentary secretary to the Minister for Justice, which incorporated the following statement: '[that] there can be no final solution of the problem created by itinerants until they are absorbed into the general community' (Report of the Commission on Itinerancy, 1963: 111). The terms of reference of the Report were therefore predetermined from the very beginning. The settlement and absorption of Travellers into the 'settled' community was set down as a prerequisite. The Report's terms of reference included the following:

> to enquire into the problem arising from the presence in the country of itinerants in considerable numbers;
>
> to examine the economic, educational, health and social problems inherent in their way of life;
>
> to consider what steps might be taken;
>
> to provide opportunities for a better way of life for itinerants;

to promote their absorption into the general community; pending such absorption, to reduce to a minimum the disadvantages to themselves and to the community resulting from their itinerant habits;

to improve the position generally; and

to make recommendations.

(Report of the Commission on Itinerancy, 1963: 110)

In reality, every facet of the 1963 Report was turned against the notion of the survival or reinforcement of Traveller culture. In fact the conclusions reached by the Report were to provide a justification for the exact opposite. The Report's goal was the settlement of Travellers on the grounds that their way of life was no longer socially or economically viable. The continuance of the Traveller way of life was seen as a hindrance to the modernisation and economic expansion of Ireland. Since Travellers inhabited land which was targeted for development, their camps were considered a hindrance to progress. Traveller camps were also thought to be a hindrance to foreign investment, and the elimination of these camps was considered a panacea for the growing tensions over land use between Travellers and the 'settled' community. The 'settlement' of Travellers therefore was seen as another rung of the national project of economic modernisation, a project initiated in 1958 by the Irish state's First Programme for Economic Expansion.

> For both social and economic reasons it is clearly undesirable that a section of the population should be isolated and follow a way of life which is harsh, primitive and of low economic value both to those who follow it and to the nation, and, most important, which tends to create a closed and separate community which will become increasingly inferior to the rest of the national population and from which it will be increasingly difficult to escape.
>
> (Report of the Commission on Itinerancy,1963: 104)

The Report therefore presented Traveller settlement as beneficial for the Irish population as a whole, the Traveller community notwithstanding. Settlement would be the first step in an inclusionary project comprising 'rehabilitation' and their hoped-for eventual 'absorption' into the 'settled community'.

The Report equated Traveller poverty with itinerancy or nomadism at every opportunity and the settlement of Travellers was presented as a boon for them, such was the perceived squalor of their existence. Arguments for settlement were supported by descriptions of Travellers' allegedly appalling living conditions. Applications for houses from Travellers were to be given priority as the Traveller community 'were living in totally unfit and overcrowded conditions' (1963: 61). The Report itself was compiled primarily by non-Travellers and did not attempt any sociological or anthropological understanding of Traveller culture. Amongst the sources of information listed as contributing to the Report were visits to itinerant encampments in Ireland and oral evidence as received from local gardaí, local officials and local residents. Most revealing of all is the fact that the Report did not pronounce judgement on any of the reasons why some Travellers lived in destitute circumstances. Neither did it critique the external factors in Irish society that contributed to discrimination against this then nomadic group in the spheres of health, accommodation and education, or the poverty of structural resources at the state's disposal so that disadvantage might be tackled. The Report noted that the Traveller way of life was different to that of the 'settled' community in so far as Travellers appeared to have little involvement in most of the major institutions of Irish society. Any charges that the conclusions of the Report amounted to a policy of settlement and absorption or were discriminating against the cultural ethos of Travellers were obviated by the assertion that the overwhelming majority of Travellers themselves were in favour of settlement, this despite the fact that no Traveller actually sat on the Commission.

Perhaps the strongest justification of all for the settlement and assimilation of Travellers lay in the Report's lack of any meaningful analysis of what constituted Traveller history or culture, particularly their long history of nomadism as evidenced in the very nomenclature the group assigned to their own community. The Report situated Traveller history and ethnogenesis anywhere between the 'last century' and a 'few centuries' ago (1963: 34). Traveller ethnogenesis was thus firmly situated within the context of colonial dispossession, thereby absolving the Irish government of any blame for the Traveller problem. Social policy in relation to Irish Travellers in the modern Irish state has been linked to their perceived status as a distinct group within Irish society. Perhaps the most significant statement in the Report then was the following, where the Commission failed to recognise that there even was such an entity as a Traveller community: 'Itinerants (or travellers as they prefer themselves to be called) do not constitute a single homogenous group, tribe or community within the nation, although the settled people are inclined to regard them as such. Neither do they constitute a separate ethnic group' (1963: 37).

Having provided extensive 'justifications' for the rightness of a settlement programme for Travellers and its mutual benefits for both Travellers and the settled community, the Report went on to outline a range of more stringent legal measures by which its proposed assimilationist policies might be enforced. The inducement for settlement would be reinforced by increased legal penalties relating to the straying of animals, begging and the use of tents and wagons. Legal penalties were also instigated to curb nomadism, including the necessity for Travellers to sign on for unemployment benefit more frequently than the settled population and increased penalties for the existence of illegal encampments, encampments in which the majority of Travellers lived at this period (1963: 104). The Report recommended the setting up of Itinerant Settlement Committees, whose remit it would be to help Travellers to settle in local communities. The Report of the Commission on Itinerancy is undoubtedly the most influential public policy document ever written about Travellers in Ireland. It marks the beginning of a purposeful 'examination' of Travellers in both the public and academic spheres. It was the catalyst for an assimilationist ethos and would prove a watershed for local government because it heralded a new penalisation of the nomadic lifestyle. The decades since the 1960s have seen the systematic blocking off of traditional campsites and a widespread failure to implement state guidelines on culturally appropriate accommodation for Travellers, factors which have in effect acted as the death knell for nomadism on any large scale. Modern sociological and anthropological studies relating to Irish Travellers have focused primarily on theorisations incorporating social identity, ethnicity, nomadism and its counterpoint, sedentarism. Ethnicity theory as applied to Irish Travellers in the modern era, and as developed by the Gmelches (1976), O'Connell, (1994a); Hancock and McVeigh (1992) and Okely (1983), has until very recently tended to follow the socio-constructionist approach as originally theorised by anthropologists such as Barth (1969) and as focusing on the social construction of difference. The most recent work in this area (Belton, 2005) has explored Traveller and Gypsy ethnicity as linked with Traveller-settled interaction, socio-economic conditions, legislative developments and the increased visibility of Traveller and Gypsy populations in the urban setting. It is noteworthy too that modern-day theorisations of anti-Traveller and anti-Gypsy racism in the European context have been accompanied by a new theorisation of the way in which Travellers have been constructed in Ireland, particularly since the foundation of the Irish state (Helleiner, 2000; MacLaughlin, 1995).

MacLaughlin (1995) links the exclusionary discourse as applied to Irish Travellers to similar discourses in the history of European nationalism and colonialism. He argues that the bourgeois nationalism of nineteenth century Ireland deliberately constructed the Travelling community as the 'Other', intentionally excluding the same community from Irish identity as defined by the emerging state.

> On the one hand, Irish nationalism, simply considered as a struggle for control of territory, has striven to control population and to produce an Irish 'people' as a political community. On the other hand the Irish nation was forged as a historical system of exclusions and dominations. It became a place where the patriarchal values of the rural bourgeoisie occupied pride of place.
>
> (MacLaughlin, 1995: 72)

An anti-Traveller racism that was once 'deeply embedded in the social fabric and agrarian history of Ireland' (1995: 73) has acquired new adherents in Irish towns and villages with the increased urbanisation of Ireland. This racism, like sedentarism, is rooted in the belief that the way of life of Travellers is an anachronism and a throwback to a less civilised era in Irish history. It is this racism, MacLaughlin argues, that is at the root of the economic, social and geographical exclusion of Travellers from Irish society.

Helleiner (2000), an anthropologist, uses archival research as well as existing biographies to reconstruct aspects of the history of Irish anti-Traveller racism. She also analyses how Travellers have engaged with this racism which acts to exclude them while simultaneously working to recreate their own identity and distinctive way of life within the constraints which society imposes on them. She reconstructs the directions taken by anti-Traveller racism from the turn of the century to the period of her fieldwork, which she undertook while living in a Traveller halting site in Galway city between 1986 and 1987. She argues that the true nature of the historical relationship between the Travelling and settled communities has been obscured by the tendency on the part of settled community spokespeople and political representatives 'to collapse the past into an ever-receding present' (2000: 50). She also questions the claims by these representatives that tensions between

Travellers and non-Travellers are a relatively recent phenomenon. The ongoing denial of a longer history of anti-Traveller prejudice has supported 'dominant models of an anti-racist and homogeneous post-colonial Irish nation' (2000: 52).

In addition to examining the dynamics of this prejudice within a modern socio-anthropological framework, Helleiner interrogates the ways in which anti-Traveller racism has been historically produced and reproduced within the wider processes of colonialism, nation-building and capitalist development. In her discussion of these processes she particularly explores how anti-Traveller racism was articulated within the wider constructions and social relations engendered by class, generation and gender. She locates anti-class-based Traveller racism within the context of changing agrarian relations within Ireland at the end of the nineteenth century and the attendant emergence of a nationalism associated with what Foster termed 'rural embourgeoise-ment' (1988: 439).

Anti-Traveller racism in Helleiner's view is an example of a long-standing and endogenous Irish racism, one which predates the more recent rise in anti-immigrant and refugee racism. Travellers differ from colonised indigenous populations elsewhere because they have not been constructed as racially 'Other'. Stories relating to the question of Traveller origins told about and by Travellers have however focused not on where they are from so much as on when and why they emerged as a distinct group within Ireland. This emphasis on the when and the why has meant that the imputed origins of Travellers as incor-porated in the many differing origins accounts have often been 'deeply stigmatising' and thus central to the reproduction of anti-Traveller racism (Helleiner, 2000: 30).

# 4 Theoretical perspectives and the Irish context

The concept of the 'Other' or Otherness has been explored through a diverse array of discourses including the historical, the socio-cultural, the anthropological, the psychoanalytic (see Freud, 1938, 1950a, 1950b, 1957, for example), the linguistic and the philosophical (see Lévinas, 1996; Volf, 1996). While the question of the 'Other' or Otherness may have not have been a term which carried much significance in Irish academic circles during the 1950s and 1960s when folklorists such as Seán McGrath were writing, it can be said with little fear of contradiction that it was the search for Otherness, albeit Irish and Gaelic and primarily through the reclamation of the folklore and tradition-rich heritage of Ireland's Irish-speaking regions, which was in reality the fundamental impulse underpinning much of the valuable work undertaken by the Irish Folklore Commission and its devoted collectors.

'Othering', 'difference' and how difference is constructed came to the fore as a question in Cultural Studies particularly during the second half of the twentieth century. It is an issue with which social and academic analysts continue to have a strong engagement, partly as a consequence of the increasingly globalised nature of the world, one where human migration is an issue of considerable social and political significance. Of particular interest to academics who have recognised the importance of this question of Otherness has been a re-engagement with the manner whereby aspects of the Enlightenment and the formation of European/Western identity were heavily predicated on the articulation and creation of the 'Other'. This analysis has included an examination of the role which ideology (see Eagleton, 1991; Said, 1993) played in the internalisation of values that accompanied colonialism and the legitimisation of ideas about the 'Other' so that these ideas appeared 'natural'.

Many theorists have identified the concept of Otherness and 'difference' as essential to the very question of meaning itself. Otherness and the way in which 'otherness' or 'difference' elucidates meaning has dominated French thought especially, where a linguistic and structural analysis of otherness was attempted by de Saussure at the turn of the twentieth century. French analyses of Otherness have focused on the philosophic, the linguistic and the psychoanalytic, in particular. De Saussure (1915) Lacan (1977) and Derrida (1974, 1978, 1982) all became dominant influences on the cultural movements known as structuralism and post-structuralism, movements for which the analysis of the relational and binary aspects of the question of Otherness were of primary importance.

The French theorisation of the Otherness question highlighted the necessity for 'difference', a difference without which meaning itself cannot exist. Meaning depends on the difference between opposites, particularly those oppositions which are binary e.g. black/white, masculine/feminine, etc. It is possible to understand what black means, because it can be contrasted with its opposite – white. This view of 'difference' or 'otherness' as an element of the human condition which exists prior to meaning came to dominate the thought of many intellectuals who attempted to theorise and conceptualise not only Otherness but the question of the human psyche and its very relationship with society in the twentieth century (see Cixous, 1975; Kristeva, 1982, 1991; Lacan, 1977).

Lacan explored the complexities inherent in any attempt to map the self, the Other and their relationship with reality as produced in any linguistic text. For Derrida, the complexities of the self meant that attempts to define meaning based on the difference between opposites were fraught with the dangers of over-simplification and reductionism. Derrida (1974) attempted to deconstruct the binary oppositions upon which much of Western literary and philosophical debate had been premised and showed that a relationship of power was inherent within the nature of these binaries. Hall (1997) outlined Derrida's deconstruction of these power relationships in the following manner: 'There is always a relation of power between the poles of a binary opposition (Derrida, 1974). We should really write white/black, men/women, masculine/feminine, upper class/ lower class, British/ alien to capture this power dimension in discourse' (1997: 235).

The theorisation of the 'Other' as encompassed through the dialogue that is language was examined by the Russian linguist Mikhail Bakhtin. For Bakhtin the 'Other' was essential to meaning because of the dialogic nature of human interaction. Meaning was dialogic because everything we say or mean is modified by the interaction with another person or 'the Other'. 'The Other' was essential to meaning because 'the word in language is half someone else's. It becomes "one's own" only when … the speaker appropriates the word, adapting it to his own semantic expressive intention (Bakhtin, 1981 [1935]: 293–294).

Psychoanalytic theory's emphasis on the formation of the self also provided certain insights into the formation of 'the Other' and the dialectical relationship that exists between the 'self' and 'the Other' (see Freud's (1938) 'object relations theory'), with a particular emphasis being placed on the unconscious dialogue that takes place between the self and the 'Other', an internalised dialogue which much psychoanalytic theory considered flawed and incomplete. Psychoanalytic theory was used by scholars such as Fanon (1986) to explain racism, arguing that a high proportion of racial stereotyping and violence against the other had its roots in the refusal of the white 'Other' to give due recognition to the black person, or he who had come from 'the place of the other' (see Bhabha, 1996; Hall, 1997).

Perhaps the most significant contribution of psychoanalytic theory to the debate concerning Otherness, however, lies in the insights it furnished into boundary mechanisms and their formation, an area that continues to be explored in the discipline of anthropology. Douglas (1966) and Kristeva (1982) described the negative feelings which accrue from boundary subversion and the disturbance of what is a perceived set cultural order. Kristeva and fellow French scholar Cixous (1975) also used the concept of the 'Other' to theorise on gender relations and what they saw as the primarily troubling discourse that is the binary opposition of man/woman. For Cixous the founding binary opposition of the couple man/woman was an exemplar of the sexist hierarchisation that constituted much of Western thought. Anthropologist Mary Douglas drew on sociological research into symbolic systems by the French scholar Emile Durkheim (1938, 1964) and the French anthropologist Claude Lévi-Strauss (1964, 1971) to argue that social groups impose meaning on the world by organising and classifying things into particular groups.

The notion of the 'Other' was fundamental to this classification process as it was normally defined in the form of binary oppositions. A disturbance of this cultural order was inevitable when hybridity manifested itself, a disturbance applied particularly to materials or groups who were to be liminal or whose status appeared ambiguous. Groups such as Travellers or mulattoes who belonged to the mainstream and were at the same time liminal to it were seen to inhabit an indeterminate, unstable or dangerous cultural locus. Since stable or mainstream cultures required that groups stay in their appointed or classified position they imposed symbolic boundaries to keep their categories 'pure' and reinforce their own meaning and identity. Douglas argued that the response to the transgression of these symbolic boundaries or taboos was an attempt to eradicate that which was considered impure, dirty or out of place. The mainstream society attempted to drive away that which it perceived as impure or abnormal.

This idea was developed further by Kristeva (1982) who saw this rejection in terms of a retreat that was in essence an attempt at purification. Many cultures simply retreated from or exhibited alienating tendencies towards the 'Other' who took the form of foreigners, intruders or those 'others' who were perceived as different and outside the norm. Babcock (1978) further developed this theorisation by analysing the seminal role of the symbolic in boundary relations between that which is considered a 'normal' part of the cultural order and that which is considered 'outside' or Other. Her insights can be seen to be particularly pertinent to the question of settled/Traveller relations as evidenced in Ireland. Babcock argued that the double bind inherent in symbolic boundaries was central to all cultural reproduction since its taboo nature made the 'Other' both attractive and repellent at the same time:

> symbolic boundaries are central to all culture. Marking 'difference' leads us, symbolically, to close ranks, shore up culture and to stigmatise and expel anything which is defined as impure, abnormal. However, paradoxically, it also makes 'difference' powerful, strangely attractive precisely because it is forbidden, taboo, threatening to cultural order … what is socially peripheral is often symbolically centred. (1978: 32)

While the question of Otherness has been theorised across a range of cultural dynamics, particularly as it applies within the realm of the symbolic, less attention has been paid to the way in which theories of the 'self' and 'Other' link to particular cultural and national contexts and within discourses such as racism, colonialism and post-colonialism. What is very evident in the work of theorists who have written on the question of the 'Other' is the primarily negative or disruptive attribution which the 'Other' holds in the development of Western thought. Cultural identities such as those which depict the Traveller, the Jew or the migrant as 'Other' have been formed and legitimated through a complex process that incorporates the representation of these cultural types in both myth and historical discourse. Historical discourse, it can be argued, tends towards the specification of social identities while at the same time frequently presenting these cultural identities in a manner which appears fixed, pre-given or immutable. Yet it can be argued that identity itself is a form of myth. Historians like Healy (1992) have highlighted the problematic that is the concept of identity as presented through historical discourse: 'History is not some unmediated story of events. It is a construct, often a narrative of interested parties who seek to prove a thesis of how events have been shaped' (1992: 15).

The 'Other' as constructed in the neo-conservative Western European tradition has generally been perceived in negative terms. The culture of the 'Other' ('their culture') is perceived as different from that of the 'us' in myriad ways including religion, race, behaviour, language, age, gender etc., traits that generally embody negativity as defined by the fictive homogeneity that is the 'us'. Contemporary studies of the 'Other' as situated within a historical or materialist context draw to a large extent on Edward Said's (1978, 1986, 1993) work on Orientalism. In this work the relationship between the Orient and the Western world rests on a discursive formation of the Orient as 'Other', a formation that was invested in both materially and culturally by the colonial powers of the West. The creation of the 'Other' as a zone of differentiation was in many ways the means by which an identity for Europe was created and installed. 'Nations themselves are narrations', wrote Said in his book *Culture and Imperialism* (1993: xiii). The formation of colonial and imperial attitudes towards the Orient was one of the methods used by both the colonisers and the colonised 'to assert their own identity and the existence of their own history' (1993: xiii). European culture and politics cooperated in the nineteenth and early twentieth century to justify the colonial project so that the identity of Europe and the Western world was, in many ways, articulated and installed through the creation of the 'Other'.

Adorno and Horkheimer (1973) used both Marxist and psychoanalytic theory to explain the central role that the Enlightenment project played in the construction of the 'Other', the development of the 'nation-state' and the establishment of European identity through a process of differentiation. In *Dialectic of Enlightenment* (1972), they exposed the double bind which, as they perceived it, lay at the very heart of the Enlightenment project. The Enlightenment promulgated humanism, universalism, rationalism and the virtue of reason. However, reason, as theorised by Adorno and Horkheimer, was a two-edged sword. It was the instrument through which humanity could free itself from nature and yet it was simultaneously the means by which Europe subjected the 'Other' to domination.

> The Enlightenment spawned both the rational and the irrational as exemplified in 'new' and discriminatory attitudes towards 'Others' such as a range of migratory peoples and the Jews. The Enlightenment of modern times advanced from the very beginning under the banner of radicalism; this distinguishes it from any of the earlier stages of demythologisation. When a new mode of social life allowed room for a new religion and a way of thinking, the over-throw of the old classes, tribes and nations was usually accompanied by that of the old gods. But especially when a nation (the Jews, for example) was brought by its own destiny to change to a new form of social life, the time-honored customs, sacred activities, and objects of worship were magically transferred onto heinous crimes and phantoms. (Cahoone 1996: 167)

While promulgated as a 'civilising' and 'radical' project the Enlighten-ment was also conservative. While all peoples could, in theory, share power, the new democracy was predicated on the premise that they abided by the rules that defined the dominant group. Rules were used to define and construct the 'Other', a process which elucidates the heavy debt that Western imperialism owes to the philosophy of the Enlightenment. Imperialism as implemented by the West involved the creation of a myth about the coloniser and the colonised, a myth that included the personae of the 'us' (the coloniser) and the 'them' (the colonised). By focusing on a range of individual works which defined the Orient, Said (1993) analysed the manner in which the Western powers overcame some of the resistance to their colonising projects. He found that a mutually enhancing relationship had been created between culture and the imposition of empire whereby countries engaged in imperialistic projects defined the superior culture as belonging to the dominant nation or state, differentiating the 'us' from the 'them' with an accompanying xenophobia. Culturally, this was achieved through the concept of the 'Other', a process whereby the colonised country was represented through the language and ideas of the coloniser. Said (1986) says that the colonised were left 'to assert a dignified self-identity in opposition to a discourse which defines them as, variously, barbarian, pagan, ape, female; but always subordinate and inferior' (1986: 7).

Eagleton (1991) elucidated the power of ideology in the internalisation of imperial values by subject peoples, a process that achieved a certain legitimacy because of its being made to appear natural, universal, obvious and unquestionable. Ideology, incorporating the coloniser/colonised myth, justified imperialism, an imperialism that was frequently couched in terms of a religious, moral or civilising enterprise. 'What persuades men and women to mistake each other from time to time for gods or vermin is ideology' (Eagleton, 1991: xiii).

The written record of the coloniser often depicted the colonised as being grateful for the imperialist project which had 'saved' them from barbarism or oppression. The imposition of imperialistic ideology and myth was also achieved by the constant repetition of certain national representations and stereotypes, as happened in the case of Ireland and the Irish people. The discursive image of Travellers as defined by the 'settled' community cannot be divorced from a tradition of anti-Irish prejudice that has strong roots in the colonial history of Ireland. As Irish people Travellers were subject to the same cultural conditioning and discursive stereotyping as others. The colonial tradition made no distinction between Travellers and other Irish people with the result that Travellers remained largely invisible in the historical record. Modern day debates concerning Travellers' cultural legitimacy and Travellers' rights return almost invariably to the question of Travellers' origins and what evidence is available in Irish historical records. The most prevalent view of Travellers' origins also situates them firmly within the framework of Ireland's colonial history. More often than not they are considered to be a people who left a previously settled existence as a consequence of the dislocation that was an inevitable outcome of the colonial project. The negative stereotyping of Irish Travellers which became dominant in the public discourse of the latter part of the twentieth century in particular can arguably be viewed as an extension of a deeply inculcated anti-Irish tradition, a more extreme version of the anti-Irish 'Othering' tradition which existed during the centuries of British colonisation. The 'Othering' of Irish Travellers as evidenced in modern Ireland can, as with the Othering of groups such as the Jews in Europe, also be linked to the formation of the new nation-state in Ireland.

A process whereby the Irish people came face to face with the self-definition of their national identity occurred with the formation of the new nation-state in twentieth century Ireland. A very deliberate political agenda had underwritten representations of Ireland, as produced by the British, and as current in the pre-independence era. The British had 'translated' the Irish using self-interested representations that were primarily negative and essentialist. Curtis (1984) and Peart (2002) have demonstrated the way in which the agents of English colonisation had both the power and authority to impose a representation of the 'Other' on the Irish that was self-interested. From the earliest times, nomadism, beggary, backwardness, superstition (later Popery), anarchy, sexual profligacy and violence have been portrayed as general characteristics of the Irish by those who 'othered' them. Strabo, whose geography dates from the first century AD and who wrote in the classical literary tradition of the time, used elements of fantasy that depicted Ireland in a pejorative light. Some of the earliest critical views of the Irish were a consequence of the Church's wish to establish greater orthodoxy in practice throughout Western Europe. This became intermeshed with more materialist, colonial ambitions. Leerssen (1996) outlines how the bull Laudabiliter issued by Pope Adrian IV in 1155 acted to condone English territorial ambitions in Ireland. The desire to reform Irish morals and imbue Irish Church affairs with increased orthodoxy meant that the English presence in Ireland under the stewardship of Henry II was envisaged as a lesser evil:

> [ut pro dilatandis ecclesie terminis, pro vicorium restringendo decursu, pro corrigendis moribus et virtutibus inserendis, pro Christiane religionis augmento, insulam ille ingrediaris.]

> that you should enter that island for the purpose of enlarging the boundaries of the church, checking the descent into wickedness, correcting morals and implanting virtues, and encouraging the growth of the faith in Christ. (Cited in Leerssen, 1996: 34)

Negative attitudes on religious grounds towards indigenous Church structures were common justifications for conquest and persecution at this juncture in Europe generally. The works of the Anglo-Norman churchman Giraldus Cambrensis who wrote his treatises *Topographica Hibernica* and *Expugnatio Hibernica* in the late 1180s acted as a religious justification for the invasion of Ireland. In much the same way as Grellmann, Cambrensis created a prototype of the negative Irish 'other' that was to last for centuries. His taxonomy of the cultural attributes which defined the typical Irish person cast a long shadow over English perceptions of the Irish. He considered the Irish to be inferior in every respect to their Norman colonisers and classified their barbarity in both economic and social terms. He considered the nomadic pastoral (herding) economy of the Irish to be inferior to that of their English counterparts and castigated their social customs, including their sense of dress and their preference for beards and long hair. The marriage customs and religious practices of the Irish came in for partic- ular condemnation, indicating that he found it necessary to undermine the widespread European view of Ireland as a centre for civilisation and learning: 'This is a filthy people, wallowing in vice. Of all peoples it is the least instructed in the rudiments of the faith. They do not pay tithes or first fruits or contract marriages. They do not avoid incest' (cited in Curtis, 1984: 5).

Other characteristic tenets of the Irish character in Giraldus's view were their animal-like natures, including slyness, nomadism, treachery and a repugnance for rules. It is fascinating to observe the consistency with which such stereotypes, as applied to Irish people generally, were subsequently transferred from the majority Irish population onto the Traveller 'Other':

> This people then is one of forest-dwellers and inhospitable; a people living off beasts and like beasts; a people that yet adheres to the most primitive way of pastoral living. For as humanity progresses from the forest to the arable fields, and thence towards village life and civil society, this people, spurning agricultural exertions, having all too little regard for material comfort and a positive dislike of the rules and legalities of civil intercourse, has been able neither to give up nor to abandon the life of forests and pastures which it has hith- erto been living. (Cited in Leersen, 1996: 35)

These aforementioned traits all coalesced in a reductionist archetype of the Irish as an essentially corrupt and sensual people who had an inher- ited propensity for degeneracy. In addition to being considered barbarous and uncontrollable, the Irish were also represented as morally suspect and criminally deviant in the writings of those tasked with the colonial project, including Sir Philip Sidney and the poet Edmund Spenser. Sidney damned the entire Irish populace in the following terms:

> Surely there was never people that lived in more misery than they do, not it should seem of worse minds, for matrimony among them is not regarded in effect than an conjunction between unreasonable beasts, perjury, robbery and murder counted allowable. Finally, I cannot find that they have any conscience of sin; for neither find I a

place where it should be done, nor any person able to instruct them in the rules of a Christian. (Cited in Johnson, 1980: 15)

Discursive techniques as outlined by Said in *Orientalism* and as employed in stereotypes such as those promulgated by Sidney can be seen as part of a technique employed to subdue the colonised. By describing the colonised through the use of rigid representations which depicted them as inferior, it seemed possible to 'know' the Irish and 'manage' them in some way. Knowledge and power were inextricably linked in this form of stereotyping, which also served to strengthen the self-image of the coloniser and justify the colonial project in terms of intervention and civilisation. The subduing of the resistance on the part of the colonised often entailed brutality and killing. Resistance to colonisation on the part of the Munster Irish, whether military or cultural – in the form of the maintenance of Gaelic customs – was met with murder, as outlined by Sir Humphrey Gilbert, military governor of Munster and a half-brother of the better-known Sir Walter Raleigh. Those massacred included many travellers and poets amongst the large population for whom nomadism was a normal part of the Gaelic way of life:

> I slew all those from time to time that did belong to, feed, accompany or maintain any outlaws or traitors; and after my first summoning of a castle or fort, if they would not presently yield it, I would not take it afterwards of their gift, but won it perforce – how many lives soever it cost; putting man, woman and child to the sword. (Cited in Ranelagh, 1981: 86)

Said charts the dehumanisation that accompanied the 'knowing' gaze of the coloniser. This dehumanisation 'justified' colonisation under the cloak of benevolent interference whereby a morally 'superior' 'race' codified a knowledge bank of ideas about a supposedly 'inferior' 'race', a 'justification' that legitimated extermination in much the same terms as the Nazi Holocaust of the mid-twentieth century:

> this Eurocentric culture relentlessly codified and observed everything about the non-European world or presumably peripheral world, in so thorough and detailed a manner as to leave no item untouched, no culture unstudied, no people and land unclaimed. All of the subjugated peoples had it in common that they were considered to be naturally subservient to a superior, advanced,

developed, and morally mature Europe, whose role in the non-European world was to rule, instruct, legislate, develop and at the proper times, to discipline, war against and occasionally exterminate non-Europeans. (Said in Mariani *et al.*, 1989: 6)

The English historian Christopher Hill links the rationalisation of English colonisation in Ireland between the fifteenth and seventeenth centuries with more modern examples of ethnic cleansing and the imposition of new forms of 'civilisation':

A great number of civilised Englishmen of the propertied class in the seventeenth century spoke of Irishmen in tones not far removed from those which Nazis used about Slavs, or white South Africans use about the original inhabitants of their country. In each case the contempt rationalised a desire to exploit. (1970: 113)

The eighteenth century saw the continuation of the Irish stereotype tradition as outlined by leading British intellectuals as a justification for colonisation and exploitation. Peart (2002) links this pattern to an internal dynamic evident in the cultural conditioning that was imposed on Ireland. Ireland and the Irish were viewed in terms of English cultural images that were considered negative – i.e. wild, uncontrollable, barbaric – mirror-images which emanated from the English hierarchical system. The English upper classes, who were the creators and controllers of this discourse, also had little time for the working class in their own country. Historian John Plumb (1969) described English eighteenth century attitudes towards the working class in the following terms: 'It was a general conviction that the working man was a savage, unprincipled brute' (1969: 158).

The English upper class frequently ascribed their alleged superiority to their ancestry and their supposedly superior bloodlines. The nineteenth century also saw the advent of 'scientific' theories of racism, theories which accompanied the British expansion into areas like the British West Indies, Canada, South Africa, Australia and India. The idea of Anglo-Saxon superiority was increasingly seen in terms of pseudo-scientific theories of race as promulgated by scholars and intellectuals and accompanying movements such as Gypsiology (described in Chapter 1 of this volume). Nineteenth century theorists divided the human population into a hierarchy of 'races', frequently on the basis of external physical features. External features were said to hold the clue not only to physically-inherited differences but also to differences in terms of 'nature' or 'character'. Inevitably, Anglo-Saxons were placed at the top of this hierarchy with allegedly more inferior races such as the Celts and the Jews further down. At the bottom of the hierarchy were races such as black people, Gypsies and Travellers. The binaries which accompanied colonial justifications for the 'civilisation' and takeover of certain peoples were part and parcel of these bizarre hierarchies. Anglo-Saxons were symbolic of traits such as thoughtfulness, emotional restraint and a propensity for abiding by the law and clean living. At the other end of the scale, less highly-ranked races such as the Celts were described by anatomists such as John Knox in terms such as the following: 'Furious fanaticism; a love of war and disorder; a hatred for order and patient industry; no accumulative habits; restless, treacherous and uncertain' (cited in Curtis, 1968: 70).

English contempt for the Irish was a part of a continuum that included the advent of a figure known in theatrical circles as the Stage Irishman, a discursive character that was to become the vehicle for the portrayal of Irish people by both Anglo-Irish and English playwrights for the two centuries prior to Irish independence. The stock character of the Stage Irishman portrayed the Irish as ingratiating rogues who encompassed a range of vices including laziness, cunning, drunkenness and mendacity. As with similar archetypal representations of the Irish in previous centuries this figure was trapped within a range of pre-determined character traits that emanated from a very old discursive tradition.

The Stage Irishman was a character who performed as outlined by the discursive tradition. He was both wild and unreliable and exuded an ungovernability that was a further justification for the exploitation that accompanied the English colonial presence in Ireland. That this anti-Irish 'Othering' discourse was exceptionally successful is attested to by Curtis (1984) who examined the evolution of anti-Irish 'Othering', culminating in the infiltration or 'naturalisation' of this discourse within the fabric of the English language itself. Curtis notes that 'The very word Irish is enough to provoke roars of laughter from television studio audiences, and is used in everyday conversation to describe behaviour that is confusing or illogical' (1984: 45). Words like 'paddywagon' and phrases like 'throw a paddy' or 'take the mickey' all attest to the internalisation of anti-Irishness within English so that this discourse has been naturalised within both English and Irish society. By tracing the stereotype tradition that locates Irish identity within a reductionist framework, I have endeavoured to examine the way in which notions of English 'identity' relied on representations of the

Irish as the English 'not-self'. The subaltern position of the Irish in this discourse resulted in their demonisation as a consequence of being discursively constructed according to a series of endemic binarisms. A discursive technique such as that outlined here employs inequities in representational power and stereotypes which become reified so as to perpetuate a sense of absolute difference between the coloniser and the colonised. The reiteration of this stereotyping process for hundreds of years morally strengthened the colonialist enterprise through the continual representation of the colonised as fundamentally inferior.

This discursive tradition can be seen as a form of cultural conditioning, one which inculcated an ideology of domination. Eagleton (1991) explained the process whereby ideology acts to legitimise a form of domination by a political power intent on promoting 'beliefs and values congenial to it' (1991: 5). The dominant power achieved this objective both by naturalising/universalising certain beliefs so that they assumed the status of universal truths and through the denigration and exclusion of any counter-hegemonic ideas that served as a challenge. The inculcation and internalisation of the values of the dominant group utilises the power of subconscious thought by incorporating enticing ideas that are constantly repeated. Tolson (1996) outlines the role of the unconscious in the inculcation of ideology on the part of a subject people:

> Ideology [is] as much unconscious as conscious, as much irrational as rational. That is, if ideology consists of arguments, containing propositions, these don't simply take the form of ideas which we may or may not find convincing. They also have the force of repeated patterns of behaviour in which we more or less unthinkingly participate. (1996: 163)

Ideology's reliance on repeated patterns as encompassed in a reductionist stereotyping tradition is evidenced in writings on the subject of Ireland and the Irish from Cambrensis's twelfth century religiously motivated images to the bizarre racialist categorisations of Knox in the nineteenth century. These writers created a myth which pertained to themselves (the dominant group) and those Others they considered subordinate such as the Irish and those people who were considered inferior on the hierarchical scale. This myth was reiterated constantly so that it became a form of cultural hegemony, internalised by coloniser and colonised alike. That this 'constructed' myth was exceptionally successful was due in no small measure to the reiterative nature of this form of cultural hegemony, a form of hegemony that came to be transferred to other subaltern groups when the project of colonisation had ended. As Gramsci (1971) put it, 'repetition is the didactic means for working on the popular mentality' (1971: 340).

# 5 Mapping 'difference': Irish Travellers and the Questionnaire

I have briefly traced the development of the Irish 'Othering' tradition as encompassed in a reiterative and reductionist discourse because Ireland's history of colonisation has meant that the 'official' version of the Irish people (including Irish Travellers) and Irish history is, it can be argued, itself a form of 'Othering'. Healy's statement regarding the 'manufactured' or mediated nature of much of the historical record can be seen to be particularly pertinent to Irish history: 'History is a construct, often a narrative of interested parties who seek to prove a thesis' (Healy, 1992: 15). That the interpretation of history and definitions of nations or self are the subject of competition or struggle on the part of various contending interests has been outlined by a number of historians. Hawthorn (1994) has outlined the way in which these competing interests condition 'processes of definition (of self and others), perception and interpretation' (1994: 116).

Competing interests in the form of the colonial discourse have also resulted in the probability that a realistic depiction of Ireland as it was in the past is extremely difficult to recreate. The only records that we have – written representations of Ireland as recounted by primarily colonial chroniclers – are confusing and suspect. Discussing the dubious nature of representations of Ireland in both the sixteenth and seventeenth centuries, for example, Kiberd (1995) has pointed out that the 'notion of Ireland' as depicted in the writings of this era can be viewed 'largely as a fiction' (1995: 83). This discursive and often false discourse concerning Ireland and the Irish can, I argue, be extended to encompass an equally discursive depiction of Irish Travellers that is available in Irish popular tradition through the lens of folklore. The primary subject of this book – the discursive image of Travellers as defined by the 'settled' community – is intimately intertwined with this anti-Irish 'Othering' tradition that I have briefly outlined. Travellers were Irish people who were subject to the same cultural conditioning and discursive stereotyping as others. The colonial tradition made no distinction between Travellers and other Irish people with the result that they are largely invisible in the historical record. Travellers are also situated within the historical framework of colonial 'othering' because the dominant view of their origins today is that they are people who left a previously settled existence and are most likely the product of Ireland's colonial past, colonial violence and eviction in particular. In addition to this it can be argued that the negative stereotypes and constructions of Irish Travellers which became dominant in the twentieth century are simply an extension of the anti-Irish 'Othering' tradition which existed during the centuries of British colonisation.

The 'Othering' of Irish Travellers as evidenced in modern Ireland can, as with the Othering of groups such as the Jews in Europe, also be linked to the formation of the new nation-state in Ireland. The formation of the nation-state in twentieth century Ireland involved a new mediation on the part of the Irish people with the question of self-definition. A political agenda had motivated the propaganda-driven representations of the Ireland of the era prior to independence. The English had 'translated' the Irish using self-interested and essentialist representations. However, a new essentialism manifested itself in the discourse of self-identity that appeared in the early years of the twentieth century and on independence. Colonialism's efforts to deracinate, assimilate, and 'civilise' the Irish meant that the new discourse of Irish identity became bound up with notions of authentication rooted in a pre-colonial, prelapsarian past that was equally essentialist. I argue here that this 'new' Irish essentialism which accompanied the discourse of the emergent nation-state employed an ideological framework of 'control' or 'representation' that was quite similar to that which had accompanied British imperialism. This new essentialism was reductive by nature and consequently it obscured the existence of heterogeneity in Irish culture including subaltern groups such as Irish Travellers. As a marginalised and stigmatised group within Irish society Travellers became a useful projective outlet for those stereotypes and types which the 'newly nationalist' Irish population wished to jettison and to categorise as 'not us'.

The 1952 Tinker Questionnaire was one small part of the emergent nation-state's attempt to re-nationalise and 're-Gaelicise' Ireland. The representations of Travellers as outlined in the Irish Folklore Commission material are thus an element of the Irish sense of self and other. They express the contradictory feelings held by those Irish people engaged with the project of nation-building towards their own society and towards the 'others' within that society. The representation of the Traveller as 'Other' can be seen as one element in the expression of the collective conscience of Irish society as it attempted to jettison a long-evolved and often-negative discourse and appropriate a new form of cultural nationalism. Leerssen (1996) has elucidated the importance of a collectively defined identity to the effort of self-definition in the form of nationhood or nationalism:

> A 'nation', which nationalism considers to be the natural unit of human society, is a group of individuals who distinguish themselves, as a group, by a shared allegiance to what they consider to be their common identity; and 'nationality' can be considered as the focus of a nation's allegiance, the idea (indeed, the selfimage) of its common identity, the criterion by which a 'nation' defines itself as such.
>
> (1996: 18)

To understand the emergence of this new cultural nationalism that accompanied the work of the Irish Folklore Commission and projects such as the Tinker Questionnaire, it is necessary to locate this nationalism's emergence within a historical framework. The end of the nineteenth century had seen the growth of Irish nationalism as promulgated by the emerging Catholic class and a consequent challenge to the hitherto governing classes of the Protestant Anglo-Irish ascendancy. This challenge was extended into the cultural sphere where both groups now competed to define what was 'really' Irish through different appropriations of Irish history.

The claims of the Protestant Anglo-Irish ascendancy class had much of their basis in the Celtic Literary Revival. In this movement a pre-colonial Celticism that played down the Ascendancy class's involvement in the structures of colonisation was put forward as the basis for a new Irish cultural nationalism. This Celticism included strong elements of the discourse of Gypsiology discussed in Chapter 1. Indeed Celtic Revivalists like W. B. Yeats, Douglas Hyde and J. M. Synge all had strong leanings towards Gypsiology and the theories discussed therein.

Both the Gypsiologists and the Celticists deplored what they saw as the death of traditional rural life. For them the Gypsies and the rural Irish were repositories of spirituality and mysticism, untainted by the materialism of urban culture. Gypsies and other wanderers as described by the Celticists and Gypsiologists were people who lived in a 'time warp'. They were survivals of an ancient past that was largely unaffected by either colonialism or industrialism. In accordance with this discourse, tinkers, beggars and other wanderers were the true heirs of an older or more traditional Ireland.

Helleiner (2000) says that the artists and intellectuals of the Celtic Literary Revival often used the figure of the wanderer to critique what they saw to be the emerging Ireland. This was an Ireland that in their view was characterised by increased materialism and repressive sexuality as encapsulated in Catholicism. The wandering life as encapsulated in the life of a Traveller was presented as a romantic symbol of escape from the perceived repression and hypocrisy of post-Famine Irish society in plays such as Synge's *The Tinker's Wedding* (1904) and *The Shadow of the Glen* (1910), and Lady Gregory's *The Travelling Man* (1905). Wanderers as depicted in these plays were sometimes a symbol for the position of the Anglo-Irish writer in the then Irish society. This position became increasingly precarious as a different and contradictory understanding of Irish history as envisaged by the hitherto dominated Catholic intelligentsia came to the fore. Irish cultural nationalism became increasingly radicalised with partition and the foundation of the new Irish state.

The new Irish state saw cultural nationalism in different terms to that of the old Anglo-Irish elite. Foster (1988) suggests that one of the central preoccupations of the nascent Irish state was self-definition against Britain in both the political and cultural arenas. Ó Gjolláin (2000) analyses the importance which these 'new' cultural nationalists placed on de-Anglicising Ireland. Douglas Hyde's seminal lecture The Necessity for de-Anglicising Ireland (1892) was a succinct summary of the direction which cultural nationalists would now take. For Ireland to assume a pre-eminent position in literature and the intellectual sphere, it was necessary for Ireland to re-Gaelicise itself. In Hyde's view, Daniel O'Connell had overseen the death of Gaelic civilisation, 'largely, I am afraid, owing to his example and his neglect of inculcating the necessity of keeping alive racial customs, language and traditions' (Hyde in Ó Gjolláin, 2000: 115). Ireland's rich Gaelic past would be the font for this new cultural nationalism, because 'though the Irish race does not recognise it just at present', it was this past that had prevented the Irish from being fully assimilated into an Anglocentric world view (Hyde in Ó Gjolláin, 2000: 115). Hyde's views on the nexus between folklore and nation-building were reflected in the contemporary thinking of the day. Orvar Lofgren says that 'cultural matrices were freely borrowed across national frontiers'. matrices that made up 'an international cultural grammar of nationhood, with a thesaurus of general ideas about the cultural ingredients needed to form a nation' (Lofgren, 1993: 217). This international 'grammar' was one that could be transformed into a specific national lexicon. Folklore was one of the means whereby people could get to know those parts of Ireland where Irish was the vernacular and where Gaelic culture was still in the ascendancy. Folklore could also act as the inspiration for a new literature, which, unlike the Anglo-Irish revival, would be an 'authentic' literature that was 'true' to its roots of origin. The establishment of structures for the preservation of folklore, then, became ancillaries to the new state's attempt to 're-Gaelicise' Ireland. The Folklore of Ireland Society (An Cumann le Béaloideas Éireann) was founded in Dublin in 1927 by a number of prominent cultural activists including the Kerry writer Pádraig Ó Siochfhradha and Séamus Ó Duilearga, the editor of its journal, *Béaloideas*. By the end of the 1930s the Society had about a thousand members, the bulk of whom were members of the emerging Catholic middle class. These included several dozen volunteer fieldworkers who in their spare time tracked down and recorded local storytellers. The focus of the Irish Folklore Commission was on the recording of Ireland's stories, popular beliefs and traditions, but the primary locus for this collecting was what were perceived to be the 'culture-rich' Gaelic speakers of the Gaeltachtaí or Irish-speaking districts.

Various possibilities for Travellers' origins and existence as a separate group were posited in the folklore of the 'settled' community as recorded by the Irish Folklore Commission's 1952 Tinker Questionnaire. What these various possibilities had in common however was that Travellers were perceived to be a group whose identity was concomitant with that of the majority Irish community. Although it was acknowledged that Travellers inhabited a separate locus within Irish society, little credence was given to the evidence that this separate existence might have included a separate and unique culture. The all-encompassing nature of the nationalist discourse that accompanied the foundation of the nation-state obscured complexities relating to the history and image of certain minority groups, including Travellers. Lee (1989) makes it evident that post-independence Ireland sought knowledge but was reluctant to seek knowledge about itself. Rather than engaging in any real analysis of Irish life, the new state participated instead in a public myth of a traditionally harmonious Catholic Ireland, a myth that was itself a response to a particular political climate and a particular historical inheritance. The creation of the Free State in 1922 held the potential for a section of the Irish people to create a new identity for themselves, one which would distinguish them and separate them from the British. The attempt to do this was flawed, however, and any expectations for extensive social and economic change in the era following partition were not realised.

It can be argued that the characteristic which defined the first four decades of the new Irish state above any other was an emphasis on continuity. Little overt change was evident from the society which had existed prior to 1922, a fact that was due in strong part to the tenuous nature of those foundations on which partition and the newly created Free State had been based. In such a climate it was almost inevitable that any radical efforts at change would be seen as profoundly threatening. Breen *et al.* (1990) who provide a good overview of the post-partition period, argue that securing the new nation-state was the most important priority in the post-1922 era where the state could 'see the potential for chaos everywhere' (1990: 2). Consequently the newly-independent state attempted to establish nationalism/republicanism on a basis of mass homogeneity and conformity. McLoughlin (1994) describes some of the negative aspects of this endeavour:

> This sense of Irishness came 'naturally' from the dominance of Catholicism and the 'shared' experience of rural living which bound all Irish people so neatly together into nationhood. The Irish state was established on this coercive basis and all those individuals and groups who did not fit the bucolic image did not belong. This coercive sense of nationhood took away from internal social conflicts and the grounds of social, ideological and political debate were effectively narrowed to issues of national self-determination.
>
> (1994: 85–86)

McLoughlin says that Travellers were viewed both as derivative and deviant from the mainstream in an Irish society whose homogeneity was often stifling. She links the assignation of Travellers as 'other' to similar depictions of other minority groups: 'Joining them in their 'problem' status were various religious groups of Protestant and Jew, as well as separated individuals, deserted wives, single parents (mostly women), homosexuals and even writers and artists. Ireland from the 1920s to the 1980s had no room for diversity, pluralism and heterogeneity' (1994: 87).

When taken as a whole the responses to the Tinker Questionnaire (I provide a copy of the Questionnaire itself as Appendix A to this volume) which I provide a brief overview of here can be seen to form a construct of a particular 'myth' or 'archetype' of Irish Traveller identity, a myth that replicates teleologically the notion of Ireland's colonial history that was in the ascendant in the Ireland of the first half of the twentieth century and a construct which subsumed Traveller identity within its framework. The written depiction of Travellers as outlined in the popular tradition and as transcribed in the Irish Folklore Commission's 1952 Tinker Questionnaire can be viewed as an example of 'Othering' that evolves whereby the subaltern or 'Other' is represented and 'translated' through the essentialist language of the dominant culture. Essentialism, involving binary articulations and stereotypes, is inevitably reductionist as it obscures any notion of heterogeneity. Essentialism consists of opposition to difference. Its insistence on the fixed or unchanging nature of certain representations is of necessity historically inaccurate as any scope for the cultural evolution of the people 'fixed' within such representations is non-existent. Cheng (1995) has outlined the manner in which nationalist movements attempting to evolve away from colonialism frequently fall into the same trap as that in which they were previously entangled. In attempting to invert the reductionist stereotypes previously attributed to them under colonialism they revert to a reverse ethnocentrism based on stereotypes which are by nature perennial and unchanging:

> This binary pattern is a trap that essentialises and limits representation to precisely its own terms, terms one must play by if one accepts the binary oppositions. In other words if you are trying to prove that you aren't what 'they' say you are, you are judging/arguing by the same rules/categories 'they' are and so you end up reifying/maintaining those categories in place as functional realities; for example if you try to prove that you are more angel than ape ... then you are only reinforcing and reinscribing the terms of a hierarchy that places angels (and Anglos) at the top and 'Negroes' and Orientals near the bottom ... In needing to prove that one is more angelic and less ape-like than the others, one ends up buying into the very terms of a binary hierarchy of Self and Other that needs to label and denigrate the Other (whether 'Negro', Oriental or Irish) as barbaric and subhuman in order to assert the Self's own unquestionably civilised 'culture' and humanity by contrast. (1995: 54)

National self-definition for the Irish becomes a form of denial by virtue of the fact that they are trapped within a discourse as initially created by the colonisers. One of the easiest options for the nativist tradition in such a situation is to direct this reverse ethnocentrism towards the

Other in its own society. Travellers were hitherto one of the few very identifiable 'Others' or subalterns onto whom this altered ethnocentrism could be transferred. The analysis of the way in which Travellers have historically been represented or 'imaged' by the settled community in Ireland is important as collective representations or the attachment of particular labels or identities to a group play a large role in shaping responses to that group even today. Today most Irish people are presented with representations of Travellers though the media and the arts. In the earlier part of the twentieth century it was primarily through the lens of the oral tradition or folklore that people formed their collective representation of Travellers and other communities who were considered as 'Other'. Mayall (2004) has outlined how important the question of representation and image-making is in attempting to understand the reaction of the mainstream community to those groups considered as marginal:

> Stereotypical images of groups affect how they are seen, how they are treated and the expectations that are held of them in terms of behaviour and abilities. Indeed, the connection between images and responses, especially in their negative and hostile forms, is a major theme and argument in host-immigrant studies in general. Many commentators have linked the hostile responses to Jews with the presence of anti-Semitic stereotypes in culture and language, and a similar connection is made between representations of the barbaric Irish and anti-Irish sentiment, and the crude racial imagery of blacks and other minority groups and overt racism. (2004: 15)

Ian Hancock (1992), a Roma activist and writer, goes so far as to say that this persistent and hostile imagery created by outsiders is at the core of the often tense societal relationship that exists between traditionally nomadic (i.e. Gypsy) and non-Gypsy communities. Not only is it the case that stereotypes give rise to hostile imagery, the reverse can happen also; and pre-existing prejudices can give rise to the further evolution of prejudice. Bohdan Zawadzki (1948) in an early analysis of the functioning of prejudice described stereotyping as a rationalisation of reductionism against the group as opposed to the individual: 'In order to rationalise one's hatred against a whole group rather than against a single individual, the prejudiced person must resort to the use of stereotypes in his thinking' (1948: 130).

The importance of representations or images lies in the fact that they may be the only source of information about a group that people who may not have direct contact with the group ever receive. Mayall (2004) outlines the responsibility that lies with the creators of a particular representation:

> Images, created for the most part by outsiders, provide a basis for how we interpret our experience, and pre-informed information and knowledge affect our perceptions and judgement by providing a normative, or standard, picture. Images themselves are rarely value-free, and the judgements they contain are often those that will generally be accepted. There can be little doubt that negative images reinforce negative responses and that there is some connection between racial stereotyping and discriminatory treatment ... Because the stereotypes of a group cover every aspect of their life, behaviour, appearance and propensities, it is possible to find confirmation and justification for any action, hostile or favourable, by calling up the required image. (2004: 17)

Labelling and representation have seemingly always lain at the heart of majority–minority relations, the imperialist expansions of the nineteenth century being a prime exemplar. Said (1978) warns of the dangers in underestimating the power of representation as incorporated in the text: 'It seems a common human failing to prefer the schematic authority of a text to the disorientations of direct encounters with the human' (1978: 93).

Representation is a core function of every written text because 'in any instance of at least a written language, there is no such thing as a delivered presence, but a re-presence, or representation' (1978: 12). Textual authority relegates reality as it really is and a textual representation is superimposed on this reality instead. The word of the stranger speaks on behalf of the subaltern or those in the subordinate position: 'this articulation is the prerogative, not of a puppet-master, but of a genuine creator, whose life-giving power represents, animates, constitutes the otherwise silent and dangerous space beyond familiar boundaries' (1978: 57).

Representations of Travellers as outlined in Irish popular tradition are therefore an element of both the Irish Self and that which is perceived as Other in Irish society. Images of Travellers as expressed in Ireland's public culture express the contradictory feelings which Irish people have towards the Other in their society and towards themselves. Since the representations of the 'Other' or Travellers are by nature a constructed 'represence' they can probably tell us a lot more about

Irish society and its attitudes than they can about Travellers. Bhabha (1990) reiterates this point when he makes the observation on this narrative aspect of representation that 'As narrator she is narrated as well' (1990: 301). In narrating the 'other', one is inadvertently narrating the 'self', including the latter's insecurities, ambivalences and contradictions. Durkheim (1954) pointed to the *sui generis* nature of such collective imaginaries. Collective representations generate an 'independent' reality that cannot be wholly explained with reference to facts about individuals. They are thus partially autonomous in nature and have the ability to 'live their own lives', form syntheses of all kinds and even engender new representations.

It is important to do justice to the compelling and (often) ambivalent nature of collective ideation or imagery in a globalised world where emerging technologies ensure that images and representations can be transferred at incredible speed. The significance of new forms of communication has combined with a number of developing traditions in the social and human sciences to ensure the increased significance of the question of collective representations. There is a growing acknowledgement of the necessity to study both language and meaning in terms of their status as cultural constructs as opposed to their position as 'natural' aspects of a material 'reality' (see Hall, 1997).

Durkheim (1954) found that the common denominator between members of a society is their collective conscience or that range of beliefs and ideas that are collectively shared by that society. These collective ideations tend to be expressed in symbols that are commonly recognised and through meanings that are collectively understood. It follows that collective ideations operating in modern society, including morality, politics, education and the mass media, ought to be seen in terms of symbolic classifications. These symbolic classifications are organised in terms of shared collective representations, 'social facts' and certain shared perspectives that make up the 'superstructure' of society. A wide diversity of sources combine to contribute to a society's collective understanding of things and events, sources that are independent of the particular societal conditions in which individuals find themselves. Making visible the invisible points to the role of stereotype as construct. Hall (1997) emphasises this facet of stereotyping which he terms the 'poetics' or 'politics' of stereotypes:

> The important point is that stereotypes refer as much to what is imagined in fantasy as to what is perceived as 'real'. And what is visually produced, by the practices of representation, is only half the

story. The other half – the deeper meaning – lies in what is not being said, but is being fantasised, what is implied but cannot be shown. (1997: 263)

Inherent in the symbolic process that stereotyping entails and outlined by Hall is a gross inequality of power, a power that is usually directed against the subordinate or excluded group. Binary oppositions such as Us/Them and Self/Other involve the exercise of symbolic power through representational practices. Hall identifies this power as representing someone or something in a certain way – within a certain 'regime of representation' as a form of 'symbolic violence' (1997: 259). Peart (2002), commenting on the way Ireland was represented or 'translated' in British colonial texts, cites Cronin's succinct summary of the symbolic power inherent in representational practices, a power that frequently has a political agenda: 'The power of representation is that it can affect the way we perceive people, events, and the past as well as the present. Representation can make the foreign familiar but it can also make the foreign even more foreign' (Cronin, 1996: 95).

Nowadays it is the media, primarily, who filter Irish public perceptions and the 'collective conscience' of Irish society. This is a relatively new vehicle for the collective ideation of Irish culture, however, and until the mid-twentieth century there is no doubt that the oral tradition played a very significant role in the formation of collective ideas and representations of Travellers and other communities who were considered as 'Other'. The reasons for the primarily discursive 'collective ideation' of Irish Travellers as evidenced in Irish culture are not immediately obvious. Travellers today score high on all indices of poverty and exclusion, a marginalisation that is often attributed in part to the long history of prejudice against this community. Why a relatively tiny indigenous group who have lived in Ireland for centuries are 'Othered' to such a degree is in many ways difficult to comprehend, as was outlined in the 1970s by S. B. Gmelch (1974), one of the few anthropologists to study Irish Travellers:

The picture that emerges .... is one of a deprived, misunderstood and powerless group living on the periphery of Irish society. Of special interest is the lack of any genetic basis for their persistent exclusion and deprivation .... their rejection by the settled community is not based on colour or 'racial' considerations as it is with American Indians, native Blacks in South Africa or aborigines in Australia. Nor is it perpetuated by notions of ritual impurity or

contamination as it is with untouchables in India or the Eta
(Burakumin) in Japan ... The Travellers' socially and economically
deprived status in Irish society is not based on or perpetuated by religious antagonisms as is the case with the Catholic minority in
Northern Ireland. And lastly their rejection is not based on economic
or political competition as it is with many such groups in Asia ... Irish
Travellers are both poor and powerless. In a society such as Ireland
where equality is a fundamental value, the persistent deprivation and
exploitation of the Travelling People appears an anomaly. (1974: 6)

The constructions of Irish Travellers as depicted in the Irish Folklore
Commission material which are considered here show the processes of
reductionism and essentialism working at their most efficient. Negative
stereotypes attributed to Travellers portray them as an 'outsider' group
whose community's traits include licentiousness, secrecy, dishonesty
and violence, to name but a few perceived shortcomings. Travellers are
represented within a discourse of difference, one which translates them
as a category of cultural 'Other'. They also demonstrate the continuation of what could be that 'surveillant' discourse of objectification that
was an extension of the broader colonial project as relating to the early
1900s in Ireland.

In essence the Travellers or the 'Other within' are now essentialised
or dislocated from their own identities and selves from the outside in.
The ideology of race, the mapping of class, the co-opting of representation, the boundarisation and cordoning off of that which is deemed
'degenerate' or 'inferior' as associated with the Victorian-inspired colonial ideology of the latter 1900s is now happening on Irish soil. Those
essentialisations of Irishness and its fixed representations – primitivism,
infantilism – are no longer circumstantial but have become inculcated
within the very natures of the oppressed themselves. The rationality and
'progressive' ideology of colonisation has already become underwritten
and unquestioned and those constructed as Other have been essentialised out of any real time or existence; from a representational point
of view their mapping or objectification denotes their de-nationalisation,
their exiling from within the frame of reference that is the emergent
nation's imaginary.

Ironically, the contradictions mapped as Other by the Travellers ultimately serve to render them invisible and insignificant on the symbolic
level. This working of discourse or knowledge is that form of repression, the functioning of which Foucault has described as 'a sentence
to disappear; but also as an injunction to silence, an affirmation of

non-existence' (Foucault 1990: 58). Within such a schema, Travellers are assigned the position of subaltern or 'cultural Other' and are subsumed within a reverse ethnocentrism characteristic of the teleological efforts and historical 're-constructionism' of early twentieth century Irish nationalism. This collective representation was reflective of the many stereotypical assumptions concerning Travellers that were common amongst the Irish settled community during the midpoint of the twentieth century, a collective 'ideation' whose central tenets continue to exert a strong influence in modern-day Ireland.

This tendency towards stereotype, reductionism and essentialism is increasingly being targeted by Traveller activists and those who advocate Travellers' rights in an increasingly multicultural Ireland, an Ireland where public calls for dialogue between both communities have become more vociferous on the part of the representatives of Traveller and non-Traveller communities in recent years. The discursive constructions or representations of Travellers contained within the Tinker Questionnaire are so detailed that a number of books could be written on this subject alone. For the purposes of this discussion therefore I highlight some primary aspects of the most significant discourse the Questionnaire's respondents constructed vis-à-vis Travellers – i.e. the signification of Travellers as a morally suspect or degenerate 'Other', a group whose socially exclusive mode of life was a cover for suspicious behaviour and crime and, associated with this, the representation of Travellers as some type of countercultural group. A wide range of reductionist stereotypes were applied to Travellers, many of which were analogous to discursive descriptions of archetypal Travellers/Gypsies in other countries. Cottaar *et al.* (1998) have described this pervasive institutionalisation of such ideas in Europe, even within socio-economic and socio-historical scholarship:

> During the last few decades the negative image of travelling groups among professional historians has only changed slowly. It is not strange to see that in more general overviews of the socioeconomic history of Europe the image is repeated time and again. A good example is the recent book by Henri Kamen (1986) on Western European history in the sixteenth and seventeenth centuries, in which 'poverty', 'beggary', 'vagrancy', 'seasonal migration' and criminality are lumped together point blank. More or less the same mixture can be found in Wehler's (1987) overview of German social history. Travelling people are depicted as aimless

wanderers, whose criminal behaviour forced authorities to adopt cruel repression. (Cottaar et al., 1998: 135)

Travellers in Ireland were accused of a wide range of vices including depravity, sexual immorality, dishonesty, primitivism, filth and violence. In short, they were constructed as the archetypal embodiments of deviance and antisocial behaviour. The discursive construction of Irish Travellers as defined in Ireland was able to draw on two principal well-springs of stereotypical reductionism. These were the negative constructions of Gypsies and Travellers in the European imaginary generally and the long discourse of anti-Irish 'Othering' that had existed in Ireland associated with colonisation, a discourse where the words Irish and Ireland were indelibly linked with immorality, violence, parasitism and deception. To see how sweepingly dismissive attitudes towards the 'archetypal' Gypsy or Traveller as defined by writers such as Grellmann (1787) have infiltrated the European imaginary so as to achieve the full sanction of scholars and the intelligentsia it is necessary only to examine the comments of a professor of psychiatry and criminology at the University of Turin in the early years of the twentieth century. His opinion concerning Gypsies was published by the American Institute of Criminal Law and Criminology in 1918 and it bears striking analogies with the construction of Irish Travellers:

> They are the living example of a whole race of criminals, and have all the passions and all the vices of criminals. They have a horror of anything that requires the slightest application; they will endure hunger and misery rather than submit to any continuous labour whatever; they work just enough to keep from dying of hunger .... they are vain, like all delinquents, but they have no fear or shame. Everything they earn, they spend for drink or ornaments. They may be seen barefooted, but with bright coloured or lace-bedecked clothing, without stockings, but with yellow shoes. They have the improvidence of the savage and that of the criminal as well ... they devour half-putrefied carrion. They are given to orgies, love a noise, and make a great outcry in the markets, they murder in cold blood in order to rob, and were formerly suspected of cannibalism ... this race, so low morally, and so incapable of cultural and intellectual development, is a race that can never carry on any industry, and which in poetry has not got beyond the poorest lyrics.
>
> (Lombroso, 1918: 40)

Stealing is a stereotype which has been associated with Travellers and Gypsies for centuries. Some of the earliest descriptions of 'Egyptians' (Travellers/Gypsies) in Britain linked the survival of nomadic people with stealing. An Acte concyng Egypsyans (1530–1531), issued by Henry VIII, maintained that 'Egyptians' survived by 'using deep, deceitful practises' and by the use of 'greate subtyll and craftye meanes to deceyve the people' including palmistry, robbery and pickpocketing (cited in Mayall, 2004: 68). A woman from County Galway gave sustenance to this stereotypical denunciation of the Travellers:

> An fhaid is a bhíonn siad sa gceanntar bíonn siad ag goid agus ag fuadach. Is fada leis na daoine nó go mbíonn said ag imtheacht.
>
> (Iml. 1256: 27)

> (So long as they are in the locality they are stealing and plundering. The people can't wait until they are leaving.)

A respondent from the Kerry Gaeltacht implied that stealing was a hereditary part of the Travellers' nature:

> Táid tugtha do ghoid, tugtha do bhruid, tugtha do throid is tugtha d'innsint bréag, mar is dual sinnsear dóibh. (Iml. 1255: 272)

> (They are given to stealing and brutality, they are given to fighting and to telling lies as was natural for their ancestors.)

This echoes the Traveller/Gypsy archetype that was created by Grellmann (1787) at the end of the eighteenth century. Grellmann theorised that idleness and laziness were inherent to the Gypsy lifestyle and that it was only through begging and stealing that the majority of Gypsies survived. Concepts such as honour or shame were anathema to them in his view except for the handful of Gypsies who practised vaguely respectable professions such as the Transylvanian gold-panners and some musicians. From the rest of the Gypsy population no one was safe:

> He considered their work to be a smokescreen that made it easier for them to be able to steal things. Gypsy women especially knew precisely how to go about their business: sales talk at the front door and children breaking in at the back. That was why, he insists, they were so eager to visit annual markets. They joined forces then in

gangs; men and women began to disport themselves scandalously to divert tradespeople while others meanwhile picked unattended stalls clean. (Willems, 1997: 54)

Hancock has pointed to the longevity of this stereotype as evidenced by its endurance in police department descriptions of Gypsy society in the US, where the innocent personage of the Gypsy woman continues to be seen as a 'cover' for more elaborate scams: 'The label of 'Gypsy' refers to any family-oriented band of nomads who may be from any country in the world ... The only measure of respect a Gypsy woman can get is based on her abilities as a thief' (Schroeder in Hancock, 1987: 112).

It is likely that there is some truth in some of the allegations regarding stealing and trickery on the part of Travellers, although the stereotype has no doubt magnified the extent of the problem beyond all realistic proportion. As Hancock (1987) has argued, survival in times of poverty has provided justification for petty stealing on the part of many social groups including Travellers and Gypsies:

> Problems which exist today are the result of a continuum of circumstances going back for centuries. Few could argue that there has not been moral justification for subsistence stealing in the past, or that in some places it continues to be necessary, although this is not likely to be taken into consideration in a court of law. Historically, stealing has meant survival, and there are many shopkeepers throughout Europe, even today, who will not serve Gypsies. There are homeowners, too, who will refuse to give Gypsies as much as a glass of water. (1987: 121)

Travellers who pilfered petty items such as a few turnips or potatoes from a field were normally only doing so to meet their subsistence needs. Cottaar *et al.* (1998), citing the German context, have pointed out that the scholarly tendency to use criminal records to construct a picture of the past has given credence to the stereotype that nomadic groups and crime were inextricably linked. They refer to recent socio-historical studies on migratory groups in Germany and Austria (e.g. Schubert and Schubert, 1983) which conclude that migratory groups in general were criminal and poor by virtue of the fact that so many ambulant professions are mentioned in the lists of 'wanted' people. Scholars such as Schubert acknowledge at the same time, however, the nature of criminalising processes and the likelihood that the historical picture is skewed:

He shows how distrustful central authorities were, trying therefore to forbid and criminalise ambulant professions. The people involved were regarded to be of a low moral standard and their professions as a cloak for begging 'and criminal behaviour'. Schubert shows that in practice many local authorities were tolerant because they knew that this image did not completely hold true.

(Cottaar *et al.*, 1998: 138)

The association of Travellers with stealing was central to one of the most frightening images inculcated in some 'settled' children from an early age. This was the image of the Traveller as a child-stealer. G. Gmelch (1977), commenting on the very early development of anti-Traveller prejudice on the part of the 'settled' population, links the fear of the Traveller 'other' with the notion that Travellers are child-stealers:

Parents often discourage misbehaviour in their children by threatening to let the tinkers 'steal' them if they are bad. One elderly Traveller recalls the alarm her family's presence created in some settled children – 'Sometimes we'd be goin' along in our pony and car [cart] when we'd come across a bunch of school children. Well, they'd drop their things and run off like they'd seen the devil himself. I'd get a terrible fright thinkin' one of them might fall and get hurt and we'd get the blame. Somebody must be tellin' them terrible stories about Travellin' People.'

(Biddy Brien in Gmelch, 1977: 203)

It is a tragic irony that this trope of child-stealing even re-emerged during one of the most widely-publicised and shocking child abduction incidents of recent years, the abduction of British toddler Madeleine McCann in Portugal. Incredible as it may seem, amongst the early raft of theories and potential 'explanations' for this girl's disappearance generated within the local media was the possibility that she had been 'taken' by Portuguese Gypsies.

Timothy Neat's book *The Summer Walkers* (1996) is the most comprehensive ethnographic work on the Scottish Travellers written to date. It links the image of child-stealing with Traveller adoption, a practice that was quite common amongst the Scottish Travellers, a group who have intermarried heavily with Irish Travellers over the past few hundred years:

adoption became .... a common fact of life. It was used by the
Travellers as a deliberate mechanism to preserve families and to
bolster the group's minority status. It did not perpetuate the north
Highland Traveller way of life but it is a phenomenon of great
human interest because, for centuries, across Europe, the Gypsies
have been feared and demonised as 'child stealers', and in Scotland,
stories about Tinker theft, abduction and purchase of children have
been an integral part of popular folklore .... it is certainly true that
some children/lovers have run away with the Gypsies – but the vast
bulk of these stories are fabricated myths, reflecting fears not reality
... Unwanted children have, almost by tradition, been given to the
Travellers and Gypsies ... Circumstance and need have encouraged
Travellers to 'adopt' unwanted youngsters. It was a natural consequence of their nomadism, their numerical vulnerability, their
traditional humanity and family-centredness. Over the years, guilt-
twisted remembrance has turned 'giving' into 'taking', agreed 'deals'
into 'theft'. (Neat, 1996: 225)

Similar allegations of child kidnap incorporating ritual murder have
been a stock trait of anti-Semitic discourse in the European imaginary
for centuries and it is interesting that this stereotype was prevalent in
the discourse of the Jew as 'Other' in many European countries prior to
the Second World War. If ever proof were needed of the discursive
power of the stereotype, even amongst the intellectual class, then this
stereotype of the Jew as 'Other' is an excellent example. For instance,
Charles Bewley, the Irish envoy in Germany during the Second World
War and a supporter of the Nazis, raised the allegation of child kidnap
and murder when defending Germany's policy of dismissing Jews from
their jobs. Reporting to the Irish government in Dublin he sent literature outlining the allegation that the Jews engaged in ritual child
murder, an allegation which had also earlier been directed at Jews in
Limerick city in the early 1900s, and a premise which was used in
Germany to support claims for the eradication of Jewish influence in
German society. Bewley reported that while the question of ritual
murder was not essential to the theory that Jewish society influence
needed to be curtailed it was nevertheless the case that 'This belief is
held, to my own knowledge, by many well-educated and intelligent
people'. Bewley also questioned Jewish denials of the stereotype,
thereby implying the possibility that there was some truth to them. He
wondered why:

in the circumstances, on the assumption that ritual murders do not in fact take place, it seems regrettable that the Jewish authorities do not deal more circumstantially with the very detailed charges made. A general denial or denunciation of 'medieval superstition' is an unsatisfactory method of meeting accusations which give dates and names, nor does it explain why at all periods and in all countries this particular charge should have been fastened to the Jewish race alone. (Bewley cited in Keogh, 1998: 102)

A Scottish Traveller named Essie Stewart provided refutation of the child-stealing stereotype by describing her own adoption and the tradition of Traveller adoption generally:

> At that time I didn't know about my own adoption – but looking back, giving children away must have been common in the Highlands, right up until the 1950s. I know myself, five people, alive today, who were given away as children to the Travellers. There were so few of us, we needed new people, and for the country folk there was nothing easier, nothing better, than giving unwanted children to Travellers. My step-brother, Gordon Stewart, he was adopted. He says if the Stewarts hadn't taken him in, he would have ended up on the dunghill! They say the Gypsies steal children! It was not stealing – but like us, the Gypsies must have been children. We gave lives and homes to many an unwanted child who might have died, been killed, put into institutions – or today, of course, not seen the light of day. (Essie Stewart in Neat, 1996: 9)

Her views are echoed by an Irish Traveller who describes the 'adoption' of a local settled child by his family:

> the other fella was named Simon Connor. He wasn't a Traveller by birth but my Mam reared him as if he was one of our own. He travelled with us whenever we hit the road. I remember the morning Simon Connor arrived in our house very well. We were living in Crumlin and the rain was lashing down outside the glazier (window). My mother saw him outside and he drenched in the pani (rain) and she asked him in for a cup of tea. He came into the house and he never went home after that. He stayed with us and went to school from our cén (house) like the rest of us. When we would go away travelling during the summer he would go away with us. And

he became as good a Traveller as any of us. He was like a brother to us. (Dunne and Ó hAodha, 2004: 4)

The irony of the stereotype associating Travellers with child-stealing is not lost on Irish Travellers who saw the state's attempts at assimilation often framed in terms of the threat to 'institutionalise' or take away their children because they were allegedly 'at risk' from the Traveller lifestyle (see Helleiner, 2000, for a more in-depth discussion of the nature of these assimilationist policies). Nan Donahue, whose autobiography *Nan* (1986) is one of the few first-hand accounts of Traveller life written in Ireland, described the dangers of turning to 'outside' help for assistance in the pre-social welfare era. Aside from the convents who supplied food to Traveller children, the only other source for food was 'the "cruelty" [National Society for Prevention of Cruelty to Children], and if you went and complained or said you had no way to keep yourself, the kids was taken from you' (Donahue and Gmelch, 1986: 81). The threat to 'take away the children' was also used by some of the authorities in Ireland in attempts to evict Travellers from certain localities until relatively recently. The notion of child 'abduction' was consequently inverted by Travellers who saw the threat as an example of the inhumanity of the settled community, as noted by Canadian anthropologist Jane Helleiner (2000) when living on a Traveller site in Galway in the 1980s:

> Another woman living in a different camp expressed outrage when city officials, in an attempt to evict Travellers from the camp, threatened to imprison her neighbour and institutionalise her children if she did not leave .... children were central to constructions of Traveller identity and Traveller/non-Traveller boundary making. An allegedly greater love for children was part of a Traveller identity defined in opposition to the alleged anti-child character of non-Travellers. Travellers often pointed to their larger families in support of this claim and cited news reports of crimes against children such as abuse and abandonment as confirmation of the hostility and cruelty of settled people towards children. I was frequently told that Travellers would never engage in such behaviour. (2000: 121)

It is known that some Traveller children were institutionalised in orphanages and industrial schools in Ireland prior to the 1960s and that others were continually fearful of this possibility (see Joyce, 1985: 48;

and Pavee Point, 1994: 26). It has also been suggested that some Traveller children were forcibly removed from their parents and placed in residential care because they were classed as being of 'no fixed abode' (see McDonagh and McDonagh, 1993: 39) although this claim requires more extensive research. The mirror-stereotype of the child-stealing state on the part of Travellers or Gypsies has a very strong resonance in the Traveller and Gypsy communities of many countries, which has been highlighted by Roma activists like Hancock (1987) who have pointed to the deliberate removal, in countries such as Austria, of Roma children from their families and their institutionalisation, as parts of larger governmental attempts to assimilate Travellers and Gypsies. The stereotype of child kidnap or adoption has also recently resurfaced in Europe (including Ireland) with new waves of Roma (Gypsy) emigration from Eastern Europe. Sensational media reporting has contributed to the image of the Gypsy 'Other' as a group who practise 'coeval' customs in the form of child-bride and arranged/dowry marriages. A number of cases of this form of arranged marriage as practised in the Roma community have received media attention in Ireland in recent times, with the Irish police instigating 'searches' for Roma girls who have allegedly been 'kidnapped' into marriage. Irish Travellers and stealing were also interlinked in the imagination by a practice which both Travellers and settled people agree was a cause of tension between communities. This was the property damage caused by trespassing horses. A respondent to the IFC Questionnaire from Navan, County Meath, had this description: 'The animals graze on the roadsides. Some of the gipsies with a number of caravans seek to turn horses from the roadside into fields during the night, unknown to the owner. This creates friction and the Gardaí are usually brought on the scene. Their removal from the district follows' (Iml. 1256: 235).

Ireland was so poor in the early part of the twentieth century that even the Traveller practice of grazing their horses along the 'long acre' – the strip of grass along the verge of the road – was resented by farmers, especially those in areas where the land was less fertile, as pointed out by G. Gmelch (1977):

> Conditions were so poor that many farmers were forced to utilise some of the same marginal resources as itinerants. Because pasturage was scarce they grazed their animals on the roadside, in direct competition with the Tinkers' horses and donkeys. Many farmers also snared rabbits; they greatly resented Tinkers doing the same, especially on private land. (1977: 22)

A respondent from the Gaeltacht highlighted the extent of the tension between the Travelling and settled Irish over the question of horses and grazing:

> San oidhche cuirid na capaill is na h-asail isteach ins na páirceanna agus bíonn gardaí is feirmeoirí ar a dtóir annsan. Is maith leo móinfhéar i gcóir na h-oidhche. Cúpla blian ó shoin bhí feirmeóir ar an dtaobh theas d'Inis, agus bhí sé cráidhte ag na capaill céadna. Oíche amháin tháinig sé ortha agus iad istigh sa choirce – chaith sé leo len a ghunna agus chuir sé piléar tré dhíon na cairte mar a raibh na tincéirí. Thugadar an feirmeóir chun na cúirte ach is beag sásamh a fuaireadar mar bhí fhios ag an ngiúistís gurbh iad na tincéirí bhí ciontach. (Iml. 1255: 58)

> (In the night they put the horses and the donkeys into the fields and the guards and the farmers are after them then. They like the meadow grass for the night. A few years ago there was a farmer on the south side of Inch, and he was tormented by the same horses. One night he found them inside in his oats – and he shot at them and he put a bullet through the roof of one of the tinker's wagons. They brought the farmer to the court but they got very little satisfaction from the court because the judge knew that it was the tinkers were guilty.)

A Traveller from Limerick city described the fear he felt as a child after being 'burnt out' of an area because of an incident concerning horses and linked with the repression of another 'Other' group, in this case the Afro-American community:

> I will never forget one incident that took place near the village of Oranmore, about seven miles from Galway city, when I was only four years of age. We had no wagon at that time and we were camped in our lúbáns (tents) in against the side of a ditch … we made camp for the night. My father left the horse into some farmer's field without asking permission. He should not have done that of course but the next thing we knew there were shouts outside our tents and we came out in the darkness to find a bunch of angry farmers standing around the camp with huge torches that were on fire. They told us to get out of the area or they would burn us out. I remember being very frightened. When you are a child and you are standing there in the darkness and all these angry faces around you roaring and shouting. It was like a scene from one of those films you

see about the Ku Klux Klan and the way that they used to attack the black people in America in times gone by.

(Cauley and Ó hAodha, 2004: 53)

The Traveller tradition of begging when calling to the houses of the settled community was also seen as a 'cover' for stealing and deception and Traveller begging was associated with fear and suspicion in the public imagination:

> The people don't trust them and many women are afraid of them particularly if there is no man about. If there is only one person about the house they sometimes ask for something, e.g. potatoes, to get the person out of the house for a time. Things have been stolen in this way. Children often steal eggs from the outhouse while the mother is begging inside (Iml. 1256: 235).

Begging by Traveller women and children was an important subsistence activity for many Traveller families and as outlined in the Tinker Questionnaire this was generally combined with the peddling of small items such as Holy Medals, Holy Pictures, pins, paper flowers, etc. Peddling was often accompanied by appeals for 'a bit of help'. Begging also proved a source of tension between the Travelling and settled communities, however, a situation which was exacerbated by the fact that for many settled people it might be one of the primary contexts in which they had communication with Travellers. This tension gave rise to other stereotypes including the image of the haranguing or 'intimidatory' Traveller woman who was never satisfied. Competition for limited resources in an impoverished country was probably a major factor in the proliferation of this stereotype. Ironically, this same stereotype has re-surfaced in Ireland in recent years with the in-migration of Roma from the former Eastern Bloc. It is noteworthy that a similar stereotype incorporating the 'intimidation' of the 'defenceless' housewife was alleged towards the Jewish pedlars, another 'Other' group who travelled throughout Ireland in the early half of the twentieth century, as indicated by these comments by a Limerick priest:

> We may notice him traversing the lanes of our cities, or visiting our country farm-houses when the 'good man' is abroad and only the woman of the household has to be dealt with. He carries bundles of cheap wares or he is laden with pious pictures, or statues of the Christian Redeemer whose name and following he abhors.

(Finlay in Keogh, 1998: 21)

A housewife from Crossmolina, County Mayo linked stealing with the absence of the 'man of the house':

> If there are no men in when they arrive – they make very bold in the demands. Only about four months ago one of the tinker women grabbed a piece of bacon which was hanging from the roof; and was away with it, but she just met the man of the house coming in and he deprived her of it. (Iml. 1256: 124)

The association of Travellers with intimidation still survives in the public imaginary in Ireland today, albeit in a slightly altered form, and it is a trope which is frequently 'dragged up' by the tabloid press. It is often rumoured, for instance, that those nomadic Travellers who travel between Ireland and England during the summer months in particular are 'paid off' by the settled community who do not wish them to park on nearby waste land or land that has been zoned for development, as indicated by the following newspaper headlines:

*'Boss held to Ransom'* (D. Lane, *Sunday World*, 2001)
*'Visitors Intimidated by Travellers'* (M. Minihan, *The Irish Times*, 2000)

The resentments and tensions between the Traveller and settled communities relating to begging requests on the part of Travellers had their roots in fearful beliefs including that of the 'evil eye' in relation to Travellers and their alleged 'magico-religious' powers. A man from the west of Ireland similarly hinted at a fear of 'denying' the Travellers:

> People believed – some still do so – that it was unlucky not to give the tinkers something asked for .... unlucky to have their curses ...
> I heard that the old tinkers were great prayers. I've heard of them begrudging a man a beast. Many would not care to buy from the tinker or refuse alms fearing their curse ... They wish all kinds of ill-luck to the house – to the crops and to cattle if they are refused their demands – and people are sometimes afraid of their curses. If they are refused milk 'that she may never again have a calf' – for often a farmer's wife might say that she had only enough milk for the household, that she was 'expecting a cow to calf'.
>
> (Iml. 1255: 47)

A female respondent from County Cork described the flipside of a Travellers' blessing:

> If they get anything they say 'God spare you' or 'The Lord keep sick-
> ness and trouble away from you' but if they are refused they curse,
> 'The curse of God may melt you'. The women carry babies to excite
> sympathy. They are generally brought on their backs and sometimes
> two together one in their arms and one strapped on the back.
>
> (Iml. 1255: 48)

It was sometimes alleged that Travellers combined the fear of their
curse with their prowess as fortune-tellers as a rejoinder to those who
insulted them.

> Ní bhfaighfeá puinn den bhfírinne ó chuid mhór aca 'á n'oirfead an
> t-éitheach don ócáid. (Iml. 1255: 20)
>
> (You wouldn't get a word of the truth from most of them, just what-
> ever lie suited the occasion).
>
> Tinkers are fond of family life when their day's rambling or work is
> over. They are affectionate to both man and beast. Their greatest
> failing is scheming or trickery. (Iml. 1255: 30)
>
> They are the greatest white liars in existence. But they enjoy being
> tripped up and caught out in their lies – and it's remarkable the
> respect they have for one who can assess their veracity. They
> approach you differently next time. (Iml. 1255: 30)

The latter-mentioned quote hints at the use of mendacity as a game or
a tactic rather than as a wilful form of deception for criminal reasons. It
is likely that Travellers, like the Irish people generally, may have used
mendacity as a method of self-defence. Historian Robert Bartlett
(1982), who analysed the anti-Irish stereotype tradition as first promulgated by Geraldus Cambrensis in the twelfth century, situated the
alleged Irish (and Welsh) propensities for mendacity within a colonial
framework. Bartlett argued that native peoples sometimes found it
expedient to make temporary surrenders or peace agreements only to
renege on them in a renewed drive for independence when they felt
the enemy's position might have weakened (1982: 13). Robert Welch
(1993) also analysed the stereotype of the untrustworthy Irish. He, too,
located its roots within the self-defence mechanisms of oppression:

> It was often said that you could not trust what the Irish will tell you
> because they will make sure that they tell you what you want to hear.

At its worst the racial slur here is that the Irish cannot tell truth from falsehood. But in another sense there is a vital cultural manoeuvre going on: it is most important that strangers feel at home, that they be accommodated within the structure, and that means adapting elements of the structure to take account of the new presence ... They (strangers) must be told what they want to hear; not to do so leaves them outside and therefore dangerous. (Welch, 1993: 279)

Jan Yoors (1967), who travelled with Gypsies on the continent during the war years and wrote an account of his experiences entitled *The Gypsies*, described the way in which Dutch nomads also seized the opportunities provided by the social incohesion and the fluidity of territorial borders that characterised the Second World War to profit from black marketeering. Dutch Gypsies became involved in the Resistance movement, their knowledge of underworld life and survival tactics proving particularly useful. American folklorist Artelia Court (1985), who recorded life histories from Irish Travellers during the 1970s, described some Travellers who spoke of having sheltered Irish freedom fighters from British authorities during the upheavals of 1900–1921. The same Travellers also mentioned wartime profiteering, although Court claimed that 'none ascribed these activities to conscious political motive' (1985: 223).

The story of Travellers' involvement in the political struggles that have accompanied Irish partition is an aspect of Irish history where much greater study is necessary. That there were certain Travelling families from the Border area in particular who had a long history of 'political' (Republican) involvement and had been imprisoned for subversive activities is well-known amongst the Travelling community. Smuggling, incorporating wartime profiteering, was linked with a very old stereotype relating to Travellers in the European imaginary, i.e. that Travellers were spies who were somehow subverting the moral order. Some of the earliest European descriptions of the Traveller/Gypsy depict them in roles incorporating sedition and treachery. Beier (1985) and Mayall (2004) link the association of Travellers with spying and sedition in Europe to the rapid social and religious changes and huge uncertainty that had accompanied the early modern era. The appearance of the first 'Egyptians' travelling in family groups fit this pattern. These groups were initially tolerated and even supported when they claimed to be pilgrims from 'Little Egypt':

Relying on the literature about the European history of persons designated in the sources as Gypsies, we find that at the time of their appearance in the fifteenth century they presented themselves as pilgrims from a country called Little Egypt. They did this in order to acquire safe conducts from higher authorities, even kings and the Pope, who assured them of safe passage through the countries of Europe … In Europe during these years, however, there was a lively trade in travel passes and many (false) pilgrims roamed about.

(Willems, 1997: 8)

When doubts about the pilgrim status of these 'Egyptians' arose, these Travellers were suspected of being spies for the Turks and were soon stigmatised. Grellmann (1783), whose Gypsy 'archetype' has held sway for centuries, claimed that Gypsies lent themselves readily to become the agents of treason in wartime. Although he found the accusations that their entry into Western Europe had been as spies for the Turks were likely to be far-fetched, he did not discount them entirely. Gypsies' indigent circumstances prompted the taking of bribes in his opinion and their happy-go-lucky character and wish to be liked could have tempted them to flirt with sedition. Mayall (2004) links the concept of sedition in a British Isles context with increased migrancy on the part of large numbers of nomadic and dispossessed Catholic Irish who were attempting to escape the war and eviction back in their native country during the Tudor era. The concept of sedition on the part of those who were 'outsiders' or dispossessed became inextricably linked in the public imaginary with pestilence and crime, two problems which increased at this period and were associated with increased poverty, itinerancy and the disruption of existing social systems:

The early modern period was a time of rapid change and extreme religious and political uncertainty, resulting in an often ill-defined fear or anarchy, popular risings and anything which might threaten or disrupt the existing social organisation. Concern about the consequences of disease, pestilence, crime and poverty was matched by the threat of sedition and the belief that Rome was sending Papal emissaries to England to provoke a Catholic revival. The link between these fears and itinerancy and nomadism was all too evident to contemporaries. Disease and pestilence were spread by nomadic carriers, various crimes were closely linked to an itinerant way of life, poverty and vagrancy were virtually synonymous, sedition was spread by itinerant colporteurs, and agents of the Pope were suspected of finding a cloak for their subversion in the camps of travellers and Gypsies. (Mayall, 2004: 60)

English colonists in Ireland made a strong link between sedition and nomadism because of the important role which the travelling bards played in the fostering of Gaelic culture and in inciting the general population to resist colonisation. Because of their nomadic lifestyle, Travelling people in Ireland, but bards in particular, were often accused of being spies and during the late 1500s many of them were executed. The British also issued many proclamations throughout the 1500s punishing both the poets and anybody who might give them a welcome in an effort to stamp out the traditional nomadism of large sections of the Irish population and the traditional system of hospitality which supported them. The proclamation of the 'President' of the province of Munster, Sir John Perrot, issued in 1571, is a case in point:

> All carrows [gamblers], bards, rhymers, and common idle men and women within this province making rhymes, bringing of messages, and common players at cards, to be spoiled of all their goods and chattels, and to be put in the next stocks, there to remain until they find sufficient surety to leave that wicked trade of life and fall to other occupation. (Perrot in Maxwell, 1923: 166)

The association of Travellers with subversive activity and spying remained strong in the Irish imaginary. One respondent to the IFC stated his belief that some Travellers were the descendants of people who were fugitives during periods of oppression in Ireland: 'Teicheoirí ón dlí cuid aca in aimsir géarleanúna' (Some of them were fugitives from justice during times of persecution) (Iml. 1256: 15).

It was also a source of prejudice in the north of Ireland where the B-Specials, a Protestant (and predominantly Unionist) force were particularly discriminatory against Travellers because of their Irish Catholic (Fenian) background. The 'double-prejudice' that Travellers encountered in the north of Ireland as a consequence of sectarianism is another aspect of Traveller history which has been hitherto severely underresearched. Traveller biographies such as Nan Joyce's (1985) and Pecker Dunne's (2004) all mention sectarian hatred and the suspicion of Travellers because of their 'Fenian' background. Pecker Dunne, a well-known Traveller musician, describes the frequent prejudice and harassment that Travellers suffered in the north of Ireland:

> Having a slag with the Garda Síochána was one thing. The north of Ireland was a different kettle of fish altogether. They had these

hornees (police) up there called the B-Specials. I can think of a few words for them, none of which I will quote here. Many of them were a cottiva (bad) crowd. The bad ones were bigots and they hated Travellers or any Irish people from the southern part of Ireland. They referred to us as Fenians and that was the most complimentary name they shouted at us, believe me! They would not let you alone all day. They harassed us non-stop. Things weren't too bad during the day. I remember coming to a town called Dungannon one time and I was busking on the street there. And people were passing up the street in cars and shouting out to me how much they were enjoying my music. That night was a different scenario though. That darkee (night) I remember being pulled out of letty (bed) at three o'clock in the morning. They dragged me along the ground and out of my tent. And they were shouting, 'Come on, get out of here, you are not camping here. You Fenians and Taigs aren't welcome.' They knew that most of the Travellers originated in the south, you see. It was as simple as that. Pure hatred. And I was only one of many Travellers who had that experience with them, let me tell you.

(Dunne and Ó hAodha, 2004: 53)

Another Traveller, Chrissie Ward, who was born in Belfast in 1947, described the suspicious death of her father while in custody in the north of Ireland. Her experience was typical of many Catholics, both Traveller and 'settled' during the 'Troubles' in the North of Ireland:

I think me father was about thirty-six when he died. They say me father was murdered but there was nothin' done about it because we were Travellers in the North an' Irish people, they didn't like people from the South. So Travellers was, they was kinda discriminated upon an' nobody ever med enquiries about it. So he was kilt in a police station. He was goin' up to see me mother one night in hospital. She was in hospital 'fore me sister was born. She was sick ... So he was comin' back and this night an' the police jus' dragged him in ....So he was found dead. They left him all night swimmin' in blood in the police station an' they say it was a haemorrhage in the brain. But he was healthy, like, he was really, really healthy, healthy man.

(Ward, 1992: 42)

Traveller activist Nan Joyce has given a good description of how both smuggling and subversion became intertwined in a divided Ireland whose border was particularly porous for a traditionally nomadic people:

The travellers used to smuggle guns for the old IRA, because they were travellers and they wouldn't be searched. One summer's day, when he and his wife were very young, soon after they were married, they were going along the road with their ass and cart looking for a camp. His wife was sitting up in the cart and they had guns hidden under the straw. Years ago the men never used to sit up, they always walked. Two Black and Tans came along and they were getting ready to search their cart. Someone had told them about the guns. It was a real hot summer's day; the flies were gathered around the donkey and its tail kept swishing them away. The man said to his wife, 'We have to make up a plan – if we don't we're finished, we'll end up our lives in jail.' He told his wife to start scratching. She didn't know what he meant and she didn't want to do it. He said, 'Scratch, or we're done out of all our happiness – here come the Black and Tans to search us', so she started scratching. He walked over to the two soldiers, scratching away, and he said to them, 'Have you got any cure for lice, sir? I'm walking alive.' He pointed over to the ass, its tail swishing away the flies and he said, 'Look at my old ass trying to beat them off and they're eating him alive.' When the Black and Tans heard this they backed away, they wouldn't come near him and they wouldn't go near the cart. When the soldiers went off he lay down in the middle of the road, he was only young, and he cocked up his two legs jeering and he said to his wife, 'Up Ireland, Mary, we won the battle that time!' It was just like the smuggling years ago because in the Free State they hadn't really got a lot.

(Joyce, 1985: 26–27)

The musicologist Thomas Munnelly gave further substance to the smuggling motif by referring to a humorous song called Smuggling the Tin which was written by a Traveller and which referred to the important role of cross-border smuggling in the lives of Irish Travellers 'during and after the Second World War when many commodities were rationed or scarce'. According to Munnelly these smugglers dealt chiefly in 'luxury items bought from bomb-damaged stores in that troubled area [Northern Ireland] and peddled in the Republic' (Munnelly cited in Court, 1985: 223).

# 6    Travellers as countercultural

And for much more might the whole island be beholden unto it [i.e. the English conquest], in case upon a certain peevish and obstinate love they beare unto their owne country fashions, they had not stopped their eares and shut up their hearts against better governance. For, the Irishry are so stiffly settled in observing the old rites of their country, that not only they be with-drawn from them, but also are able easily to draw the English unto same.

(Cited in Leersen, 1996: 46)

Aside from the construction of Travellers as 'degraded' or 'threatening/dangerous' Other, the second primary discourse that serves to delineate Travellers within the Tinker Questionnaire material is that which 'frames' them as a culturally exclusive group, one who function completely 'independently' of the major organs of Irish society and who actually function as a countercultural group, forming 'a society within a society'.

This depicts Travellers in terms of a countercultural threat. They are seen to disturb the moral order because they are perceived to inhabit an exclusive and secretive society which operates in symbiosis with and yet on the margins of the settled community. This discourse implies the existence of a mutually exclusive 'society' which has a certain internal structure incorporating leaders/kings and a range of customs, superstitions and ceremonies that exhibit an absence of coevalness. This belief system incorporates constructions of Travellers that place them 'outside of history' and frozen in certain folkways that have been abandoned by the 'civilised' or 'progressive' settled community. According to these constructions Travellers are 'Other' because they are nomadic and allegedly engage in cultural practices that are considered anachronistic by the settled community, including a range of beliefs and taboos associated with social organisation, death, marriage, the use of a 'secret' language, and a refusal to integrate into the wider community, etc.

Many respondents to the IFC Questionnaire constructed the 'aloofness' and lack of integration of Travellers as indicative of the existence of a separate and mutually exclusive society with a distinctive internal structure and a form of leadership that involved kings. The notion that Travellers, Gypsies and other nomads had their own kings went back to the very first archetypal images of Travellers and Gypsies in the European imaginary. The German 'gypsiologist' Heinrich Grellmann considered this belief to be a projection of the social structures of the 'civilised' world: 'Since their initial appearance in Europe Gypsies were said to have travelled about in bands under the leadership of chiefs. Down through the years these headmen were referred to in annals by such titles as woiwoden (a Polish term for governor or leader), knights, counts, dukes, and kings' (Willems, 1997: 51).

In Ireland similar notions of a historical Travelling 'aristocracy' were linked more with the concept that the Travellers were the remnants of 'fallen nobility' who had lost status during the various periods of dispossession associated with the conquest, confiscation, and colonisation of Ireland. The following rather romantic description of some of the 'Simey' Dohertys, the famous Traveller musicians from Donegal, indicates as much:

> Tig bean tincleora isteach agus dhá pháiste léithi agus mála líonta d'áráistí stain ... Mar is gnách lena leithéid labhrann sí go deas séimh le bunaidh an toighe. De threibh na nDochartach í. Sin na 'Simeys' nó tá Simon mar ainm coitianta sa teaghlach i gcónaí. Bhí said i gcónaí ag obair ar an stán agus bíonn said uilig go maith ag seinm ar an bhfideal agus an seancheol ar fad acu. Siúlann said go stáitiúil ar an mbóthar agus deirtear go bhfuil siad síolraithe ó na ríthe.

> (A tinker woman comes in accompanied by two children; her bag is filled with tin items. As is usual for her type, she speaks in a nice gentle voice to the occupants of the house. She is one of the Doherty clan. One of the 'Simeys,' as they are called, because Simon has always been a common name in the family. They were always tinworkers, and they are all good at playing the fiddle, many of them being experts on the older tunes. They walk along the road in a stately fashion, and it is said that they are descended from the kings.)
> [my own translation]

The marginality of Travellers and Gypsies to the dominant social order was partly a consequence of the fact that they appeared to have their own political structure that operated independently of the politics of non-Traveller society. This separate society rendered Travellers 'apolitical' regarding developments in settled society, a conviction displayed by this survey respondent from County Mayo:

> In their society, among the people, the tinkers are a very exclusive set. They have never merged into the fabric of the general population through marriage or affinity ... Neither have they been known to absorb any outside individuals into their own pattern of society. Political or social questions never seem to trouble them. Problems such as emigration or falling population never worry them. They never participate in public amusements such as athletic sports, football, dances, etc. They are not, of course, popular with the people, and the aversion is equally reciprocated by them ... They are a distinct people following their own exclusive way of life.
>
> (Iml. 1256: 119)

It is no coincidence that the notion of a separate and 'exclusive' class with its own social structures and organisation seems to have come to the fore generally in contexts in which large groups of Travellers gathered together in one place. Funerals, weddings, patterns or fairs seem to have been occasions for the proliferation of the 'king' stereotype, and the well-documented connections of Travellers with such occasions are possibly indicative of the countercultural threat in the subconscious of the settled community prompted by large assemblies of this 'Other' group:

> The groups had a king or leader whose word was law, but since his death a few years ago, I do not know if a successor was appointed.
>
> (Iml. 1255: 239)

> Paddy Maughan was king of his tribe. Had a wealth of horses and left legacies when he died ... Since Maughan died, the local groups didn't bother going to Ballinasloe, and they had no king since.
>
> (Iml. 1255: 222)

> They have no local 'king' here, but a few years ago, hundreds came to a tinker's funeral in Tullamore, and the 'king' travelled from Galway and was royally received. (Iml. 1255: 232)

Interestingly, Irish oral tradition had for many centuries a range of beliefs concerning the existence of countercultures made up of beggars and various types of wanderers. According to this discourse, beggars and nomadic people generally were allegedly divided into well-organised communities akin to trade unions, some of which mobilised themselves so as to keep 'foreign' beggars from their own area of operation. Countercultural motifs such as 'fraud,' the use of an anti-language or 'canting' jargon, and organised groupings under a specific leader or 'king' remained remarkably consistent over long periods of time, as shown by the testimony of witnesses from the West of Ireland given to the pre-famine poor law inquiry, an investigation that produced the *First Report of His Majesty's Commissioners for Inquiring into the Condition of the Poorer Classes in Ireland* (1835). Certain witnesses from County Galway reported seeing the following occurrence among the 'begging' community at country fairs:

> That man gave his daughter [a] £30 fortune. He is like a king over the others, and people say that he has a tribute from each of them. I saw him at the fair of Kilcreest take off the bandage in a drunken fit and defy any man in the fair to try him at the stick. [The travellers or *bacachs* were said to wear bandages while soliciting alms from the general body of fair-goers.] (1835: 478–9)

An IFC respondent from County Monaghan linked the concept of 'nobility' with ritualised fighting – a linkage that persists as one of the most prominent vehicles for the construction and dissemination of the king stereotype in the public imaginary of modern Ireland:

> Once when I was at the Connemara show in Ballinasloe in October, I saw hundreds of gipsies or tinkers there. It seemed to be a real re-union of the tribes from the various parts of Ireland. On that occasion the new king of the gypsies had to be chosen, for the previous one had died. The choice was made when the eligibles from each family fought for the kingship. The champion who was successful in overcoming all his rivals was declared 'King of the Gypsies' as long as he lived. (Iml. 1256: 227)

The comments of another 'settled' person who responded to the IFC Questionnaire make reference to the alleged existence of rulers amongst the Traveller community and can be seen as a 'projection' of the class structure that existed among the settled community:

> Here is an account of what a gipsy told me in reply to my questions.
> In reply to tinker society. Yes, we have a chief or king to whom we
> give allegiance. I can't mind his name but I think he is Ward. No,
> there are no classes within our ranks. Yes, some of us are richer than
> others. We are mostly Roman Catholics. We practise our religion.
> Keshes, Lockes, Stewards, Prices and Whites are mostly Protestant.
> No, they do not practise their religion. (Iml. 1256: 257)

These sentiments were repeated by a Traveller from Munster who
implied the existence of democratic structures in the election of a king:

> The old lady said that there would not be an election for a King, and
> that nothin' would happen for a long time. I think that a selection
> would be made from some of the King's family if some of them
> showed outstanding merit and gained the good will of the rest –
> otherwise things would be put on the long finger. (1255: 234)

The idea of a separate society with its own class structure was
mooted by a range of Questionnaire respondents. As with the settled
community, class divisions were often perceived to fall according to
gradations of wealth: 'They seem to have greater and lesser social
status within the gang for a member of the Wards was asked about a
brother of his and the answer he gave was, "I know nothing about him,
he married into the Gavins and we don't recognise him"' (Iml. 1255:
214).

The notion of kingship was also linked to a stereotype that implied an
alternative or 'pagan' form of marriage operating outside the sanction
of the Catholic church. A retired schoolteacher from County Kerry who
responded to the Tinker Questionnaire described Traveller marriage in
the following way:

> Marriages do not take place before a priest, and the common belief
> is that when a pair wish to become man and wife, they meet some-
> one in authority; an authority that they believe in – such as a king or
> queen appointed by themselves, and that a part of the ceremony is
> the 'jumping over the budget' ['budget' refers to a bag of tinsmith's
> tools]. (Iml. 1255: 60)

This teacher's comments were given some support by the following
description from County Westmeath: 'I was told of a tinker wedding

which took place on the roadside, an old member of the clan performing the ceremony. He stood between the shafts of an unyoked cart, the young man on his right hand and the young girl on his left. I could not get further information about it, as regards words said, etc.' (Iml. 1255: 216).

A similar practice incorporating countercultural motifs and marriage of a casual nature was ascribed to those people referred to as 'beggars' or *bacachs* who met at fairs. An observer from the 'settled community' gave the following description of *bacachs* to the poor law inquiry in 1835: 'There is a place near Strokestown where they assemble every year in immense numbers; at this fair, called the fair of Ballinafad, the beggars are married for a year. The ceremony is performed by joining the hands of the parties over a pair of crutches, and hundreds return to have the rite renewed year after year' (1835: xxxii: 513).

These countercultural motifs incorporating the idea of a 'pagan' marriage ceremony provided a link connecting the construction of Travelling people with an imagined sexual licentiousness and a romantic concept of 'freedom,' as revealed in the folklore tradition. The association of Travellers with sexual immorality in the European imaginary has deep roots. One need only consider the image of the 'fiery' Gypsy as depicted in Spanish culture and as associated with flamenco (see Mitchell, 1994).

That the image of the Gypsy and Traveller woman as an object of sexual allure has been central to artistic impressions of travelling life is unquestionable. The allegedly 'casual' attitude of Travellers concerning marriage, courtship and sexual congress gained popular currency partly through the medium of the theatre. The Anglo-Irish playwright J. M. Synge based his play *The Tinker's Wedding* on popular perceptions of Traveller marriage incorporating 'pagan' wedding rites as recounted to him by country people in the East of Ireland. Synge described how a man had told him of a 'tinker' couple who had never been married. The folklorist, writer and Abbey Theatre-founder Lady Gregory collected similar accounts in the West of Ireland during the same period. One country person allegedly told her that 'the tinkers sell their wives to one another; I've seen that myself … [and] as to marriage, some used to say that they lepped [leaped] the budget [bag of tinsmith's tools], but it's more likely they have no marriage at all' (Gregory, 1974: 94).

The notion of a 'pagan' marriage that involved the jumping over or passing of some sort of boundary was mentioned by respondents to the Tinker Questionnaire as well:

Another vague custom re: a marriage of tinkers in 'the quarry hole' in Crockanboy, one side of Donnelly's. Only information so far available is that the couple being married 'had to jump in and out of a ring'. (Iml. 1255: 64)

There used to be a story told when I was young that a tinker's marriage [had] taken place by extending hands over the Cross on a donkey's back – the ceremony being presided over by the Tinker king or family head. (Iml. 1255: 244)

There are evidently various classes in the tinker world considering all the bartering and bargaining that usually precedes a tinker's wedding. Negotiations go on for a considerable time before the match is finally fixed.
(Iml. 1255: 241 - IFC respondent from County Carlow)

Notions of separateness, a countercultural 'exclusivity,' and licentiousness in the sexual sphere were linked to the concept of disorder as applied to Irish Travellers. This concept had strong affiliations with Travellers' ascribed 'status' in the world, as outlined in the Irish folktale tradition, where their apparently aimless, unsettled and unconventional lifestyle was seen as a punishment for an offence against some holy person or deity.

This notion of disorder was most obviously manifested in the stereotype of Travellers as a people inordinately given to fighting. Their repeated fights were held to be a clear demonstration of their allegedly 'primitive' or uncivilised lifestyle. While the 'countercultural' image of a separate society or 'kingship' raises its head today less frequently than it did in the past, the association of Travellers with fighting and feuding strongly persists. It is one of the strongest images of Traveller life in the Irish 'settled' imaginary today, and is steadily beamed through the lens of the Irish mass media. The phenomenon has a long pedigree. Many IFC respondents gave in-depth descriptions of Traveller fights, utilising the same imagery that had been ascribed to the faction fights common in Ireland in the late eighteenth and early nineteenth centuries. Many of these respondents described Traveller fights in terms that echoed the ritualised nature of earlier faction-fighting in Ireland. Like the faction-fighting of the pre-famine era, the fights mentioned by IFC respondents were perceived as a marker for the separate or distinct nature of Traveller society:

I remember the wholesale use of sticks, stones, soldering irons, and even iron bars, and the wholesale wounding of men and women, whose shouts and curses made a bedlam that roused the whole neighbourhood ... Those who were the best fighters, always the least wounded, hobnobbed over pints of stout in one of the local pubs and spoke of the wounds they inflicted on their opponents ... In such rows there was much blood to be seen, and afterwards many bandaged heads and limbs, but somehow it struck me that they started such rows to keep up their credit in the country and to instil the fear of the Tinker in the neighbourhood, with the usual result of getting a better reception through fear in their usual daily, weekly, or yearly rounds to the farmhouses. (Iml. 1952: 60)

An IFC respondent from County Wexford declared: 'After a horse fair the tinker clans sometimes fight, but only among themselves'.

(Iml. 1255: 362)

The ritualised nature of Traveller fights and the fact that women also joined in them was highlighted by some IFC respondents as further evidence of the Travellers' perceived outcast status as a socio-cultural group. References to the way in which Travellers were often friendly to one another after a fight, and descriptions of their 'single' combats, all reinforced this idea of ritualised fighting as a form of separateness[1]: 'Tinkers are very violent – when they fight among themselves. No-one would interfere in a tinker's fight. People say "tinkers tear each other to pieces tonight and are great as pickpockets tomorrow"' (Iml. 1255: 362).

Interestingly, apart from the Tinker Questionnaire, most of the IFC references to fighting by Travellers pertain to challenges and single combats. This is consistent with the 'one-on-one' bare-fist fighting and the challenges in which some Traveller families reputedly 'specialise' today. One of the major cultural attributes which was deemed to assign 'exclusivity' to Travellers and situate them within a countercultural discourse was their use of 'secret' forms of communication. According to the IFC respondents, Travellers utilised two forms of secret communication. One involved a spoken language known as Cant or Gammon. The second form of secret communication was a sign language that took the form of physical 'markers,' which were left out in such a way as to communicate with other Travellers. These markers, including rags, sticks and embers, were left in a highly particularised manner so that 'readers' would immediately know certain types of information, such as the direction that another family might have taken on the road, the attitudes of locals in relation to almsgiving, the arrival of a new horse, or the deaths of family members.

> It is said that they have a means of following each other from signs left by the first party. Broken twigs or marks on trees or crossroads.
> (Iml. 1256: 262 – IFC respondent from Enniskillen, County Fermanagh)

> I am told that they tie a red cloth or string to the willow or alder bushes that they used, and other gypsies or tinkers who came that way were supposed to not cut any of those bushes.
> (Iml. 1256: 277 – IFC respondent from County Cavan)

Relatively little modern research has been undertaken into the functions of Travellers' spoken language, known in academic parlance as Shelta but referred to by Travellers as Cant or Gammon. Opinions vary as to the exact functions of Shelta, whether it was primarily a 'secret' language or a trade language, and whether it should be defined as a language or a linguistic register (Binchy, 2002; Ó Baoill, 1994). That Shelta is acquired by children in infancy and is employed unselfconsciously (as an alternative to English) within the community indicates a broader range of usage and the importance of Shelta as a marker of Traveller identity. But none of these aspects of Traveller language use was noticed by the IFC respondents to the Tinker Questionnaire. Instead, they generally saw Shelta as an example of the conscious and deliberate separateness of Travellers, who wished to exclude those who were not able to understand their special tongue. Shelta, as described by the few IFC respondents who mentioned it, was generally defined in terms of an 'anti-language' – in the sense employed by Michael Halliday and John Yinger. Halliday described an anti-language as a form of language generated by an anti-society – that is, 'a society that is set up within another society as a conscious alternative to it' (Halliday, 1976; Yinger, 1982).

As examples of anti-languages, Halliday cited the 'pelting speech' of the vagabond counterculture[2] that characterised the poor of Elizabethan England, the argot used by the Calcutta underworld, and an anti-language used in Polish prisons. The few IFC respondents who noted the existence of Shelta placed their emphasis on this perceived anti-language function of Shelta, highlighting its secretive and 'exclusive' aspects, a practice that served to emphasise the cultural 'othering' of Travellers as a separate or countercultural group:

The tinkers are supposed to have a language known as 'gibberish,' which is told as being mostly a concocted Irish. They break into this when unwilling to be heard at their business. I heard them more than once in my parents' shop when I was a little girl, but of course never understood. (Iml. 1255: 266)

Tinkers have a certain language which they use when they do not want others to understand the meaning of [it], especially when they are making bargains. I spent some time about a year ago with a Tinker who was making saucepans at the entrance to one of those picturesque Killarney lanes, and I wrote down a good deal of it. I put it aside and must have hidden it too well, as I cannot put my hands on it right away. (Iml. 1255: 61)

The notion of a separate 'Travelling society' that was presided over by its own rulers and was the subject of separate and secretive practices and taboos had very old roots in the European imaginary. Fears over the countercultural threat posed by the nomadic 'dispossessed' go as far back as the early modern era. Changes in population structures and the transition from feudalism to capitalism resulted in greater migrancy and more repressive attitudes towards nomadism on the part of governments tending towards the centralisation of the state. The litera-ture of Gypsiology stressed the marginality of Travellers and Gypsies to the dominant social order, as indicated by Mayall (1982), in relation to British Gypsy Travellers:

Few commentators were able to write about the gypsies without stressing the marginality of this separate and secretive race to the dominant political and social institutions. Essentially, the gypsies were said to be uninvolved in the politics of the wider society of which they were a part, and had instead their own organisations that depended on dark and mysterious meetings, which called to mind freemasonry practices. (Mayall, 1982: 208–209)

Related to the belief that Travellers were an aloof and 'exclusive' group, then, was the notion that they had their own political structure that operated externally of the politics of the host society. The fact that Travellers in Ireland were considered to be similarly 'apolitical' regard-ing developments in the political spheres in which the 'settled community' engaged only added to the strength of opinion with respect to these stereotypes. While this discourse of difference with respect to the Irish Traveller minority may not have the same strength today as it did in earlier decades, when Ireland was transitioning from a rural economy to one that was primarily urban, the ramifications of this 'othering' discourse nevertheless continue to exert a strong hold on the Irish imaginary.

## NOTES

1   There are references in the IFC archive to group fighting at fairs between Travellers and settled people. One description that I came across related to Turloughmore in County Galway and involved a large group of country people and Travellers fighting against one another (Iml. 1255: 45).

2   In a 1567 pamphlet Thomas Harman described the counter-language function of the 'pelting speech' as follows: Here I set before the good reader the lewd, lousy language of these loitering lusks and lazy lorels, wherewith they buy and sell the common people as they pass through the country; which language they term the pedlars' French (Harman in Salgado 1972, 146).

# 7 Narrative and the Irish imaginary: Contested terrains

> Things fall apart; the centre cannot hold
>
> (The Second Coming – W. B. Yeats)

Traditionally post-colonialism has read Irish culture through its inherited dichotomy of colonised/coloniser and empowered/disempowered thereby replicating imperialist power structures of old; the reading of the two primary strands within the representative discourse explored here points rather to the atypicality, the nomadic qualities, of Ireland's postcolonial configurations and the subaltern histories of social groupings which Gramsci characterised as 'fragmented and episodic' (Gramsci, 1971: 55). My discussion seeks to underscore the importance of rethinking and re-interpreting nationalist ideology and praxis within the Irish (post-) colonial context. Emphasised in the narratives explored here however is the 'radically undecidable nature of the text' and a general re-appraisal of our assumptions with respect to colonial textuality. In narratives such as those explored below contested ideas of Irish identity and nationhood as relating to both the Traveller and settled communities are played out through a deconstruction of textual authority whereby the discourse is shifted laterally, opening up a dimension beyond the binaries of traditional or 'contested discourses'. In these exemplars the Irish colonial text is 'strained between representing the other and denying Otherness, giving authority and giving it away, the text becomes both the refuge of colonial ideology and repeated sign of its own ambivalence and incapacities as a discourse' (Hooper and Graham, 2002: 38)

The text *is* the limen. It is that special point of tension, the margin which is simultaneously the border and the crossing point. Viewed from the perspectives of scholars such as Bakhtin and Bhabha this is the place where textuality and discourse are in a constant state of tension between that which exists inside and outside the text. It is a text which oscillates between that which is apparently stable and one which is hybrid, restless and disruptive and where it cannot be firmly 'contained' within the bounds of ideology. This is Bakhtin's 'absolute Other' or Bhabha's 'Third Space', a space which 'though unpresentable in itself ... constitutes the discursive conditions of enunciation that ensure the meanings and symbols of culture have no primordial unity of fixity; that even the same signs can be appropriated, translated, historicised and read anew' (Bhabha, 1994: 37). It is evident that the 'Othering' of Irish Travellers has been influenced and energised by a range of discourses, whether folktales, narratives or other texts, each of which can be said to form elements within this 'Third Space' and which have assimilated Irish oral tradition including a range of folktales which encompass both hegemonic and counter-hegemonic impulses and which constitute a discourse of 'othering' regarding the Travelling community. In the following chapters I explore the central attributes of this discourse which incorporates both affirmative and negative 'constructions' of Travellers from within the Irish tradition.

The liminal margins of the text present exciting new opportunities for textual analysis; in particular, they offer places where agency in the form of oral traditions influence the discourse, where the text is decentred, loosened and re-contextualised. The text begins to operate as a nexus where political resistance and social agency preclude any single meaning. Such a process is in line with the 'new' function of the literary or cultural critic as delineated by Barthes (1977) whereby the focal point is on the reader/audience – those who read/hear and interpret the text, as opposed to those who generate text: 'to mix writings, to counter the ones with the others in such a way as never to rest on any one of them' (Barthes, 1977: 146). Texts are placed one against the other in order to challenge and alter the prevailing orders of power. As delineated by Foucault, such a process involves contextualising the circumstances of narrator and audience and reader, in short everybody who generates and 'receives' the text, whether in oral or written form: 'Perhaps it is time to study discourses not only in terms of their expressive value or formal transformations, but according to their modes of existence. The modes of circulation, valorization, attribution, and appropriation of discourses vary with each culture and are modified with each' (Foucault, 1984: 117).

The 'modes of existence' I explore here relate to both vernacular culture and the juxtaposition that is the 'local struggle'. The contingency of power dictates that the liminal historical discourses I explore here were muted yet tenacious. The fact that it is only very recently that the oral histories of the Irish (majority) population itself have begun to be retrieved is symptomatic of the problematic nature of all historical versions of the past including ongoing attempts to ascribe such identities in line with homogeneous or linear processes.

Attempts to 're-present' or recuperate the history of marginalised groups such as the Irish Travellers have their own difficulties. The contingency of power dictates that the linkages between self-representation and representations of social groups imposed from the 'outside' by way of the dominant culture are complex and can never be fully delineated from one another. When one adds the longevity and complexity associated with the colonial project in Ireland including the large-scale switch from the Irish language to English the difficulties of confirming any definitive 'truth' with respect to the representation of cultural minorities and 'outsiders' in Ireland is made manifest. Exacerbating the situation is the fact that many marginal groups who were objectified by long-held tropes and representative strategies frequently complied or exaggerated these constructions as acts of resistance and mimicry.

Since I am dealing with texts which were originally spoken aloud in front of an audience, and primarily in the Irish language, the insights of a rhetorical theoretician such as McGee (1982) seem particularly apt here. Developing his theorisation, in part, on the works of Aristotle, Marx and Kenneth Burke, McGee explores the material approach to text and distinguishes between what might be termed the more idealist history of ideas and material history as it is really engendered. While idealist history has a tendency towards the prescriptive approach and a certain reification of text, McGee emphasises a material history of rhetoric, one which is established and rooted in what people understand and know. 'A material history of rhetoric ... begins with real speeches which are demonstrably useful to an end or are failures. Such an approach to theory would not aim at making rules of composition, but rather at the description, explanation, perhaps even prediction of the formation of consciousness itself' (McGee in McKerrow, 1982: 25).

McGee's approach is particularly appropriate when considering the folklore-inspired texts explored here. Performance and the performative function is essential to the construction of materiality through text. A text which is symbolically ineffective or which does not function towards a perceived 'end' is a failure. A text is also something which can be physically felt or (sometimes) viewed. It is an entity that is materially evident. Not only is each text or discourse a product of its own environment, it is also a product of the material relations which occur between real people and between human beings and their immediate environment. Each text is henceforth a 'discourse' in itself and will of necessity 'have to be characterized as material rather then merely a representation of mental and empirical phenomena' (McGee in McKerrow, 1982: 25).

Postcolonial and postmodern modes of questioning and resistance, particularly those which delineate certain minorities as 'outside history' are those which inform the analysis here, particularly in rela-tion to the manner whereby language, text or image serve to construct an 'identity' for the Travellers and gradually assume a 'factual' status, the category of some apparent or objective identity. The intention here is to approximate in as far as possible to the role of 'critic' or reader, that audience which 'receives' the texts, he or she who is most often at the vantage point where the individual is – 'with-out history, biography, psychology; he is simply that someone who holds together in a single field all the traces by which the written text is constituted' (Barthes, 1977: 24). It is evident that the oral traditions and discourses explored here complicate our notions of authenticity and 'truth' and question the efficacy of many dominant European cultural paradigms as inculcated in the nineteenth and twentieth centuries. A postmodern critique of representation as undertaken here rejects the totalising perspectives and apparent social 'coher-ences' of old. Ultimately, the myths and folktales explored in the following chapters reject causality in favour of fragmentation and indeterminancy. What initially appears a rational or unified subject or identity, i.e. the image of the Traveller as 'inferior Other' or 'outsider', is resisted and the frame of representation is usurped.

As evidenced in the previous chapter, Irish public discourse as expressed within the oral tradition is characteristic of a primarily pre-urban (pre-1960s) Ireland and was frequently delineated by a nexus of power relations as predicated on the binary which was Self and Other. That these representative tropes and stereotypes were specific to a particular time and cultural milieu is clear. Such Othered constructions and representative strategies have a long and well-established history in Irish literature as written in the English language, particularly as relating to the Anglo-Irish literature of the Literary Revival or the literature of the 'Celtic Twilight'. The English literature produced in Ireland during this period, in particular that produced by the Anglo-Irish, highlights the acknowledged truism that Travellers have never 'been themselves' in the literature and culture of the Irish mainstream. Not unnaturally, as the long-established quintessential 'outsider,' the figure of the Traveller held a fascination for Irish writers, a fascination which flourished in the

English language particularly during the late 1900s (Delaney, 2000, 2003, 2007; Lanters, 2008).

Irish writers working in both the Irish and English languages and whose work is as diverse as that of J. M. Synge, W. B. Yeats or Pádraic Ó Conaire have employed Traveller characters and Traveller tropes from time to time, the vast majority of which have been made to fit generic images based on what Robert Rhodes has called a 'received lore' (Rhodes in Delaney, 2007: 32). This construction that is the Traveller ironically provides one of the clearest nexus points between the colonial and postcolonial Irish literature, since images of Travellers mirror those of the colonial 'stage Irishman', the happy-go-lucky vagrant, the criminal, the drunk, the storyteller, the fighter and the outcast (Delaney, 2000, 2003, 2007; Lanters, 2008; Walsh, 2008).

Indigenous and transnational literary representations of Travellers and Gypsies (Roma) have in common the fact that they are nearly always related to an obsession with cultural legitimacy but more particularly with origins – whether linguistic, ideological, racial, personal or national. As Deborah Nord (2006) points out with respect to English Romani (Gypsies), a people without historically identifiable origins often come to 'stand for the question of origin itself and to be used as a trope to signify beginnings, primal ancestry, and the ultimate secret of individual identity' (Nord 2006: 8). Literary representations of Irish Travellers also fit within this paradigm as much as they do within the nineteenth century quests to describe and categorise racial and cultural groups as discussed earlier in this volume. It is no small irony that it is almost always from the 'outside' that the first interest in these numerically small cultural groups is first evinced. In the case of Irish Travellers it was in Britain and within the Gypsilorist tradition, a tradition which itself emerged from a culture with a long-established stereotype tradition with respect to Ireland and the Irish more generally. This confluence of representative strategy and type serves to situate Irish literary categorisations of the 'other' within a broader European literary framework where the Roma people also have frequently found themselves enmeshed within the literary and representational tradition incorporating the exotic 'other' that is Orientalism. As with Irish Travellers, this 'othering' process was a form of 'other within an other' whereby Roma were seen as 'Orientals' who were established within European borders. This form of exoticism ensures the assignation of travelling peoples whether Irish Travellers or Roma to a place that is 'outside of historical record and historical time, outside of Western law, the Western nation state, and Western economic orders, outside of discursivity itself … in an eternal present, a self-continuity that transcends context and time, they seem able to remove and replace the memory of others at will' (Trumpener, 1992: 180).

As evidenced in this volume Irish Travellers hold in common with other traditionally migrant and diasporic peoples the fact that they have witnessed the construction and permeation of a wide range of reductionist representations and stereotypes (Bhreathnach, 1998) in relation to their community, many of which have assumed the status of 'fact' within Ireland's collective conscience. These have coalesced over time into what Foucault defined as a 'regime of truth':

> Each society has its regime of truth, its 'general politics' of truth – that is, the types of discourse it accepts and makes function as true; the mechanisms and instances that enable one to distinguish true and false statements; the means by which each is sanctioned; the techniques and procedures accorded value in the acquisition of truth; the status of those who are charged with saying what counts as true. (Foucault, 1977: 131)

So reified and 'fixed' have these constructions become over the course of time that scholars such as Paul Delaney have queried 'whether it is possible to recognize and depict another culture as also Irish' (Delaney, 2003: 163). Other scholars of Otherness have considered this same difficulty in the broader European sense, given that more often than not the representations of marginal groups have been formed within an imperialistic paradigm, one incorporating subordination as an aspect of a difference that is at its roots perceived as negative and is a subject for surveillance or control. Dyer (2003) puts this quandary very succinctly when he says that the representation or study of marginal groups has the effect of 'reproducing the sense of the oddness, differentness, exceptionality of these groups, the feeling that they are departures from the norm' (Dyer (2003) in Lanters, 2008: 189).

While outlining the undoubted limitations of representation, whether literary or visual, Dyer also admits that they (i.e. representations) are 'also what makes saying possible at all' (Dyer, 1993: 2). Given that dominant cultures have the ability and (frequently) use representations of marginalised groups in ways which bolster or justify oppressive practices or systems it is the case that subjugated or subaltern groups are thrown back upon creative ways to resist such constructions and definitions. This is quite true in the case of Irish

Travellers whose growing written canon reveals the clear understanding that 'conflicts over representations are struggles over meaning' (Rakow and Wackwitz, 2004: 174). Recently, a small body of Traveller literature has emerged to challenge this static and stereotypical way in which Travellers have been reproduced culturally, politically and ideologically. This small yet emerging canon comprises primarily life histories that seek to forge a 'place' for Travellers in modern Ireland that is no longer marginal. Autobiographies, 'life histories' and memoirs as produced by Travellers themselves (Cauley and Ó hAodha, 2004; Donahue and Gmelch, 1986; Dunne, 2004; Gorman, 2002; Joyce, 1985; Warde, 2009) challenge the traditional Western mode of self-representation in historical terms and signify a change of genre and approach whereby diverse and multi-voiced texts, autobiographical practices and testimonies have emerged into the public sphere. From different traditions and histories, these texts do justice to what Spivak has defined as 'the subaltern giving witness to oppression, to a less oppressed other' (Spivak, 1998 in Phelan and Rabinowitz, 2005: 352). A small yet important aspect of these life histories includes the attempt to identify the specificities of Irish representational practices as relating to the 'constructed' Traveller Other and the usurpation of stereotypes, attitudes and perceptions, whether current or historical.

This as-yet small canon of literature is one thread in the increasingly multicultural tapestry that shapes public discourse in Ireland. Given that the past decade has witnessed large-scale immigration to Ireland for the first time in centuries including myriad new ethnicities and communities (whether Eastern European or from Sub-Saharan Africa), it can be argued that one of the most fundamental values inherent in such 'new' discourses is the challenge they pose to long-standing perceptions, within both the official and public spheres, that Ireland was always an ethnically homogeneous monocultural state or that it was a nation devoid of any seriously overt and long-standing prejudices (see MacGréil, 1996; McVeigh, 1992b, 1994, 1997; Ó Síocháin et al., 1994; Power, 2004; etc.) Homi Bhabha (1994) has highlighted the role of literacy as a homogenising impulse in the modern nation-state and the fact that oral forms represent a counter to those homogeneous or unifying trends which characterise the development of the modern state. In many ways the recent and growing canon of life histories as produced by Travellers is also a usurpation of those national narratives which have been 'elevated' or long privileged. They are representative too of those covert cultural forms (Gibbons, 2006: 72) which are remarkably tenable despite their marginalisation or occlusion.

The discussion here has drawn to a large extent on post-colonial theoretics. This type of criticism incorporates a strong focus on the use of textual constructions of historical contexts and events. In the case of Ireland, the Self/Other relationship establishes a context in which moral evaluations are predicated on a colonial relationship encompassing an identity or space which is appropriated – and in which the subject is conquered or controlled against his/her will. The textualisation of Irish identity resulting from this historical framework comprises a teleological impetus, one where the narrative is celebrated in a utopian realisation of Self, one which assumes the end of the anti-colonial struggle and a triumphant self-determinism. One of the drawbacks of this teleological impetus, however, is the stasis which accompanies the culmination of discourse; the self/other split remains, a historical legacy which is re-established through the elision of those narratives and expressions of identity which are liminal, hybrid or in-between. These energies frequently challenge those apparently indefatigable configurations which are the authority of the national language or official text. The indeterminacy of Ireland's colonial position and its ramifications have been theorised by a number of scholars including Graham (1994, 2002) and Kiberd (1996). Graham (2002) describes the peculiar satisfaction linked with the tensions of Self/Other and the straining of the coloniser/colonised distinction as associated with analysis of the Irish text:

> This is the joy of reading the Irish text, since its embodiments are multiple and always overlain with these tensions between self and other, the tendency to the archive and the tendency out of the archive to an Other which would destroy the archive. And yet this is not a simple act of destruction – indeed it is a destruction always threatened, always happening, near-silently. It is what Roland Barthes calls a 'subtle subversion … not directly connected with destruction, [which] evades the paradigm and seeks some *other* term: a third term. (Graham, 2002: 45)

The discourse which is examined in the following two chapters and as elucidated in Irish oral/folk tradition (as delineated in the Irish language) is an example of the 'multiple' indeterminancy of Self and Other in the Irish context. That history is both a site of struggle and a point of political discourse and ambivalence is a well-acknowledged truism. With this in mind, theorists including Foucault have advocated the obligation that is the study of discourse, in particular those discourses which have the potential to alter the relations of power through the narrative process (Foucault in McHoul and Grace, 1997: 121). The 'Othering' of Irish Travellers has been influenced and energised by an ambivalent and often dichotomous discourse internal to Ireland as encompassed in folktales, narratives and texts that have assimilated both hegemonic and counter-hegemonic impulses. The Irish oral tradition includes a range of folktales which can be seen to constitute a discourse of 'othering' regarding the Travelling community, one which is deeply ambivalent however. In the following chapters I explore the central attributes of this discourse which incorporates both positive and negative constructions of Travellers as evident within the Irish tradition. In one set of folktales (*The 'Nail' Legend*) Travellers' liminal status as a very small and marginalised group is 'justified' in the text on the basis of perceived 'mythical' transgressions while in another (*Ortha an Ghreama* – The Stitch Prayer) they are considered 'outsiders' (outsiders who are simultaneously within and without the moral and textual economy) – a people who have been 'chosen' to act as moral arbiters of the actions of the majority (settled) community. As with the Irish traditional music tradition (Mac Aoidh, 1994; Ó hAodha and Tuohy, 2008) Traveller folk narratives and stories incorporating Traveller characters and tropes are an element of both the larger Irish (settled community) tradition and the narratives of the Travelling community itself (Court, 1985; Zimmermann, 2001). Given that these narratives where Travellers are the main protagonists are an element of both the settled community's (mainstream) Irish storytelling tradition, and Travellers' own tradition they are at a very fundamental level important examples of the power base of native Irish culture as set against British colonial traditions and the 'talking back' that is redolent of long-subjugated peoples. These texts highlight the disarticulation of textual representation and the subversion through irony, imitation and colonial mimicry of prevailing power systems. It is a movement into those spaces characteristic of 'the liminal undecidability of Ireland's colonial position, producing a sense of dilemma within colonial discourse, within Irish textuality' (Graham, 2002: 45). Here the text proves inadequate in its regulation of that postcolonial boundary that is other/Other. The ideological deadlock induced by the teleologism of the 'same' (i.e. national language) is subverted and 'in the very practice of domination the language of the master becomes hybrid – neither one thing nor the other' (Bhabha, 1994: 33).

The fact that they are a people indigenous to Ireland has made it possible to situate Traveller 'othering' within the framework of imperialist and colonial 'othering' as theorised by Said (1978, 1986, 1993) and Miles (1989). Travellers have been 'Othered' in Ireland in an uncannily similar way to the way that the Irish and other indigenous peoples were 'othered' as part of the English colonial project. Traveller 'othering' differs in nature however from the 'othering' of colonised indigenous populations elsewhere because they have not been constructed as racially 'Other'. Within Ireland itself, Traveller 'othering' has historically been placed within the framework of colonial 'Othering' since the dominant view of their origins is one where they are perceived to have left a previously settled existence and are most likely the remnants of Ireland's colonial past. It as if the stockpile of negative imagery that accompanied the British 'othering' of Irish people was simply transferred from one 'Other' to another. Traveller 'Othering' can be seen to have been influenced and energised by an ambivalent discourse internal to Ireland.

The Irish folk tradition includes a range of folktales which when taken together can be seen to constitute a discourse of 'othering' regarding the Travelling community. The 'othering' incorporated in these myths situates Traveller origins within a degraded or inferior discourse. Traveller origins are attributed to moral transgressions. These alleged transgressions render Travellers a 'disordered' community, a community who are perceived as 'Other'. In the following chapters the themes and tropes of a number of these folktales are explored and the argument is made that they served to reinforce strong 'anti-Traveller' sentiments or attitudes amongst the mainstream or settled community. I argue that these tales validated at a deep psychological and socio-cultural level a suspicion of Travellers. They also provide a mythic basis not only for the marginalised status of Travelling people, but also for their origins and their social evolution as an outcast group. As was the case with other Travelling groups, Irish Travellers were seen as a threat to the country's internal boundaries and order as Ireland, like other European countries, firmed up its political and administrative boundaries with the emergence of the nation-state. Certain attributes of the 'Other' as theorised by Miles (1989) are useful for examining the framework of the unique form of 'Othering' that took place in the case of Irish Travellers. Notions such as civilisation, private property, the control of nomadic workers, the threat of economic competition and the use of pseudo-religious tenets to legitimate pathologisation and control are all intermeshed in the history of anti-Traveller 'Othering' in Ireland as evidenced in the imagery of the folktales which I discuss here. In the following chapters the way in which this anti-nomadic strand of the Irish folklore tradition operated is considered, as is the link the between the assignation of Travellers as 'negative Other' and the stereotyping accorded to those people formerly known as tinkers.

I discuss three discourses as encompassed in various versions of three folktales that were once widely known in Ireland. These are the 'Nail', 'Pin' and 'Bar of Gold' legends. All three include a number of tenets which were central to Irish (particularly Catholic) and Christian self-identity (see Ó Héalaí, 1985), including The Crucifixion, Charity to the Blessed Family who are frequently in exile or in flight, and the traditional Irish concept of hospitality/charity which had a central place in Irish society in both the pre-Christian and Christian eras. These tales depict one group of Travelling tradesmen (often represented by an individual (i.e. the tinker) who morally transgress by behaviour that is perceived as unusual, churlish or outside the norms of society. The transgression of these norms is depicted as particularly serious in these tales as they are transgressions which include accusations such as deicide and the display of immoral behaviour in relation to holy people or saints. The analysis of these transgressions includes an examination of the concepts of good and bad luck as inscribed in binary oppositions between tradesmen such as the blacksmith who are depicted as highly respected members of the community and those who are perceived in a more negative light i.e. nomadic tradesmen.

I also examine two other intertwined discourses in the Irish tradition which are seen to be linked to one another and related to these tales. One is the discourse which depicts Travellers in conflicts with the saints, particularly in relation to their flexible working practices and their ignoring of shibboleths regarding working on the Sabbath. The other is a part of the satirical Irish tradition and is a discourse where the poet/Traveller is seen to be in a verbal dispute with a highly respected and educated member of the majority community, i.e. the priest. Reductionist views and stereotypes relating to Travellers and their origins have such firm roots in Irish popular belief that they even influenced the iconography and belief system of the settled community in relation to traditional trades like smithery and the forge. I discuss the internalisation of the tenets of this pathologising discourse on the part of the settled community, a discourse which points to the sometimes fraught relationship that existed between the travelling and settled communities and between travelling and sedentary workers in particular. The analysis of each of these discourses has as its outcome the conclusion that Travellers and their cultural values are judged according to the norms of the settled community and are defined by certain stereotypes and attributes which continue to be ascribed to the Travelling community today. Reductionist ascriptions include the allegations that Travellers are dishonest, prone to violence and poverty, belong to a different and lower class in society and are representative of a dysfunctional culture. This culture is rendered dysfunctional because poverty is seen to be the outcome of the Travellers' outcast status encompassing self-employment and nomadism. I devote the final section of this chapter to an examination of the way in which this pathologising tradition as encompassed in the folktales has been internalised in Traveller self-identity. I examine the way in which the pseudo-religious aspect of these tales has been particularly damaging to Traveller self-identity and use the comments of a number of Traveller intellectuals to attempt to describe the process whereby a minority group internalises feelings of shame and inadequacy.

# 8 Anti-Traveller prejudice: The narrative within the Irish imaginary

The folktales explored here are no longer as widely known or as widely disseminated as they once were. However their *raison d'être* – i.e. the 'accursed' or 'disordered' status of Travellers as a consequence of their perceived 'punishment' – continues to resonate strongly both in Irish popular belief and in the general public discourse concerning Travellers in Ireland. I argue that reductionist stereotypes as applied to Travellers in the folklore tradition and in Irish popular belief generally continue to have an impact upon the way in which the popular image of Travellers is constructed in Ireland. For the settled community reductionist stereotypes as elucidated in the folklore tradition have also become part of popular belief concerning Travellers, including current beliefs as to their origins and the origins of certain cultural attributes associated with them, in particular their nomadism.

While little literature to date exists on the question it is generally accepted by both Travellers and the settled community that Traveller self-identity has been heavily influenced in a negative manner by the reductionism and stereotyping which has been attributed to them. Writers of Traveller and Gypsy background such as Hancock (1999) and McDonagh (1994) have only recently begun to discuss the stigmatising effects of the pathologisation of Travellers, a stigmatisation which as they point out often leads to an unwillingness on the part of Travellers to acknowledge their own identity. More damagingly still, popular (negative) beliefs concerning Travellers including possible explanations of their origins are likely to have influenced the official discourse of modern public policy makers and state policy vis-à-vis Traveller settlement and possible assimilation.

In this chapter I show how the derogatory status associated with the term 'Traveller' but more especially 'Tinker' as outlined in the folklore tradition has also influenced in a negative way the culture of Travellers themselves. The pseudo-religious nature of these folktales which provide an explanation or alleged justification for the outcast position occupied by Travellers in Irish society has had a profound effect on Traveller self-identity and on the self-confidence of Travellers and probably acted as a partial explanation as to why they were, and continue to be, the subject of prejudice from Irish society.

My primary goal here is to discuss the influence of these folktales in the Irish tradition and their influence on popular beliefs and attitudes regarding the Irish Travellers. I also make links to similar folktales as they exist in the European tradition. The mythic demonisation and ostracisation of nomadic people like the Travellers is not confined to the Irish tradition. Irish Travellers are only one of a pantheon of pan-European nomadic groups who have been travelling in Europe since at least the seventeenth century and probably well before this date (see Acton, 1974, 1994; Beier, 1985). Kenrick (1972) notes that as early as 1243 an English law was passed aimed at curtailing the 'wandering Irish' then in England. It is also known that Gypsy (including Romanichal and Roma) groups travelled and worked in Ireland periodically. It is safe to assume then that reductionist or 'negative' stereotypes as outlined in the European folklore tradition were interchangeably applied to a range of different Travelling groups.

This present chapter explores the folklore evidence for the depiction of the Traveller as 'negative Other'. It acts as an important foil to a later chapter where I discuss an opposite strand of the folklore tradition, one where this negative depiction of Travellers is challenged. The assignation to Travellers of the status of 'negative Other' is only one facet of the tradition. The counter-tradition includes a number of folktales where Travellers are seen to subvert their ostracisation by the majority community and defend cultural values of particular importance to them including their nomadism. The folktales discussed here are tales which I refer to as the 'Nail', 'Pin' and 'Bar of Gold' tales. The Irish folklorist Pádraig Ó Héalaí is the first Irish scholar to have examined these 'anti-Traveller' folktales. In his seminal article 'Tuirse na nGaibhne ar na Buachaillí Bó' (1985) he examines the way in which elements or motifs from these different folktales influenced one another.

The composition of this chapter is much indebted to this seminal work, and is in many ways an attempt to expand on many of the themes first outlined in Ó Héalaí's article. Ó Héalaí (1985) concentrates particularly on motif transferral in the above-mentioned tales and emphasises an internal dynamic within the tales whereby the denigration of the ambulatory tradesman led to the elevation of the figure of the *gabha* or blacksmith. By taking Ó Héalaí's analysis a stage further it is possible to view these tales in an even more radical or reactionary light. Whether read singularly or in conjunction with one another, they can be said to form a discourse whereby anti-Traveller or anti-nomadic prejudice is justified and validated by the settled community, a validation that is (apparently) logical in its exclusion of Travellers from mainstream society. Travellers are portrayed as a negative 'Other' because they have disturbed the social order of things. Their crimes as outlined in these folktales include deicide, the ultimate disturbance of the natural order.

The focus in these tales on where the Travellers came from is also a central plank in the logic which serves to exclude them from the discourse of the mainstream. Their imputed origins as recounted in these tales are deeply stigmatising and may in fact be where the real power of these tales lies. This is because they imply a falling from grace which culminates in a 'falling out' from the settled community. The latter tenet has probably served until very recently to bolster the justification for assimilationist approaches and policies with regard to Travellers and their culture as implemented in Ireland. The versions of the 'Nail', 'Pin' and 'Bar of Gold' tales which I discuss here I located on the archival reels of the Irish Folklore Commission material in the library at the National University of Ireland, Galway. My method for finding these tales was to search the indexes referring to the different *Imleabhair* (Volumes) of material held on the microfiche of the IFC material. These tales are listed in the index under a range of sobriquets including:

*'Ceardanna agus Ceardaíthe'*, *'Lack of Charity punished'*, *'Charity rewarded'*, *'Holy Family'*, *'Ár Slánathóir'*, *'Virgin, smith and tinker'*, *'Smiths'*, *'An Gabha'*, *'An Mhaighdean Bheannaithe'*, *'An Mhaighdean Mhuire agus an Tincéir'* etc.

It was not always straightforward to locate material pertaining to these folktales. Some versions of these folktales are not listed in the index. Others can be found bearing no particular title or are listed under a topic which may not seem directly related to the subject in hand on an initial search – e.g. *'An Gabha'* or *'Ceardanna agus Ceardaíthe'*. There is a huge quantity of material in the IFC archive. All that one can hope to do is to compare a range of different versions of the folktales as accessed from different reels in the archive using the index as a basic guide. In locating and copying examples of the folktales (i.e. Nail, Pin and Bar of Gold tales) from the archive I am satisfied that I accessed a fairly representative selection of the tales as they appear in the archive. These tales seem to have been found throughout Ireland, or at least anywhere in Ireland where the IFC folklore collectors gathered material and there did not seem to be any obvious regional variations in either the frequency of the tales or the content of them. A large number of the tales were written in Irish and I translated the excerpts of these for the purposes of this analysis.

It is important to recognise that the roots of anti-nomadic and anti-Traveller/anti-Gypsy prejudice are very old indeed; they can be traced to biblical and apocryphal myths rooted in the Judaeo-Christian tradition, myths which sedentary society has been able to call upon from time to time in an effort to justify exclusionary practices against nomadic peoples and their lifestyles. The French scholar Jean-Paul Clébert (1963) was one of the first to discuss some of these myths of origin. He identifies an 'exoticist' folkloric discourse of the 'Other' whereby Gypsies and Travellers are said to have originated in the 'foreign' or 'exotic' lands of the Far East (hence Egyptians for Gypsies) or to have descended from characters like Vulcan whose association with metallurgy was a source of disapproval.

The most powerful 'pseudo-religious' myth about Travellers or Gypsies is what I will term the 'Nail' legend i.e. the story of the travelling tinsmith/tradesman who as a punishment is cursed to a life of wandering. The legend says that when Jesus was being crucified the Romans asked a blacksmith to make the nails for the Cross. He refused and they then asked the Tinker or Gypsy instead. The Tinker agreed to make the nails and consequently the Tinker/Gypsy or travelling tradesman is cursed for ever to a life of wandering. This punishment is the tinkers' lot because the Roman and Jewish blacksmiths when asked to make the nails for Christ's crucifixion refused, whereas the tinker/Gypsy is said to have agreed. As punishment for their part in the deicide, the descendants of the tinker are cursed to wander, running (in part) from any reminder of their part in this crime.

The Jewish people, in parallel, have suffered a similar 'punishment' for their 'role' in the same deicide. They too, are also condemned to wander for 'killing' Christ. These myths, where nomadism is seen as a punishment, have strong allusions with two other powerful myths, whose currency is even wider. The first is the seminal biblical myth of the Garden of Eden, where as a punishment for defying/insulting God and succumbing to the temptations of the serpent (the Devil), the human race, as represented by Adam and Eve, is excluded from the Garden of Eden. The human race suffers as part of the earthly journey, a suffering/punishment that manifests itself through the 'mark' of Original Sin.

Another myth which encompasses elements analogous to the 'nail' legend, including those of the 'mark', the punishment, and the wandering/exclusion from mainstream society is the biblical story of Cain and Abel. Cain and his descendants are also cursed to wander as a punishment for Cain's act of fratricide.

The existence of 'biblical' myths such as these are indicative of the fact that nomadism, since the earliest times, has been perceived in association with themes that carry a negative import – exile, banishment, flight. All of these apocryphal myths also have redemptive features however. The legend of Cain is both a blessing and a curse. While the process of banishment makes outcasts of his followers, the wandering in the desert is nevertheless a journey to a new liberation. The *Book of Exodus* indicates that the Jewish 'scattering' which gave rise to the stereotype of the 'The Wandering Jew' also has redemptive qualities. It is both a punishment and redemption for the unfaithful Israelites. Stories relating to Travellers and Traveller origins in the Irish folklore tradition also include this duality. While on the one hand nomadism is seen as a punishment for alleged misbehaviour on the part of the Travelling community, their 'Other'/'outcast' status also empowers Travellers, who, in a direct reversal of roles, act as moral arbiters on many aspects of the social life of the settled community including the possession of 'emotional magic'. That this duality between good and evil is one of the central energies of the myth is confirmed by Leach (1969). He writes of the dualities that are to be found in the myths of the Book of Genesis. These myths encompass within them a number of binary oppositions, dualities that are both complex and simple at the same time – the binary oppositions between the good people/chosen people and the wicked/Other. He argues that the cultural force of these 'religious' myths lies in these binary oppositions and that these myths could have validated their exclusion not only for the Travellers/Gypsies, themselves mainly Christian, but also for those who act to exclude them. Burke (1964) situates the existence of these binary oppositions within the context of developing hierarchical power structures in Western society. He argues that the imposition of laws controlling land and property are underpinned by the ideology of Western Judaeo-Christianity: 'If the great pyramidal structure of medieval Europe found its ultimate expression in a system of moral purgation based on the two "moments" of "original sin" and "redemption" … the "guilt" intrinsic to hierarchical order … calls correspondingly for "redemption" through victimage' (Burke, 1964: 284).

Travellers and other nomads have disturbed the theocratic social order which is said to have existed previously. Their nomadism challenges the progress towards order and hierarchy and their 'punishment' is consequently 'deserved'.

This theme of *'Order/Disorder'*, *'Anarchic/Conventional'* (my italics) has also been touched upon by a number of scholars writing about Travellers. Okely (1983), who has researched Travellers/Gypsies in Britain, says that Traveller nomadism in modern society is a powerful symbolic challenge to notions of fixity and order. Traveller nomadism represents an 'ideological and symbolic disorder' (1983: 2). Gmelch (1977) and McVeigh (1992b) situate anti-Traveller prejudice in Ireland within the context of nomadism's challenge to fixity and order and Gmelch specifies the roots of this prejudice in the suspicious attitudes of peasants to those who are landless. McVeigh goes further and terms anti-Traveller prejudice a form of racism, a racism which he terms sedentarism. Sedentarism, he argues, is a phenomenon premised on the Travellers' rebellion against attachment to land and especially capitalist property and notions of community. The suspicion of Travellers so widespread in the 'majority' community he attributes to their subversion of the selfsame majority's norms: 'the refusal to work for others, the refusal to be "settled", and the refusal to recognise capitalist definitions of ownership and control remain profoundly subversive acts' (McVeigh, 1992: 43).

A number of themes and motifs commonly found in both Irish and international folktales have had a major influence on these binary oppositions. Seminal amongst these is the folktale known as *The Various Children of Eve*, a didactic story which seeks to explain the existence of different classes in society and the different levels of social status associated with each class (Ó Héalaí, 1985: 87). This story attempts to justify the inequalities between societal classes on the grounds that Eve hid some of her children from God's blessing: 'Eve has so many children that she is ashamed when God pays her a visit. She hides some of them and they fail to receive the blessing that God gives those in sight. Thus arises the differences in classes and peoples'.[1]

A number of folklore narratives have in common the idea that the actual origins of Gypsies/Travellers are accompanied by an inherited collective guilt, a guilt that can be linked to the biblical myth that is the story of Adam and Eve. Kenrick and Puxon (1972) mention folktale narratives where biblical allusions attribute unnatural and incestuous origins to the Gypsies. According to one folktale variant they describe, Gypsies are an unnatural result of the 'disorder' that accompanied the Garden of Eden. Eve is said to have lain with Adam after his death, thereby producing the first Gypsy. Although the actual story *The Various Children of Eve* is not found in the Irish oral tradition, the central point of the tale is evident in a number of Irish narrative tales. Many of those tales which assign the status of negative 'Other' to Travellers and nomadism show the delineation of different levels of social status and material prosperity, a particular binary opposition being that between the 'established' or local tradesman and the 'stranger' or travelling tradesman (Ó Héalaí, 1985: 91).

Motifs which explain such delineation are apparent in a number of Irish narrative tales which seek to explain how status, good fortune and material prosperity accrue to some tradesmen – particularly 'established' or non-ambulatory tradesmen – more than others. Derrida (1974) and Hall (1997) have deconstructed the binary oppositions that underpin much of Western literary and philosophical debate and have shown that a relationship of power was inherent within the very nature of these binaries. These binaries appear to be very clear-cut but are in fact complex. Their ambivalence lies in the way in which they function in the ordering of society as a whole, both sedentary and nomadic.

Bhabha (1990) and Freud (1938) have analysed the ambivalence that is central to the operation of binary oppositions. They argue that society as a whole cannot function in mutual solidarity unless there is an 'Other' or non-conforming group within that society onto whom hatreds and negative perceptions can be transferred. The narrative mechanisms employed in these stories are the essence of this binary process since they portray one highly-respected and well-established group in Irish society – i.e. the blacksmiths – in a very positive light by contrasting them with the alleged improper and feckless behaviour of the Travelling community who are depicted as the negative 'Other'. The Nail legend depicts the Tinker/Gypsy being cursed while the blacksmith is the recipient of everlasting good fortune. Not only does this 'Nail' folktale operate to categorise people according to different societal classes, it also justifies their assignation to such classes in a very 'logical' manner and provides an explanation for the harsh conditions and low status that are alleged to accrue to those who follow certain trades.

In these stories the ostracisation of the Travelling community from the 'majority' community and their nomadism is a 'normal' aspect of the 'order of things' because they are said to have behaved improperly towards a holy personage, in this case Jesus Christ. The hardship which is the Traveller's lot is accentuated by a direct contrast with the lot of the blacksmith. As the tinker's nemesis in the settled community, the blacksmith is rewarded with seemingly everlasting strength or energy while the tinker is 'cursed' with the inconstancy of having to wander forevermore so as to make a living, as evinced by this variant from the Irish folklore tradition recorded in Rinn, County Waterford:

> When the Jews were going to crucify our Lord they went to the blacksmith so that he would make the spikes to nail Jesus to the cross. The blacksmith refused to make them. They went then to the tinker and he made the spikes for them. They say that this is the reason that the blacksmith is as strong at the end of the day as he is at the start and that this also explains why the tinkers are wandering vagrants and will be forever. (Iml. 809: 471–472)

The blacksmith is further rewarded by having a regular stream of customers while the wandering is seen as part of the tinker's punishment that he has to constantly travel in an effort to seek out new work opportunities:

> *Our Saviour and the Blacksmith*
> Our Saviour said to the blacksmith … 'Everyone to your door and you to no-one else's door.' And the poor tinker made the nails and Jesus said – 'You to everyone's door, he says, and no-one to your door.' That is the way it is ever since. Everyone comes to the black-smith and there is no better trade than it, and the tinker has to go from house to house. (Iml. 809: 471–472)

It is the Gypsy or Roma (in European countries other than Ireland) who is primarily associated with the Nail legend in the folklore tradition. A Greek Easter carol identifies the Roma Gypsies (who also worked as smiths) as the makers of the nails for Christ's Cross and curses them for using their skills to make Jesus die in a particularly savage manner:

> And by a Gypsy smith they passed,
> a smith who nails was making.
> 'Thou dog, thou Gypsy dog' – said she,
> 'What is it thou art making?'
> 'They're going to crucify a man

And I the nails am making.
They only ordered three of me
but five I mean to make them.
The fifth the sharpest of the five,
within his heart shall enter.

*(Journal of the Gypsy Lore Society*, 3. II, 175)

Liégeois (1987) alludes to a folktale variant found in Europe which blames the Gypsies for having forged the nails used to crucify Christ. Only three of the nails are used in this version however. The fourth becomes a red-hot piece of iron, iron that can never be cooled, one which has pursued the Gypsies and their descendants everywhere ever since, thus explaining their nomadism.

It is the tinker/smith, above all tradesmen, who, by virtue of his trade is primarily associated with the nail legend in folkloric discourse. However there are many variants of the 'Nail' legend where a wider range of Travellers are accused of improper behaviour. De Meyer (1921) mentions a folktale found in Europe which explains why misery and misfortune are the fate of the weaver. In this story it is he who supplies the nail for the Crucifixion. In the European folktale tradition as a whole, the Crucifixion is often the context within which travelling tradespeople are castigated for their alleged derision, laziness or lack of generosity, their role in the Crucifixion resulting in an accursed status[2] being attributed to them. In a Romanian folktale it is the carpenter that is cursed because he makes a large heavy Cross for the Crucifixion despite being asked to make a light one. His opposite number in the settled community, the blacksmith, finds favour because he makes small nails for the Cross despite being asked to make large ones (Gaster, 1923). In another version from England it is the shoemaker who is cursed as he spits at Christ on his way to Calvary. A shoemaker from Devonshire, when admonished for his shiftlessness is said to have answered his accuser like this:

Don't 'ee be hard on me. We shoemakers are a poor slobbering race, and so have been ever since the curse that Jesus Christ laid on us' … when they were carrying Him to the cross they passed a shoe-maker's bench, and the man looked up and spat at Him; and the Lord turned and said, 'A poor slobbering fellow shalt thou be, and all shoemakers after thee for what thou hast done to Me.

(Henderson, 1879: 82)

The Irish tradition also includes variants of the 'Nail' legend where rather than spitting the shoemaker actually makes the nails for the cross, indicating that the improper behaviour towards a divine personage was attributed to a wide spectrum of tradesmen and not confined exclusively to the tinker or the cowherd. That the same 'Nail' legend had a deep psychological and even sociological import for those who heard it can be gleaned from the fact that the story even affected the working practices of certain metal-workers. Even the hammering methods employed by blacksmiths were affected by the psychological import of the 'Nail' legend. The blacksmith's habit of striking the anvil before striking the iron is explained by this variant on the 'Nail' legend: 'The Jews came to a blacksmith and asked him to make the nails for the crucifixion. The blacksmith struck the anvil three times with his hammer but did not make the nails … That is why a blacksmith always strikes the anvil before he strikes the iron' (Iml. 815: 50).

Blacksmiths in County Tipperary also had another work practice which related directly to the 'Nail' myth:

> When the Jews were about to scourge Our Saviour they came to the blacksmith to make the spikes. The blacksmith made the spikes but he put a twist like a hook in the top of them and this meant that they were useless. They couldn't get any of the Jews in Jerusalem to straighten the spikes again so they went to the tinkers. Liam Ó Lúbaigh remembers that when the blacksmiths in his own place were making spikes it was their custom to put a twist at the top of the spikes and then to straighten them again. They used to do this as a reminder of the time the blacksmith did this trick for the Jews. That custom was in southern Tipperary until about twenty-five years ago when the blacksmiths gave up making spikes. (Iml. 630: 240)

A metalworker recorded by the IFC was made to feel uncomfortable about the fact that he made nails, even though the same nails were only for a statue of Jesus that was to be hung in a Catholic Church as part of the Stations of the Cross.[3]

> I done all the iron work at the monument. I had to make four hundred iron clasps for jointing the stones. The stones in the floor are from the old jail in Downpatrick, you know. If they could only speak. I put up the iron railings long ago when Francis Bigger asked me to do it. I made the nails for the stations too. One man said I'd have no luck, making the nails to crucify Christ. It was a shoemaker

first of all made the nails that crucified Christ, for the smith refused. That's why a shoemaker will never make money and never have no luck. (Iml. 1220: 278)

While the 'Nail' legend is one of the most well-known 'anti-nomadic' myths internationally and undoubtedly had a significant role in the perpetuation of anti-nomadic prejudice both abroad and in Ireland, there are a number of other narratives common to the folklore tradition which may have also contributed significantly to anti-nomadic preju- dice. As with the 'Nail' legend the principal mechanism whereby anti-nomadic prejudice is elucidated in these narratives is through the explicit contrast implied between the respective behaviours of the sedentary and travelling tradesman towards a sacred personage. Once again the steadfastness of the blacksmith, a revered personage in Irish tradition, is contrasted with the alleged improper behaviour of that negative 'Other', the travelling craftsman. The title of the most common of these stories in the Irish tradition is *Tuirse na nGaibhne ar na Buachaillí Bó* (lit: The Tiredness of the Smiths that falls on the Cowherds). This story often depicts a Travelling woman, usually the personage of the Virgin Mary travelling through the countryside while reliant on the 'hospitality' of the country people. The Virgin asks a Tinker (and/or cowherd) to give her a pin with which she can tie her cloak. He refuses and is consequently cursed and despised whereas the blacksmith obliges and is once again rewarded with 'a good name' and good fortune. Occasionally the Virgin Mary is alone and in the guise of a Travelling woman as in the following version of the 'Pin' tale where the origins of the blacksmith's unique supernatural powers are explained as a reward for his generosity:

> They say that the blacksmiths have a gift that other people do not have. That's how I heard it ... until recently nobody would annoy in any way someone who had any drop of the blacksmith's blood flow- ing in their veins. They used to say that it was the Blessed Virgin who gave this gift to the blacksmiths the first day ever. The day that she lost the pin from her breast ... after the tinker had refused her request ... I forgot to tell you that she went to the blacksmith then. The blacksmith didn't know who she was. He just thought she was some poor travelling woman and of course she was, but not exactly. 'Come down to the fire and warm yourself', says the blacksmith. She sat down by the fire and got warmed herself with it. 'Maybe you would make a pin for me' she says, 'to put in my cloak where I lost

the other one.' 'I'll do it and you're welcome' says the blacksmith. The blacksmith started on making a pin for her then despite the huge amount of work he had already had on hand. When he had it made he gave it to her. She thanked him and she wished happiness and good luck on himself and his trade. She also prayed that he might possess gifts that other people didn't possess. The black-smiths have these gifts ever since. (Iml. 770: 69–70)

In some variants of the 'pin' legend the Virgin Mary is travelling with the Baby Jesus and the 'pin' is required to protect not only the Virgin from the elements but also the Baby Jesus. In an ironic reversal of the 'stereotypical' role of the Tinker/Traveller wandering the world in search of hospitality/lodgings, it is the selfsame Tinker who refuses 'hospitality', in this case, the 'pin' to the travelling holy personages.

A noteworthy aspect of the variant on the 'Pin' legend (transcribed below) is the fact that the Tinker is depicted as working within his own home. Irish social policy relating to Travellers, hitherto primarily assim-ilationist in nature, has for the best part of the twentieth century been formulated along this very premise i.e. the view that the Travellers were originally settled people who took to the road for a variety of reasons. Since they were allegedly originally a settled people the assimilationist viewpoint sees it as a worthy enterprise to 're-settle' or 'rehabilitate' the Travellers back into 'mainstream' society.

The fact that the Tinker is too busy to make the pin is also perhaps indicative of the function of these stories in articulating tensions or jealousies between sedentary and nomadic tradesmen and can be linked to those stories where Travelling tradesmen and those who practise a flexible economy are castigated, in many cases by a respectable 'representative' of the 'sedentary' community such as the priest for working outside the normal 'sedentary' working hours i.e. working at night or on a Saturday or a Sunday etc. The final line of this variant on the 'Pin' legend, – '*Ní maith an rud a bheith doicheallach*' (It is not a good thing to be churlish) – can also be read as a simple endorsement to Christian charity, an endorsement that can be found in any number of morality tales:

The Mother of God was walking around with her Son once. It was a very dark night and the rain was torrential. Not alone was it raining heavily but the wind was blowing off the shawl that was around herself and Our Saviour. He was only a child at the time. The two of them were drowned wet so that anyone would surely have had pity on them. She was walking along until she came to a little cabin on the side of the road. She heard a sound inside, the sound of someone beating the tin with a hammer. It was only the beginning of night and the door was not closed. She stood at the door and she said hello. There was a tinker inside and she asked him, for God's sake to make a pin for her that would keep the shawl around herself and the child. The tinker was impolite to her and ordered her to leave. He told her that he had better things to do than making pins for everybody who came the way … She walked until she came as far as the forge. There was a blacksmith inside and he was working the bellows. The Blessed Virgin said 'God bless the work' and she asked him, for God's sake to make her a pin that would keep the shawl around herself and the child. 'I will make it and welcome, good woman,' said the blacksmith … 'It's a bad night for anyone to be outside.' The blacksmith wasn't churlish like the tinker.

(Iml. 117: 182–184)

Another context in which the 'Pin' legend is frequently situated is the flight from Egypt where the Virgin Mary and the baby Jesus are travelling hastily through the countryside in an effort to evade Herod and his soldiers. The pin on the Virgin Mary's cloak goes astray, such is the haste of their departure. In these narratives the Virgin Mary is frequently depicted carrying the Baby Jesus on her back or in her arms. Mary asks for 'charity' in the form of a request for a specific item – i.e. a pin with which to fasten her cloak. The response which she receives from the differing craftsmen from whom she requests the pin determines the esteem in which the differing craftsmen are henceforth held and what becomes their lot in life. In the variant below Saint Joseph is in company with the Virgin and the Baby Jesus on the flight from Egypt. The fact that in addition to the cowherd it is the woodcutter in this variant who refuses 'charity' to the Holy Family is indicative of the fact that, like the 'Nail' legend, it is not always the tinker who is cursed but travelling tradesmen generally. The fact that Saint Joseph is a tradesman who is refused 'charity' by other tradesmen only adds to the offence inflicted on the saintly personages who make up the Holy Family and emphasises the worth of respective tradesmen. Part of the folktale's irony lies in the fact that the Holy Family are migrating or travelling and are at the mercy of the sedentary community while the moral power within the tale finds the traditional figure of the nomadic tradesman – in this case the tinker – depicted as morally culpable:

When Herod thought to kill the Child Jesus, Our Lord and St. Joseph, as we know, fled with him into Egypt. As they went on their way with great haste Our Lady lost the pin of her cloak and she could not keep it wrapped around the Child Jesus. St. Joseph was very distressed at this for he himself, being only a carpenter knew nothing about iron. Accordingly he asked a wood-cutter whom he met to make a pin. The latter replied, however, that the winter was near and that he was so busy cutting wood that he had no time to waste. Next they met a cow-herd and St. Joseph asked him also to make a pin. But he likewise refused. His herd had strayed he told them and now he was busy seeking them. At last they came to a forge where the smith was busily engaged at his trade. Seeing that the man was so busy he hesitated to go near him with his request. The smith however noticed the couple and perceived that they were in distress ... St. Joseph told him of their trouble in getting a pin for Our Lady's cloak. The smith told them to worry no more. He himself would make one immediately. This he did and that in spite of the fact that he was very busy. When he brought the pin to Our Lady she smiled on him and blessed him. She told him that henceforth anyone who should bathe in the water in which he cooled his irons would be restored to health. Accordingly, to this very day these waters have the power of restoring to health people who suffer from various diseases. (Iml. 1270: 498–500)

As a consequence of their respective behaviours, the blacksmith is rewarded with supernatural powers while the woodcutter and the cowherd are not. When any blacksmith feels tired at his work from then on, the tiredness disappears: 'The smith got that gift from Our Blessed Lady – the tiredest day the smith'll wash his hands and face in the trough, he'll be as fresh as he was in the morning' (Iml. 629: 67).

As recompense for his generosity the blacksmith is rewarded with prosperity, good luck, increased energy and the qualities of stability and perseverance whereas the Traveller's lot is one of violence, hardship and wandering. As indicated by the most common title by which this story is known in the Irish tradition, *Tuirse na nGaibhne ar na Buachaillí Bó* (lit: The 'Tiredness of the Smiths that falls on the Cowherds') – in itself a proverbial saying in the Irish language (Ó Héalaí: 1985) – part of the blacksmith's recompense is exemption from the tiredness that allegedly afflicts other nomadic/less highly-regarded tradesmen like travelling tailors, weavers, tinkers, woodcutters and cowherds, a tiredness that is in fact transferred onto the ambulatory tradesmen. The concept of transferral here is a common one both in folklore generally and in the pre-twentieth century Christianity of many countries.[4] It also ties in with the concept of the binary and the traditional belief in the idea of 'limited good' as outlined in popular tradition. This is the idea that there is only a 'limited' amount of good in the world and that consequently the badness or suffering of the world is apportioned to different people according to their station in life and the appropriateness of their moral actions. The following variant which outlines this apportioning of hardship/good fortune specifies the role that the outsider in the form of a holy personage has in the balancing of the moral order. It also implies a previous 'golden age' when the travelling tradesman lived in harmony with the moral order and consequently did not experience hardship:

> She didn't take her two eyes from the blacksmith as long as he was making the pin for her and she took pity on him and blacksmiths like him. It is said ever since that the blacksmith never gets as tired as other tradesmen no matter how heavy his workload is, the reason being that she prayed to God that some of the blacksmith's hardship would be taken away from them and that it might be given instead to those who did not have any hardship. They say ever since that the blacksmith is never the one who is first to complain about the day's workload. (Iml. 97: 51–52)

Both the 'Nail' and 'Pin' legends influenced one another heavily and the central themes of both – betrayal by the Travelling craftsman, elevation of his counterpart in the settled community etc. – mean that they could arguably be classed as the same story. The 'Nail' legend's association of the nomadic tradesman with deicide gives this story a stigmatising power that is far stronger than that seen in the 'Pin' legend however. What both tales undoubtedly have in common is their didactic functions. Elements of each were occasionally combined in order to explain the good luck which was associated with certain tradesman and the insecurity and bad luck which was perceived to accompany others. Elements of both also had a great influence on how the iconography and 'belief system' of the smithery and the forge developed, an iconography that was a reminder and a bolstering mechanism for the values of 'steadfastness' and sedentarism as encompassed in the figure of the blacksmith. The following anecdote based on a variant of the 'Nail' legend indicates the value of the horseshoe nail as fashioned by the blacksmith, a value that is both practical and didactic because the story of its fashioning carries a deeper and more profound meaning:

> When the Jews were going to hang Our Saviour they went to the blacksmith and asked him to make the nails so that Our Saviour could be tied to the tree. Devil the nails I will make for you, said the blacksmith. They went to the tinker then and asked him to make the nails. The tinker made the nails for them. Our Saviour gave his blessing to the blacksmith and he cursed the tinker. That money and a good livelihood may always be yours forever, he said to the blacksmith. And that you may be searching for a living forever, he said to the tinker. The special power of the blacksmith is in the horseshoe nail ever since. (Iml. 627: 31–32)

Since the blacksmith encompasses the qualities of steadfastness and generosity it is no surprise that his elevated status as outlined in the 'Pin' legend influenced some of the traditional belief system relating to smithery and the forge. Even the instruments used by the blacksmith were said to be influenced by the blacksmith's character as recounted in both the 'Nail' and 'Pin' legends. One variant of the 'Pin' legend actually explains that the shape of the smith's tongs is a direct consequence of the smith's generosity towards the travelling Holy Family, a generosity that challenges the scorn with which others hold the selfsame Travellers. It is said that the reason why one leg of the tongs used by blacksmiths is shorter than the other is that the smith had no metal with which to make the pin when the Virgin Mary arrived at his door. Consequently he used some metal from his tongs and ever since the legs of a smith's tongs are unequal in length.

> When the Blessed Virgin was 'flying' from Bethlehem with the Child Jesus, as Herod wanted to kill him, she called at a blacksmith's forge for a pin to pin the wrap 'round the Child. People that were in the forge at the time laughed at her with scorn. The blacksmith said to her: 'My poor woman, what is it you want?' She told him, so he put the end of the tongs in the fire and made a pin out of one of the jaws of the tongs. That is why the jaws of a blacksmith's tongs are never even – one of them is always a bit longer than the other. When the blacksmith gave her the pin she went up and washed her hands in the trough and said: 'A blacksmith will never be tired after his work if he washes himself in the trough in his forge.' And a blacksmith is never tired after he does this. (Iml. 815: 48–49)

As is the case with the 'Nail' legend the above variant on the 'Pin' legend indicates the supernatural nature of the blacksmith's reward. Substances associated with the blacksmith – in this case his forge-water – henceforth exhibit the properties of everlasting rejuvenation, a rejuvenation that is the direct result of the blacksmith's kindness in fashioning the pin for the Virgin Mary: 'When he put the pin into the forge-water he felt very refreshed in himself. From that time on, when he puts his hands into the forge water he feels very refreshed' (Iml. 602: 229).

Ó Súilleabháin (1970) explains how the blacksmith in Ireland, as in many other countries, was held in high esteem by the local community. This status was predicated firstly on his vital role as a maker of implements for the local agricultural economy. However the blacksmith's status was further elevated by the belief that as a consequence of his constancy and steadfastness, as outlined in folktales such as the 'Pin' legend, both he and the forge were the conduits of supernatural powers including the power of healing.[5] It was not the blacksmith alone who as an exemplar of the 'steadfast' was rewarded. The community which surrounded him were also rewarded. The forge itself was said to be a lucky place as a direct consequence of the blacksmith's role in the 'Pin' legend. One variant on the 'Pin' legend attributes good luck to the pregnant woman who visits the forge during her confinement, the good luck being a direct consequence of the blessing imparted to the blacksmith/forge by the pregnant Virgin Mary:

> In thanks for that Our Lady left a blessing on the forge. She was expecting our Lord at the time. When I was young I heard my grandmother speak of the forge to another woman. They were telling a woman that was expecting that it was lucky to go into a forge. It would bring her safe through her delivery. They told her to go into the forge on some excuse or other – ask for a nail or something like that. It was a lucky thing to do, they said, as Our Lady left her blessing on the forge. (Iml. 1429: 225–226)

The curative properties of the forge were a part of the recompense due the smith for his kindness to the Virgin Mary in supplying her with a pin:

> The Blessed Virgin thanked him and taking the pin dipped it in the forge water and made the sign of the cross on the water with it. 'This

will kill or curse anything', she says. She left a cure in the forge water
and it is in it ever since. (B.S. Iml. 642: 364–366)

and

Ever since the blacksmith is blessed and there are several cures in
the forge, particularly in the iron and in the water which the iron has
been cooled (B.S. Iml. 1157: 529)

The 'reward' which was the blacksmith's often became a permanent
boon to the local community as his healing gift became a hereditary one
in many cases. As the following anecdote, recorded in County Clare,
indicates it was believed that the blacksmith's 'gift' was one which was
passed on from generation to generation as a recompense for goodwill
as exhibited towards the Holy Family or other saintly personages:

*Galar Buí (Liver Complaint)*
The cure is said to have been given by a saint to the Curtis family.
They were blacksmiths. They shod the Saint's horse shoes back-
wards so that he was able to escape from his pursuers. When
applying the cure people had to lie flat on the anvil, the smith had
the sledge-hammer in hand and he sounded the anvil and swung it
around the person a number of times whilst saying the words of the
charm. The sign of the cross was made on the person's breast with
the anvil. Three drops of water from the forge had to be drunk. The
smith made the sign of the cross on himself a number of times. He
had also to say a certain prayer which was in Irish. The patient was
given also certain prayers to say. Mondays and Thursdays were the
days for working the charm. There was no charge. (Iml. 1517: 157)

While the blacksmith was a tradesman of elevated status in most
communities, so too was his locus operandi, the forge. In many rural
areas the forge was the focal point of the community and was the location not only for smithing and healing, but also a place where socialising
and recreational pursuits such as card-playing, storytelling and sports[6]
took place. A variant of the 'Pin' legend indicates the sacrosanct nature
of the forge. Like other sacrosanct places such as holy wells, interference
with the forge was liable to have negative consequences including the
attribution of bad luck to the guilty party. 'And ever since the Virgin
prayed that a blacksmith's door might never have to be closed – the
forge was not locked. The old people would tell you that it was not lucky
to steal anything out the forge' (Iml. 1039: 551–554).

This belief that the forge ought not to be locked is ironically one of the few instances where the blacksmith and the forge depart to some extent from their symbolic roles in the majority community bulwarks of sedentarism, steadfastness and as a vehicle of anti-nomadic prejudice. Despite the role of the forge and that of its principal actor, the blacksmith, as a foil to the alleged vagaries and misery foisted on Travellers as part of their nomadic life, the forge was nevertheless left unlocked because it was seen as a legitimate place of sanctuary for any passing Traveller who might need shelter for the night. In some variants of the 'Pin' legend the Virgin Mary allocates a duty of hospitality/lodging to the blacksmith as part of her recompense to him, a duty which may be seen as a didactic 'inversion' of the lack of hospitality she received at the hands of the 'nomadic' tradesmen:

> And she prayed then that neither himself nor any tradesman like him would ever be without a fire or without shelter, or that there would be shelter for anybody that he wished it for as well as himself … It was and still is the custom of many blacksmiths in County Galway that they don't put any lock on the forge in case anybody might be going around at during the night who might be looking for a refuge for the night. And none of the blacksmith's tools were ever stolen and many are the people that travelled all over the county and found a night's shelter in a forge. (Iml. 795: 122–126)

Ó Héalaí (1985) says that the 'Pin' legend itself appears unique to Ireland. Its principal motif – the Virgin Mary requesting a pin with which to fasten her cloak – does not appear in the folklore tradition of other European countries.[7] The importance of the 'Pin' legend lies in the fact that it is only one segment of a larger anti-nomadic discourse. The basic motif whereby different tradesmen refuse/grant hospitality to a holy personage/personages and are rewarded/punished accordingly is a common one in the folklore of many European countries (see Degh, 1965 – included in Appendix B as a sample text from the Hungarian tradition – or Rokala, 1973). In a story from Greece the ploughman is rewarded for his truthfulness and humility towards Christ while the curse of never-ending work is put on the weaver because of his deceit and pride (Klaar, 1963) while another often nomadic craftsman, the mason, is the subject of opprobrium in a Portuguese story. Misfortune is said to follow the mason's craft because of his derisive attitude to the Holy Family or because of the lack of attention to detail in the work which he undertakes for the same Holy Family (Cardoso, 1971).

It is very likely that there was cross-fertilisation between the story-telling of different countries on this same theme just as it is likely that both the 'Nail' and 'Pin' legends, as told in Ireland, influenced variants on the same theme where, in the absence of either the pin or the nail, certain tradesmen were nevertheless cursed because of the impropriety of their actions towards holy personages. A good example is the following recorded in County Kerry. In this story it is the mason, a craftsman who like the tinker was particularly associated with nomadism in Ireland, who is again cursed, in this instance by the Virgin Mary:

> It was always said that the stonemason would never have any luck. This was said and that he would never be comfortable. Because when they were working at the masonry in the old days the Virgin Mary passed by carrying Our Saviour. She was inside under a ledge sheltering from the rain, a sort of a rainshower. And she went in to shelter under the ledge. The masons were up above her working away. One of them saw her and didn't he throw some of the mortar down on her and she cursed him ... that he might never have any luck. (Translated from citation in Ó Héalaí, 1985: 122)

While in Ireland it is the Virgin Mary and the Child Jesus who are the principal holy personages associated with the 'Nail' and 'Pin' legends, their nemesis most frequently being the tinker or the cowherd[8], there additionally exists a corpus of folktales (or variants on the aforementioned folktales) whose central motif is the refusal of generosity on the part of an ambulatory tradesman towards a sacred personage other than one of the Holy Family i.e. one of the saints. There also exist not only variants on these tales, however, but in addition a corpus of folktales whose central motif is the refusal of generosity or the exhibition of a churlish attitude on the part of an ambulatory tradesman towards a sacred personage other than one of the Holy Family.

The consequences of these actions on the part of the ambulatory tradesmen are similar to those in the 'Nail' and 'Pin' legends. In Irish tradition it is Saint Patrick, the patron saint of Ireland, who is most frequently depicted in 'confrontation' with travelling tradesmen. The fact that such an important saint and iconic emblem of Ireland is seen to confront the nomad only serves to highlight the binary opposition which sets sedentary against nomad. The 'Nail' legend situated the nomad outside the boundaries of civilised behaviour because of the Traveller's part in deicide. Improper behaviour as exhibited towards Saint Patrick also serves to marginalise Travellers and validates the perceived justness of their marginalisation within an Irish context. It is interesting that a pivotal role in relation to both the origin and rejection of nomadism itself is assigned to Saint Patrick, the patron saint of Ireland, by one respondent to the IFC's Questionnaire on Travellers (then known as Tinkers) issued in 1952. This respondent from Omagh attributes the nomadism of the West of Ireland Travellers he encounters to the fact that they were cursed by Saint Patrick for eating his goat. That Travellers bear the mark of this curse physically manifests itself to the respondent in the fact that he cannot understand the Travellers's West of Ireland (and presumably Irish-language-laden) accent: 'They ate Saint Patrick's goat and can't speak right since' (Iml. 1256: 257).

This comment also hints at further layers of 'Othering' within Ireland itself, an othering that was not solely confined to Travellers. Prejudice against migratory people generally was widespread including those *spailpíns*[9] or migratory labourers who frequently came from the west of Ireland people (see O'Dowd, 1991).

S. B. Gmelch (1974) has pointed out that Travellers were a sizeable minority within this migrant worker population, joining Irish people from the settled community who worked annually on farms on Ireland's east coast and on the west coast of Scotland. The fact that a very sizeable proportion of the Irish Traveller community have surnames originating in the west of Ireland such as Joyce, McDonagh and Ward also gave credence to the fact that they were originally west of Ireland people who had lost their land through some historical circumstance or transgression. Accusations regarding interference with Saint Patrick's goat[10] or otherwise irritating the Saint while he was engaged with his spiritual duties were not confined to Travellers in the Irish folklore tradition. These 'allegations' often had their origins in rivalries between different parishes who were seen to have competed for Saint Patrick's favour. Indeed it was commonplace in the medieval era, both in Ireland and abroad, for different areas of the country to dispute[11] their claims to the relics and memorials of saints. The suspicion that, in addition to certain regions of the country, the Saint favoured certain classes of people also appears in Irish folklore. This is a possible echo of the way in which the divine personages of Jesus and Mary are said to have favoured certain classes of craftsmen e.g. the blacksmith as outlined in the 'Nail' and 'Pin' legends. Patrick often appears as chief protagonist in another folktale which, like both the 'Nail' and 'Pin' legends depicts Travellers in a very negative light. This is the 'Bar of Gold' folktale, a story in which Travellers are accused of 'sharp practice' towards Saint Patrick or on occasion divine personages like Jesus or Saint Joseph. This story can be seen as another variant on both the 'Nail' and 'Pin' legends as it continues with the basic theme of punishment as recompense for the nomadic tradesman who displays a lack of generosity or – in this case – 'sharp practice' in his dealings with Christ or one of the saints. In this story a holy person such as Saint Patrick finds a bar of metal. The saint, or on occasion Christ himself, asks a Traveller or cowherd to value the item. The Traveller, who secretly hopes to acquire the item for himself, states that the metal is of little value. Christ/the saint refuses to accept this valuation however and goes to the blacksmith to ask his opinion. The blacksmith informs him that it is in fact a bar of gold and is very valuable. As a consequence, the blacksmith is assigned everlasting prosperity while the tinker or cowherd is consigned to a life of wretchedness. In the following variant of this tale it is the Holy Family who are the attempted victims of the Travellers' sharp practice:

> ### The Tiredness of the Smiths Transferred to the Cowherds
> Our Lord, Saint Joseph and the Virgin Mary were travelling along the road one day. Saint Joseph had a gold can. They met a blacksmith. Where is the can of gold said Our Lord to Saint Joseph. We can show it to the blacksmith. Is that worth anything so that we could sell it to you? The blacksmith looked at it. That's pure gold he said. You're set up for life now. I'll give you a bit. No, I won't take any of it from you said the blacksmith. They went on their way. They met a cowherd. Look at this fine can of gold says Our Lord. I would sell it to you if you gave me a good price for it. Give it to me said the cowherd and I'll have it for chasing the cows. He didn't give it to him. They went on their way and who did they meet but the tinker. The tinker looked at the can of gold. He said he would give them a penny for it. He gave him the can and his wish for the tinker was that he should never have a specific place of lodging but that he would forever be searching for somewhere to stay. He gave as a Gift to the blacksmith that he should be as fresh after a day's work as he was in the morning. He transferred the tiredness of the blacksmith onto the cowherd and 'wished' that the tinker would always be wandering.
>
> (Iml. 1277: 123–124)

While the above variant of the tale makes reference to the Holy Family as the finders of the gold, it is more common to find Saint Patrick mentioned as the chief protagonist in the story, as evidenced in this variant recorded in Limerick. The fact that this variant actually names and accuses what was a well-known Limerick Traveller family of cheating behaviour towards a saintly personage only serves to underline the 'moral' power of these narratives to bolster anti-nomadic prejudice.

> *Eachtraíthe ar Naomh Pádraig (Stories about Saint Patrick)*
> Saint Patrick was herding pigs an' the pig sorted up a lump of gold an' Saint Patrick brought it to the tinker. 'Ah', says the tinker, 'that's nothing'. He said it was no good. He gave him his 'blessing'. 'Go mbí d'aghaidh ar gach tig agus do chúl leis an dtig a bheug id' dhaig'. He's travelling around ever since. Tis the tinker too that made the nails that crucified Our Divine Master. Hartigan he was called. Saint Patrick then went to the smith. The smith said that it was solid gold and not to believe that ruffian. He blessed the smith then and he lightened the work on the smith and put a portion of it on the tinker and on the herder. A smith is never tired since. (Iml. 613: 106–107)

Folk anecdotes or what some people might term 'urban legends' circulate amongst Irish people today which can be seen as a continuation of this stereotype of 'sharp practice'. One of the most common is the following which I recorded from an elderly neighbour from County Limerick and concerns the alleged sharp practice of those Travellers who specialise in trading antiques.

> A young fella called there one day. He was well-dressed with a nice shirt on. A shirt and a tie like any other salesman. And he was well-spoken too. He had the gift of the gab. It was only afterwards when he was gone that I realised he was one of the caravan crowd, you know – the Rathkealers. I had hardly opened the door when he was inside in the hallway and what did he spot only the grandfather clock that's on the wall ... Anyway, straight away doesn't this fella ask me whether I'd be willing to sell it. Before I had a chance to answer him doesn't he offer me 200 euro for it. I said to him that I had never really thought about selling it, that it was just always in the family. He asked me then whether it was working and I said it did if it was wound but it would lose a few minutes every day. Ah, it's probably past it he said. Sure, I'd be doing a favour for your Mam by taking it off your hands. I'll tell you what – I'll give you 250 euro for it. That's not a bad offer and it's hardly worth that, in fairness. It must be worth a few quid more than that surely, I said. I mean it's very old ... He was telling me it wasn't worth much but he was still having a good gander at it at the same time. He had a good look at

the hands of the clock and rubbed his hands along the front case of the clock. He shook his head and said, 'To tell you the truth, this clock is hardly worth the guts of 200 but sure I'm in a generous mood today. What do you say to 250 euro? No one else will offer you the same. I can guarantee you of that. I don't want to rush you but I better get going as I have to meet a fella up the road' ... something inside me had clicked at that stage and I told him I wasn't interested. I told him I'd have a think about it. He kept asking me was I sure over and over again and I told him I was. It was hard enough to get rid of him. The next time my son was down didn't we go into town and get a fella out to examine the clock. I was shocked. Didn't he value the clock at 8,000 euro ... If I had sold it to that dealer fella, I wouldn't have got half of what it was worth. He would have got a bargain and I wouldn't have been any the wiser. Sure those caravan people, they'd buy you and sell you.

(Interview with M. H., Limerick City, November 2002)

Stories in the 'Bar of Gold' tradition depict Travellers ignoring the rules of 'fair play'. That they are willing to indulge in sharp practice even when dealing with Saint Patrick or Christ himself makes them appear untrustworthy. The reductionist stereotype of sharp practice as relating to Travellers and the belief that 'they cannot be trusted' became part of the fabric of anti-Traveller discourse in Ireland as the twentieth century progressed. In Irish folklore, Saint Patrick above all the Saints is frequently seen as the upholder of Church ordinances and the castigator of those who deign to work independently of the 'established system'. In many variants on the 'Pin' legend Saint Patrick is seen invoking his wrath on the sharp practice of those travelling tradesmen who work outside normal hours or subvert what are seen as the norms of the mainstream or settled community. These variants on the legend articulate an aspect of Traveller-sedentary relations which has hitherto been relatively ignored in the socio/anthropological analyses of the history of anti-nomadic prejudice – i.e. the tension between the Traveller whose ethos of self-employment allows him to 'undercut' his sedentary rival by virtue of his more flexible working practices. In Irish folktales, Saint Patrick is often depicted upholding the religious prohibition regarding work on the Sabbath:

Saint Patrick was making his way along the road one Sunday. He saw three stonemasons making a house. He asked them why they were not at the Mass. They said that they were too poor and that they could not afford to go. Saint Patrick put his hand in his pocket and he gave them a shilling and eight pence, and he told them to go to the Mass and to refrain from any more work that Sunday. When Saint Patrick was passing by that afternoon, he saw them working again and he became really angry. He put curse on the lot of them and the curse he put on them was the following – 'a long life and broken shoes', and this curse is on the stonemasons ever since.

(Breathnach, 1947: 115)

Another common tale in the Irish tradition states how Saint Patrick came across a group of carpenters who complained to him that their trade was proving very unprofitable to them. Saint Patrick said nothing, but observed them at work on Saturday evening and again on Monday morning. He noticed that they gave 'the late blow' with the hammer on Saturday night and 'the early blow' on Monday morning, and then he upbraided them severely for not showing more respect for the Sabbath and for behaving in such a mean and calculating way. Ever since, it is said, a workman should avoid these two 'blows', for otherwise his work will not prosper (Ó Hógáin, 1985). This idea also appears in some variants of the 'Pin' tale where it is the Virgin Mary rather than Saint Patrick who speaks out against working on Sundays. Having received the 'Pin' from the blacksmith she advises him that good luck and prosperity will follow his trade if he avoids 'the late blow' on the anvil on the Saturday night and 'the early blow' on the Monday morning.[12] This relates to a traditional motif also found in the folklore of other European countries where the constancy of the blacksmith is rewarded by the 'gift' whereby his hammering on the anvil is said to keep the devil away. It is difficult not to see these tales admonishing tradesmen who work outside the 'normal' hours as indicative of something deeper than simple religious exhortations to keep the Sabbath. It is very likely that economic competition or economic jealousy between the sedentary and the nomad was at the root of much of the tension between the sedentarist and nomadic viewpoints. When one considers that flexibility and self-employment encompassing different time-management practices were characteristic of the nomadic craftsman's economy it is easy to see how the propagation of tales where those who work outside the 'normal' hours are admonished might well be in the interests of the sedentary craftsmen, who often had extreme competition from their nomadic equivalents.

This theme whereby a tension exists between a religious figure such as Saint Patrick and a travelling tradesman is commonplace in Irish folklore. It is not surprising then to find that the folklore of the Travellers themselves includes an opposite discourse whereby the Travellers are seen to have a particularly close relationship with Ireland's patron saint and help the saint in his life's mission – the conversion of Ireland to Christianity. In the next chapter I discuss one aspect of this discourse where the Travellers are intimately identified with saints and other holy people through a symbolic inversion whereby they travel in the guise of holy people or healer-shamans who provide a balancing force on the action of the settled community through their role as moral arbiters. This theme whereby the Traveller and a holy personage are in conflict extends into another and related discourse, however, in Irish folk tradition. This is the discourse whereby the Travelling tradesman and the local 'authority figure' of the priest, as opposed to a saint, are seen to be in conflict. Many anecdotes relating to Travelling poet/tradesmen such as the legendary Munster poet/mason Eoghan Rua Ó Súilleabháin depict the poet/craftsman engaged in verbal duels with priests, often in response to the priest's criticism of their 'flexible' working hours. In the following anecdote it is the poet Eoghan Rua Ó Súilleabháin, better known as a journeyman mason and labourer who is depicted defending his work as a shoemaker against the priest's accusation of laziness. It is interesting that two of the most frequent stereotypes as applied to Travelling craftsmen and Travelling poets i.e. that they are fond of drinking and are indolent are the very same stereotypes which the Traveller uses to strike back:

> One day Eoghan Rua was fixing shoes and a priest passed by. The priest spoke to him in a half-verse:
> > 'The poet working slowly.
> > A blow of the hammer struck by him only here and there!'
> > This is how Eoghan replied:
> > 'The priest his head full of Latin,
> > But his stomach dancing with punch!' (Iml. 253: 563)

That Travellers themselves had an internal discourse within their own communities where they challenged this type of scapegoating is indicated by the following anecdote recorded from some travelling stonemasons[13] in County Cork. Here the mason is seen taking the very serious step of pursuing the priest as far as the Confession box in order to extract payment from him because the priest has 'short-changed' him. This anecdote is unusual because it includes a written example of

*Béarlagar an Saor*, the language of the stonemasons, a language very little of which was ever written down:

> *The mason and the priest*
> There was a priest who had a mason working for him and when Saturday came the priest did not remember to pay the mason before he went off to the church to hear confessions. The mason followed him to the church and he became impatient waiting for an old woman to finish her long confession. He lost his patience and he spoke to the priest in the loud voice of the Mason's Cant. 'Come out here, priest, and pay me and don't be listening to that old woman and she talking rubbish' i.e. making up stories. (Iml: 1455: 230)

These folk tales and their variants had a great impact on the popular mind. These legends and their perpetuation had a huge influence in moulding popular prejudice against Travellers and their nomadic lifestyle. The central motifs of all of the tales we have examined portray Travellers in a negative light. The Traveller is accused of inhospitality and a lack of courtesy in the 'Pin' legend. The 'Bar of Gold' legend depicts the Traveller as an untrustworthy good-for-nothing who is always capable of sharp practice while the 'Nail' legend accuses the Traveller of complicity in the worst crime anyone can commit, deicide.

Ó Héalaí (1985) notes that these well-known and widely-disseminated folktales are not the only tales in the Irish tradition which foster anti-nomadic prejudice. They are also bolstered in their central thesis by other aetiological tales which provide alternative rationales for the 'accursed' position of Travellers and the perceived wretchedness of their nomadic way of life. Like the 'Pin' and 'Nail' legends these narratives lend support to reductionist and stereotypical views of Traveller culture, views which frequently cast them in the role of scapegoat. An example is the tale where the archetypal theme of the Traveller who requests lodgings is inverted. In this tale the alleged accursed state of Travellers is elucidated by their supposed origins. They are described as the descendants of a man who refused to give Christ a night's lodgings (see Iml. 412: 7–8). Another example repeats a common stereotype employed against nomadic peoples generally i.e. the accusation that the Travellers operated as spies and in the process betrayed Ireland during a rebellion against British rule (see B.S. Iml. 907: 5). These same reductionist explanations have also been applied to other nomadic people including the Gypsies in the European folk tradition, explanations including the allegation that the Gypsies were Christ's guards but that they got drunk and were unable to defend him (Liégeois, 1987). Yet another proposes that Gypsy nomadism is a punishment, the consequence of their refusal to shelter the Virgin and Child during their flight from Egypt (Liégeois, 1987).

The 'accursed' or 'disordered' status of Travellers, a consequence of their 'punishment', lends support to the perpetuation of a wide range of reductionist stereotypes as applied to Travellers in Irish popular belief, stereotypes which still have wide currency in Ireland today. In Irish folklore generally the symbolic disorder of Travellers is often symbolised by fighting and trouble. Traveller feuding and their alleged propensity for fighting continues to be applied as a scapegoating stereotype to Travellers even today. Of all the negative stereotypes that have been applied to Travelling people this alleged propensity for disorder as symbolised by ritualised-type fighting is probably the one which remains uppermost in the minds of the settled community as illustrated by some the responses to the 1952 Tinker Questionnaire:

> No sooner than they have a drop taken they start arguing. They set to one another and start hitting and planking each other until they are cut up and injured badly. You'd hear women shouting and giving each other a mouthful of abuse – children roaring, men hitting each other. When the fight is over they gather together their belongings and move on
> (Iml. 1255: 269 – IFC respondent from County Kerry)

The utilisation of Travellers as 'negative Other' or 'mirror-image' for the disorder that takes place in the majority community is a common device in the Irish popular and literary culture. Many of the descriptions of the stereotypical 'fighting Tinkers' as recorded by the Questionnaire bear an uncanny resemblance to the descriptions of faction fighting that occurred between large groups of the settled community earlier in the twentieth century and particularly at the end of the nineteenth century:

> They crowded to the 'fair field' and to the locality around some days before the fair driving their droves of unbridled asses before them, except those which were attached to carts for the conveyance of their women and children. Their weapons of offence and defence were ashen 'plants' – young trees about three feet long trimmed and 'seasoned' for the purpose. The tinkers' free-fights was a particular feature of the fair and of the most spectacular' ... There was often a

good deal of enmity between certain groups or families of tinkers and on occasions on which the several groups came together, such as Bartlemy Fair, this enmity frequently showed itself in general free-fights in which the whole tinker community often got mixed up, even the women fought throwing babes aside ... old custom assigned them the exclusive possession of a particular quarter of the field, a spot that wise men well might shun.

> 'For no man once could know or tell
> When tinkers' war-cries there might swell
> o'er clashing fight or fray,
> Where tribes in mustered strength were met
> From wide Deasmumhan' length and breadth
> Whose weapons once in motion set
> But fallen foes could slay'.
>
> (Iml. 1255: 139 – IFC respondent from County Cork)

The very word 'tinker' became associated with fighting in the minds of some of the settled community according to this respondent from County Kerry: 'B'ionann tincéir i n-aigne na ndaoine nó duine ólthach imirtheach bruighneach' (Tinker was synonymous in many people's minds with someone who was a drunkard, a trickster or a violent person) (Iml. 1255: 20) and the very surnames of local tinkers were often used as a byword for troublesome people, as indicated by this respondent from County Tyrone: 'The Dowds were also a feared tribe. It used to be said to quarrelsome children: You're as bad as the Dowds' (Iml. 1256: 254).

In folklore narratives this predilection towards fighting is seen to be a part of their status as negative 'Other' and an inevitable consequence of their punishment for their roles in the 'Nail' and 'Pin' legends. This is clear from the Virgin Mary's recompense to the tinkers in a variant of the 'Pin' legend:

> 'Níl aon áit choíche', ar sise, 'a mbeidh gabha nach mbeidh rath agus rathúnas air agus níl aon áit choíche a mbeidh na tincléarannaí nach mbeidh gach uile bheirt acu ag troid agus ag marú a chéile'.

> ('There will be nowhere from now on', she said, 'that the blacksmith won't have luck and prosperity but there isn't anywhere that the tinkers will be that every pair of them won't be fighting and killing each other'). (Iml. 990: 477–478)

In today's Ireland the stereotype of Travellers and fighting is probably the most powerful reductionist view of Travellers that continues to be widely held. Indeed it can be said that perhaps the only aspect of Travellers' lives which many settled people are aware of is this alleged propensity for fighting as it is frequently an object of morbid fascination for the shock-hungry media. Headlines such as the following occur frequently today in the Irish newspapers:

'Clash between Travellers averted' (*The Irish Times* 10 September 1998)
'Family feud leads to bill hook attack' (*The Irish Times* 21 April 1999)
'Traveller shot in feud over land' (*The Examiner* 25 March 1999)
'Travellers in hiding as vicious clan war erupts' (*Sunday World* 27 June 1999)
'Traveller feud causes tension' (*The Irish Times* 26 August 1999)
'Feud Between Traveller Cousins' (*The Connacht Tribune* 7 June 2002)

The 'accursed' or 'disordered' status assigned to Travellers as part of their function as negative 'Other' in these narratives is not only symbolised by the 'disorder' of fighting. Poverty, including hunger, strife, homelessness/nomadism and unemployment are also perceived attributes of the same disorder. The didactic force of these narratives is elucidated in the contrast between the social and economic conditions as experienced by the bulwark of respectability – the smith, and the outsider or 'negative Other', the Traveller[14] (in this case a travelling tailor).[15]

> What do you want, says he to Saint Patrick
> I was wondering whether you might put a patch on my cloak.
> I don't do work for the likes of you, said the tailor
> I do work only for the gentry.
> Hungry and arrogant you will be forever, says Saint Patrick.
> And that's the way it is since then for all the tailors
>
> (Iml. 977: 405–406)

In contrast with the blacksmith a lack of 'steady employment' is as part of the Travellers' status as exemplar of the 'disordered' or negative 'Other'.

> 'Go dtaga airgead a's beatha isteach sa teach agat arís go brách!', deir sé leis an ngabha.
> 'A's go dtuga tusa a' tóruigheacht do chodach arist go brách', deir sé leis an tinncéiridhe'

('That money and a good livelihood will come into your house for
ever', says he to the blacksmith.
'And that you may be searching always to make a living', says he to
the tinker.) (Iml. 627: 32)

The power of these folktales as explanations for the status allocated to
different classes of people is perhaps best exemplified by the reasons
they promulgate to explain Traveller nomadism. Traveller nomadism,
when not romanticised by the Irish literary tradition has been one of
the least understood and most vilified aspects of Traveller culture as
perceived by the 'majority' community. In these folktales Traveller
nomadism or their 'homelessness' is frequently defined as another
negative consequence of their assigned 'punishment':

agus chuir sé an taighncéir gan ao' chunaí go brách ná tara teine
d'adhaint ar an aon teighnteán amháin. (Iml. 977: 510)

(And he made the tinker homeless forever so that he might never
kindle the second fire on any hearth).

Deirtear gurab é sin an chúis go mbíonn an neart céudna i lámhaibh
an ghabha um thráthnóna thiar is a mbíonn ar maidin agus go
mbíonn na tinncéirí ar fán is go mbeidh go deo. (Iml. 630: 247)

(It is said that that is the reason why the blacksmith has the same
strength in his hands of an evening as he has in the morning and it
is also the reason why the tinker is wandering and will be forever.)

Chuir sé tuirse an ghabha ar aodhaire na mbó agus ar an dtinncéir a
bheith sa tsiubhail i gcomhnuí. (Iml. 1277: 124)

(He put the tiredness on the cowherd and the tinker so that they
always have to be walking (wandering)).

That this 'negative' belief as to the origins of Traveller nomadism was
not simply confined to the folktale tradition but was a widely-held belief
by settled people generally was indicated by many respondents to the
Tinker Questionnaire when questioned regarding possible Traveller
origins, as indicated by the following:

Tradition is that the tinkers and the blacksmiths are the two oldest
trades known or extant. Story heard locally, but not now clearly

remembered (I recorded a version from a smith in Beragh, in Omagh) that tinkers made nails for the Crucifixion when blacksmith refused; were cursed and have to keep travelling since.
(Iml. 1256: 258 – IFC respondent from Omagh, County Tyrone):

The local tradition is that the gipsies stole one of the nails and Our Lord condemned them to a wandering life for doing so. Local tradition has it that the gipsies came from either Spain or Egypt.
(Iml. 1256: 268)

*The origin of the tinkers*
The most popular version goes back to the time of the Crucifixion. When the blacksmith refused to make or sharpen a spear for the Jews, the tinker did so, and for his perfidy his tribe was condemned by Divine ordinance to wander homeless through the world till the Last Day. Being so despised and ostracised by mankind generally they formed gregarious groups or communities, each tribe or body appointing its own King or head to whom they took an oath of allegiance (Iml. 1256: 116)

These tales then can be seen as part of a popular tradition which 'justifies' the alleged 'wretchedness' of Traveller's lives, a wretchedness which is the fruit of alleged misconduct. When looked at in an Irish context Traveller culture is further denigrated because the sub-text of these legends hints that Traveller nomadism rather than being a cultural marker is a 'punishment' or a by-product of dysfunction. The implication here, although it is not articulated, is that Travellers were originally settled people who had to 'go on the road' because of a misfortune which they brought on themselves. Collins (1994), O'Connell (1994b, 1995), McDonagh (1994) and McVeigh (1992a) among others have described the strong assimilationist thrust of Irish social policy as implemented by the Irish state in relation to Travellers in Ireland for the last fifty years. This assimilationist effort can be linked to a conceptualisation of Travellers as 'drop-outs' in the Irish imaginary, a notion which modern-day Traveller activists are particularly anxious to refute (see McDonagh, 2000b). It is clear how damaging this supposition of 'punishment' or 'falling out' from settled society as promulgated by the folktale tradition is. The steadfastness and constancy of the blacksmith is lauded constantly by way of contrast with the wandering and alleged fecklessness of the Traveller. As an honoured representative of the majority society the blacksmith's role sheds light on the construction and maintenance of sedentarist values in Irish society. While he represents order and steadfastness, the Traveller by virtue of his nomadism is symbolic of a disorder which is perceived as a hindrance to material progress and fixity. That this perception of Traveller culture as elucidated in the 'unofficial' discourse of folklore permeated the 'official-speak' of the emerging European nation-state is no coincidence. Liégeois (1994) notes that for the better part of the twentieth century state policies in relation to Travellers, in both Ireland and Europe, have focused on settlement and assimilation – i.e. attempting to control Travellers and impose order on them. Anthropologists such as Burke (1964) and Okely (1983) have also touched on this theme whereby Travellers represent the anarchic, a symbolic disorder that must be controlled or repressed through fixity and assimilation. Indeed it can be argued that Travellers, as portrayed in these folktales are 'punished' in great part because they are seen to disturb progress towards order and hierarchy.

It would be dangerous to underestimate the significance of anti-nomadic narratives like the 'Nail', 'Pin' and 'Bar of Gold' legends in the moulding of popular prejudice in Ireland. These narratives undoubtedly had a certain psychological power for their audience because they provided mythic explanations or 'justifications' for the existence of different classes within Irish society, their positions vis-à-vis one another and the tensions that accompanied the interaction of these different relationships. The wide influence of these narratives is indicated not only by the fact that these narratives were common currency in Ireland but also by the fact that many phenomena perceived as everyday experiences were explained by reference to events recounted in these narratives. Indeed a good deal of the Irish belief system pertaining to smithery and the forge was actually corroborated by reference to these narratives. The moral dimension to these tales is also clear. They praise the qualities of generosity and charity and warn that punishment and bad luck attend those who are perceived to be miserly or over-opportunistic. What is not so clear but may be of equal significance, however, are the ramifications of such exhortations. Any history of Traveller/sedentary relations/tensions and the accompanying stigmatisation of Travellers necessitates an examination of the relationship between migration and the labour market and how the work of Travellers fitted into an Irish economy that was primarily rural from the Middle Ages until the middle of the twentieth century. A range of different indigenous Travelling groups all appeared in Europe more or less contemporaneously from the 1400s onwards. Their appearance and their subsequent stigmatisation can be attributed to some extent to the structural and economic developments which Europe underwent from the Middle Ages, in particular the change from a feudal to a market-oriented capitalist system, an economic revolution which meant that many workers either chose or were forced to become migrants. This new-found mobility meant that self-employed itinerants were increasingly viewed with suspicion and stigmatised as 'drop-outs' and vagabonds. The overall result of these structural ideological and economic changes was the emergence of increasingly repressive policies towards those people looked upon as vagrants, *gens sans aveu*, masterless men, and those craftspeople who travelled in groups including indigenous Travellers and Gypsies. Increasingly repressive policies towards travelling people came into force in many European countries from about 1500 onwards (Acton 1974, 1994; Beier, 1985). These policies were repressive and yet flexible in the sense that they targeted all sorts of mobile people, including seasonal labourers, self-employed pedlars and those categorised as Travellers or Gypsies. This repression and stigmatisation was particularly directed at travelling groups because being on the move with one's family without an apparent aim to settle again symbolised an anti-social lifestyle.

The appearance of the first 'Egyptians' (Gypsies) travelling in family groups in Western Europe (1419) fits well into this categorisation. When they claimed to be pilgrims from Little Egypt, they were tolerated and their nomadism was sometimes even given tacit approval. When doubts about their pilgrim status arose, however, they were suspected of being spies for the Turks and were consequently subjected to increasing stigmatisation.

The fact that economic competition or economic jealousy between the sedentary and the nomad was at the root of much of the antagonism between both groups has tended to be ignored in much socio-historical and socio-anthropological literature to date, however. Instead historians throughout Europe have tended to study Travellers and Gypsies only from the perspectives of criminality, marginality and poverty, thereby ignoring the social and economic function of these travelling groups. Recent academic commentary on Travellers by both Travellers like McDonagh (1994) and non-Travellers like Ní Shúinéar (1994) has tried to redress this situation by elucidating the differing attitudes towards work, economy and family which delineate Traveller culture from sedentary norms. The Traveller economy has traditionally been entrepreneurial and flexible. Travellers have tended to reject the sedentary entrepreneur's interest in building up plant and have selected trades that allow them to fill niche markets in the majority community. Flexibility and self-employment[16] are phenomena that entail different attitudes towards work practices and time management from that of the majority community. The propagation of myths like those concerning the 'Nail', 'Pin' and 'Bar of Gold' and the attribution to Travellers of traits like laziness, shoddy workmanship and sharp practice may have been in the economic interests of certain sections of the community (e.g. sedentary tradesmen like blacksmiths, sedentary tailors etc.) who may have been in competition with nomadic craftsmen. Travellers often had severe competition[17] from their settled equivalents for the niche markets that they filled. For most of the trades and services performed by Travellers, there were sedentary equivalents, whether these trades involved chimney-sweeping, furniture making, horse dealing, veterinary work, playing music or hawking. While some Irish Travellers travelled over a wide area, for many of them their nomadism was more localised and involved travelling a circuit which encompassed only a small number of towns. Many Travellers, perhaps the majority, camped on the edge of a large town or took a house in winter when weather conditions were harsh and when the roads were frequently impassable. In both instances they posed a serious threat to tradesmen who performed similar functions in the local sedentary community. The very flexibility of Travellers' occupations and their 'jack of all trades' skills, when combined with their bargaining and possible undercutting of prices, made them a real threat to a wide range of workers in the 'settled' community. Even when Travellers engaged in begging to supplement their income they found themselves in competition with sedentary beggars and the poorer cottier class, many of whom also begged on a seasonal basis depending on the success or failure of the harvests. When these factors are taken into consideration the fact that the sedentary competitors of Travellers might denigrate the work of nomadic tradesmen as inferior by spreading false accusations against them is not surprising.[18] The economic competition that was at the root of some of this jealousy also infiltrated the culture of Travellers as outlined by west of Ireland Traveller Pecker Dunne (2004):

> Calling a man a blacksmith is one of the worst insults a Traveller can
> give to any man. That is because in the old days there was always a
> tension between the Traveller and the blacksmith. The Traveller was
> a travelling blacksmith and so he and the 'settled' blacksmith were
> in competition with each other for work. Naturally enough the

'settled' blacksmith never liked to see the Travelling tinker come into his village as it was bad for his business. So the two of them used to be spreading stories about the other. The blacksmith had the advantage when it came to spreading stories because his forge was a place where people would meet in the evening to chat and tells stories. This was in the time before television. (Dunne and Ó hAodha 2004, 25–26)

The nucleus then of many of the allegations directed against Travellers as incorporated in the mythic tradition of folklore was probably economic. The age-old stereotype that Travellers were working under the cloak of begging and stealing or refusing to work was a frequent accusation which undoubtedly had its genesis in the sedentary envy of Travellers' competitors. One of the better-known variants of the 'Nail' myth is said to have issued from the lips of the blacksmith himself:

Beirt ghaibhne de na Connors a bhí ann – beirt deartháir. Do bhí gasra againn istigh sa cheárta tráthnóna agus do ghaibh an-dhream tincéirithe thar bráid. Agus dúramarna gur ghreannmhar an cúrsa a bhí acu san agus go raibh fir bhreátha láidre orthu. 'Ó, tá sé sin mar chúrsa ceaptha dhóibh,' a deir duine de na gaibhne agus d'inis sé an scéal dúinn ansan. (Iml. 238: 45)

(Two of the Connors were smiths – two brothers. A group of us were in the forge one evening when a large band of travellers passed by. We said how odd an existence these people lead and that there were fine strong men among them. 'Oh, that lifestyle is assigned to them,' said one of the smiths and then he told us the story.)

While the propagation of 'anti-nomadic' folktales with a didactic-type message as above may have been in the economic interest of certain sections of the majority community it is probably the case that the tales also had a didactic function for the Travelling community as well. The internalisation of the sentiments expressed in these folktales by Travellers must have provided them also with an explanation, albeit a sad one, for their marginalisation from the mainstream and their lack of social acceptance by the majority community. This, perhaps, is where the prejudicial power of these narratives resides.

Some commentators on Traveller culture have downplayed the role of these legends in anti-Traveller prejudice and suggested that such folktales be dismissed only as 'charming legends' (Ní Shúinéar, 1994:

60). It is argued that the search for theories of origin are neither relevant to Travellers nor do they do anything to justify their latter-day claims to ethnic status (Acton, 1994; Ní Shúinéar, 1994; Okely, 1994 etc.). This is to underestimate the significance of the legends in the moulding of popular prejudice. It is also to underestimate the central role of Travellers as storytellers[19] in Irish society and the degree to which they may have internalised the prejudice elucidated in these narratives.

The importance of Catholicism to Irish Travellers has been well documented (Gmelch, 1977; Liégeois, 1994; McCarthy, 1971; O'Connell, 1992a, 1994b etc.). The effect on the Traveller psyche of their mythical attribution to a role in the Crucifixion and their perceived churlish behaviour towards sacred personages in narratives like the 'Bar of Gold' and 'Pin' legends can never be accurately gauged. The psychological damage inflicted must have been further exacerbated by the importance of religion in Travellers' lives and the guilt engendered by the myth's implication of their involvement in the persecution of Jesus Christ. The devotional dimension to these stories had powerful resonances for both the Travelling and majority communities.

> Is é sin an fáth a bhfuil an tádh riamh ar na gaibhne, is go bhfuil an tincéirí le fán agus seachrán an tsaoil, mar ní maith an rud a bheith doicheallach. (Iml. 117: 182–184).

> (That is the reason why the blacksmiths are always lucky, and the tinkers are wandering and lost in the world, because it is not a good thing to be churlish.)

These processes lent strength to opinions and institutions that had wide acceptance particularly within the majority society and to a lesser degree within the Travelling community. The portrayal of the Virgin Mary and the child Jesus in the stories holds devotional significance as it emphasises the wretched state that the Virgin Mary and Jesus assumed so as to redeem mankind. The moral function of the stories is clear and unequivocal in its assignation of blame. The recompense for the two contrasting types of behaviour is dramatically illustrated. Those who practise hospitality are rewarded with God's blessing and worldly success whereas those who do the opposite suffer God's disapproval and are cursed to a life of wretchedness. The feeling of shame or being 'cursed' in some way as a consequence of some mythical indiscretion looms large in the few Traveller biographies produced to date:

> At one stage I felt that those on the road were a people cursed by God. (Maher 1971: 68 )

> There are no more tinkers, Daughter, no more. If there was, you'd have to go and make a spleen over it. Some say we took to the road with a curse that hung over us since Cromwell. (Anonymous Traveller in O'Fearadhaigh and Weidel, 1976: 22)

This alleged 'accursed' status even impinged on the very nomenclature by which Travellers were once known – i.e. tinkers – and the way in which they define themselves today. As indicated by the following examples from various respondents to the 1950 IFC Questionnaire on Tinkers, the very term 'tinker', which from the late 1800s was used increasingly by the settled community to refer to all Travellers travelling Irish roads, became of itself pejorative:

> This word Tinker is used as a term of contempt and a derivative (beltinker)[20] is used in local language, meaning evil-tongued or ill-spoken. (Iml. 1256: 234)

> Sometime people call a very bold scolding, arguing person in a temper, a Tinker. – 'Sure she's only a Tinker'.
> (Iml. 1256: 216 – IFC respondent from County Monaghan):

'Tinker' became a pejorative that was applied to more than just people. The counter-cultural 'Othering' of Travellers as a group who were defined in terms of 'negative' behaviour tenets e.g. secrecy, dishonesty, licentiousness, violence etc. and 'a society within a society' was theologised in a range of sayings that mapped Traveller 'Othering' as a form of intersignification for the settled community. The following examples are taken from the IFC Tinker Questionnaire:

> Ar séideadh na mbolg do doirteadh an goradh,
> Is do chuirfidís cogadh ar an aonach.

> (Blowing the bellows and heating the iron
> And they'd make war at the fair). (Iml. 1255: 18)

> It is no odds among tinkers who carries the budget. (Iml. 1255: 247)

> Drunk with hunger like a tinker's dog. (Iml. 1255: 247)

Light on his foot as a Tipperary ragman. (Iml. 1256: 268)

'B'fhearr an réiteach', mar a dúirt an tincéara nuair a bhí an catha thart.

('Agreement is best', as the tinker said when the war was over).

An bata agus a bothair, páighe asail a' tincéarai

(The stick and the road, they are the wages of the tinker's donkey).

As cross as Puck tinkers.[21] (Iml. 1255: 52)

'Is fusa bualú ann ná éirí as', mar a dúirt an tincéarai sa troid.

('It is easier to join in than to stop', as the tinker said in the fight).

In Puck they should be (to describe people who are always arguing).
(Iml. 1255: 52)

'A tinker's damn' is taken to mean something trivial or of little account. (Iml. 1255: 20)

Bata agus bóthar mar fhás capall an tincéara.

(The stick and the road – the upbringing of the tinker's horse).

Airgead na n-óinsighe a chuireas bróga ar bhean an tincéara.

(It is the stupid woman's money that puts shoes on the tinker's wife).

Ar nós na dtincéaraí, ag troid ar maidin 's mór le chéille tráthnóna.

(Like the tinkers, fighting in the morning and the best of friends in the afternoon).

Chomh dí-náireach le cailleach tincéara. (Iml. 1255: 20)

(As shameless as a tinker witch).

Níl luach tufóg tincéara de mhaith ann (rud éigin gan rath).

(Iml. 1255: 20)

(It isn't worth a tinker's fart (something that is worthless)).

As 'settled community' respondents to the IFC Questionnaire from both Kerry and Tyrone outlined, local Travelling families became instituted as a 'negative Other' in the minds of the prejudiced settled community:

Ní raibh aon meas ag a lán daoine ar thincéirí. Is minic a ghlaodhfadh fear 'tincéir' ar fear eile le tarcuisne. Bhíodh oiread de dhroichtheist ar na Coffeys (muintir Cathbhuaidh) chun bruighne go nglaodhtaí Coffeys ar dhream a bheadh tugtha chun bruighne.

(Iml. 1256: 226)

(A lot of people had no respect for tinkers. Often a man would call another man a 'tinker' in a contemptuous tone of voice. The Coffeys had such a bad reputation for fighting that any crowd that were fond of fighting would be referred to as 'Coffeys').

Another Tyrone respondent describes how the Traveller status of 'negative Other' was used as a point of reference or 'projection' for the alleged differences between the people of different townlands or parishes: 'You might as well as draw a tinker-woman's tongue on you as a Charman (Carrickmore) woman's' (in vituperative or invective) (Iml. 1256: 257).

Some Travellers began to shy away from the term 'tinker' because of its negative allusions. The Tinker Questionnaire records settled people who said that Tinkers/Travellers expressed upset when referred to by the pejorative word 'tinker':

Hogans; tinkers of this name frequented this district and were well-known around. Old Hogan carried a budget[22] on his visit to houses but arrived per ass cart. Like some of the others already mentioned he resented the title of tinker. He was in a house one day. He had been told to call as there was work for him. He arrived early and the missus hurried to get the breakfast for him. The servant wasn't in and the 'missus' says 'Where is that 'tinker' (meaning the girl) gone? Hogan took great umbrage at this remark and lectured the bean an tighe[23] telling her that his trade was the ancient and respectable one of tinsmith etc. All these were honest characters and held in respect by the people ... The Hogans 'circulated' around Kilmallock, Bruff, Knocklong and Kilfinane. (Iml. 1255: 95)

The same is true today. Many younger Travellers are upset when the term 'tinker' is applied to them, even when the context is not a pejorative one, as recounted by Traveller musician, Pecker Dunne:

> Well I was doing a benefit gig for one of those Traveller groups in Dublin a year or two ago – you know one of those groups that helps younger Travellers through education and all that. And I went up to sing a song. And I said that I was a tinker and proud of it. That my father and mother were tinkers and the people who went before. But a couple of the younger Travellers there weren't happy with me. They didn't like me saying the word 'tinker'. Y'see they are ashamed of the fact. They don't want anyone to call them the 'knacker'. (Dunne and Ó hAodha, 2004: 51)

S. B. Gmelch (1974) describes the internalisation of the pejorative meaning associated with the word 'tinker' by Travellers themselves. She says that during the early 1970s when she undertook her anthropological fieldwork amongst Travellers in Dublin they themselves used the term 'tinker' when arguing amongst themselves.

> In moments of stress and anger Travellers often direct the pejorative labels of the settled community against each other. When one teenager refused to carry out his mother's request she yelled at him, 'You tinker tramp! You tinker tramp!' While drinking, Travellers may call each other, 'You dirty knacker!' ... During a fight with her husband one woman screamed, 'My father wasn't a knacker. My mother was a Traveller right enough but not my father. You should treat me with respect. My father wasn't a knacker.' (1974: 216)

This usage has similarities with the way other 'marginalised' groups have used 'internalised' terms of contempt to describe one another – for instance the usage of the word 'nigger', once a term of abuse that has today been reappropriated as an in-group reference term amongst Afro-Americans in the United States. Notwithstanding the above examples where the very name by which they were known – i.e. 'Tinker' – became a pejorative, there is ample proof that the internalisation of their allegedly negative roles as outlined in narratives like the 'Nail' legend left a deep scar on the Traveller psyche, one which appears to resonate even today. An Irish television documentary entitled *Traveller*, broadcast in February 2001, showed the well-known Traveller storyteller Patrick Stokes recounting the 'Nail' legend and giving it as an 'explanation' for the marginalised status of Travellers in Ireland today. A range of sociologists and folklorists who have written on the subject of Travellers including McCarthy (1971), Barnes (1975) and Ó Héalaí (1985) all heard the 'Nail' myth as recounted by Travellers themselves. McCarthy (1971) reports the upset response of Travellers on hearing the 'Nail' myth as retold by a sedentary woman on a bus journey thus:

> [a Traveller man, wife and son were on a bus. A woman] noticed that he was a tinker … She said that she was a blacksmith's daughter and that the blacksmiths refused to make the nails for the cross of Jesus but that the cursed tinker did … [He] became very upset at this … Travellers are very sensitive about [this well known myth]. He tried to argue with her but [his son and wife] intervened, apologising for him … [His son] started to sing for the company. (1971: 85)

Anti-Traveller rhetoric, one strand of which is evidenced in the folklore tradition, when combined with assimilationist policies and almost continuous efforts (both coercive and inducive) to abandon their nomadic lifestyle, has undoubtedly played a part in undermining Traveller culture. In the past decade or so Traveller activists have touched on this theme and have described the discrimination inflicted on Travellers in Ireland as a type of cultural genocide. Various commentators on Traveller issues in Ireland have also increasingly drawn parallels between the history of Irish Travellers and other indigenous peoples like the Australian aborigines.[24] Nan Joyce (1985), author of one of the first Traveller autobiographies, has described how discrimination has led to feelings of shame or low esteem amongst Travellers:

> I would like all the travelling children to have self-confidence and to grow up proud of what they are because they are very special people with their own traditions and their own way of life. But the way they've been treated and discriminated against they grow up ashamed of their own parents. It used to be that the one time you heard about travellers was when they did wrong; nothing about us was ever taught in schools and when children came by our camp

they would just run by – they were afeared of the travellers. Even today some people are afeared to come near us and chat with us – it's a fear of the unknown. (1985: 118).

Michael McDonagh (2000a), another Traveller activist, has also high-lighted the shame that Travellers felt in the past concerning their identity and the inferiority complex that accompanied the denigration of their nomadic tradition:

> In a way Travellers were ashamed of their identity because for years we were told to give up our traditions and ways. As it is many of our traditions are gone forever. When you take away a person's identity, as has happened to many Travellers, it causes unbelievable prob-lems … Many have a fierce inferiority complex … a couple of years ago they were hiding the fact that they were Travellers. Many were trying to 'fit in' … Could you imagine not being yourself or having to deny that your grandparents ever existed because they were Travellers and you no longer wanted to be a Traveller? We were expected to assimilate. (2000a: 30)

McDonagh also describes the social consequences of this Traveller infe-riority complex or low 'self-image' and the damage it has done to Traveller identity. He argues that the internalisation of their perceived 'negative Other' status has aided the Irish state in its attempts to impose assimilationist policies on the Travelling community:

> It's not simply about having nomadism taken away. The policy-makers who do this also ensure that Travellers are getting a great deal of 'help' to 'integrate' into 'the community' … And once you do that, you're lost, because settled people won't accept you, and Travellers won't want you any more than you want them to. Where does that leave you? Without your identity. Many Travellers find themselves stuck in limbo, with parents ashamed of their relatives and children ashamed of their parents. (2000a: 33)

In this chapter I have examined the themes of a number of folktales existing in the Irish tradition, all of which reinforced an anti-Traveller mindset amongst the settled community. These folktales assigned to Travellers the status of 'negative Other' and acted as a justification or validation for their marginalisation from mainstream society. I have argued that the negative stereotyping and reductionist view of

Travellers that accompanies these folktales has had a significant effect on both the settled and Travelling communities. With regard to the former it has functioned as a vehicle for prejudice against Travellers and even bolstered popular beliefs that have influenced social policies with an assimilationist bent. In relation to Travellers the discourse inherent in these folktales has served to undermine their self-identity and validated their exclusion from mainstream society. This mythic tradition is part of an internalised discourse which validates the sedentary community in its prejudice and persecutes the Traveller community and its nomadic cultural attributes on both a social and psychic level.

Perhaps the most damaging belief articulated by these narratives is that the wretchedness of Travellers' lives is justified[25] because of their alleged misconduct. They 'deserve' their punishment because they brought it upon themselves. The marginalisation of Travellers from the majority society is 'justified' and the assignation of Travellers to the role of negative 'Other' is bolstered. These folktales are seen to serve a similar function to mythic stories of monsters, foreigners or 'the stranger ... who operates as a limit-experience for humans trying to identify themselves over and against others' (Kearney, 2002: 3).

These folktales recall the fact that the self is never secure in itself. The Traveller image highlights the fracture inherent in the human psyche, the fear of the 'Other' which as Foucault (1981) pointed out, is ever-evolving – 'There are monsters[26] on the prowl, whose form changes with the history of knowledge' (1981: 26). The institutionalisation of this anti-nomadic prejudice within the Irish folklore tradition is made manifest in the phrase whereby recompense is assigned to both smith and Traveller, a phrase which itself has become a proverbial refrain in the Irish language: 'aghaidh an tincéara ar gach doras agus aghaidh gach éinne a bheith ar thigh an ghabha' (Iml. 267: 507–508) (the face of the tinker at every door and everyone else's face at the house of the blacksmith).

How great an effect their 'mythic' role of 'negative Other' as encompassed in these folktales has had on the Travelling community will always be difficult to gauge. Travellers themselves have resisted attempts at their 'mythic' demonisation and unsurprisingly have helped to propagate narratives which portray themselves in a non-prejudicial light. Irish folklore also includes a countervailing 'mythic' tradition which countenances that charity and hospitality be displayed towards Travellers. In this tradition Travellers are frequently seen as 'Others' who maintain a certain balance in the majority society by virtue of their 'Other' or outsider status as moral arbiters on the actions (e.g. generosity or otherwise) of the majority society. They are also the instigators of a powerful form of symbolic inversion where their 'Other' status is shown to be a disguise for their function as 'holy people' or shamans. This countervailing narrative tradition will be the subject of the next chapter of this volume.

## NOTES

1   Summary of Folktale Number 758 from A. Aarne and S. Thompson, *The Types of the Folktale*, Folklore Fellows Communications 184, Helsinki 1973.

2   It is worth noting that certain animals in the Irish folklore tradition were also assigned an 'accursed' status because they allegedly betrayed a holy personage or a member of the Holy Family. One of these animals is the wren, a bird who is hunted on St. Stephen's Eve in Ireland by the Wren-boys who go from house to house with the dead wren while playing music. As an IFC respondent from County Kerry outlines: 'The wren is known as the devil's bird because she betrayed Our Lord. When the soldiers were looking for Our Lord, they asked the wren did He pass this way. She told them He went this way. Then the soldiers arrested Our Lord' (Iml. 242: 18). Another animal assigned an accursed status in Irish folklore is the *deargadaol* or beetle (lit: Devil's coach-horse), an insect which is also said to have betrayed Jesus when he was fleeing from the Romans.

3   The Stations of the Cross are a form of devotional prayer to be found in Catholicism. This practice originated with the visits of Catholic pilgrims to Jerusalem to see the 'way of the Cross' or those sites particularly associated with the suffering of Jesus. Following in the footsteps of Jesus along this 'way of the Cross' eventually became a part of the pilgrimage process itself. The actual devotion known as 'The Stations of the Cross' is said to have been instigated in the 1500s when villages all over Europe began creating replicas of the way of the Cross with small shrines commemorating the places along the route to Jerusalem. Eventually these shrines became the set of fourteen stations that are now known as the Stations of the Cross and which are to be found in almost every Catholic Church worldwide.

4   The idea of transferral here also has a strong basis in the 'native' healing traditions of many peoples. In Ireland people who were seen as 'outsiders' including Travellers and beggars who specialised in healing, were often seen as (liminal) intermediaries who could transfer suffering from one place to another. Healing itself involved the transfer of energy

and it was believed that some healers, including healing priests, died quite soon after they had performed a cure. That the energy associated with some healers survived death is shown by the fact that the cures were attributed to the graves (or clay of the graves) of certain healing priests even after they were dead (see Iml. 1276: 311). It was also believed that sicknesses could be transferred from human beings to animals or inanimate objects such as stones or trees. This concept of transferral was until recently a major feature of the Irish folk belief system.

5    Mac Cana (1970) alludes to the antiquity of those beliefs attributing curative properties to the blacksmith and the forge, beliefs which may even have their roots in pre-Christian Irish tradition. In pagan Irish tradition the mythical blacksmith Goibhniú was alleged to have had curative powers and the forge was seen as a locus for good luck and the healing of many illnesses.

6    One sport which folklore anecdotes frequently refer to as taking place in the forge was weight-throwing, weight-lifting or other tests of strength.

7    This motif is not listed in Stith Thompson's Motif-Index of Folk-Literature, i–vi, Copenhagen, 1955.

8    The role of the outcast whose exclusion is 'justified' is most frequently assigned to the tradesman whose occupation is that of a tinker or a cowherd in these stories. Both of these occupations, in common with the migratory worker, appear to have had a lowly status in the eyes of certain sections of Irish society.

9    The *spailpíní*, like Travellers, were perceived as landless and rootless since they generally didn't own their own land, and as a consequence they sometimes – like the Travellers – found themselves the objects of prejudice, derision or poor treatment. Rural Irish communities had many different names for the *spailpíní* (migratory workers) including a number which (like the word 'tinker', 'hawker' or '*bacach*' (beggar)) were sometimes used in a contemptuous or derisive way. These included *cábóg* (clodhopper, clown), *cornermen, Connies/Cunnies, Culchies, Westies* to name but a few (see A. O'Dowd *Spalpeens and Tattie-Hokers.* 1992).

10   Ó Hógáin (1985) says that this story of the malappropriation of Saint Patrick's goat is likely to have been a development from the biographies of Tíreachán who states that Patrick cursed a band who stole his horses (1985: 14).

11   Ó Hógáin (1985) elucidates how current folk tradition concerning Saint Patrick in Ireland makes play of a similar psychology. One common joke or jibe directed at residents of the poorer western regions of Ireland is that Saint Patrick never visited their area. The conceit is that having stood on a height on the border between two regions so as to survey the new

mission territory he decided it was better not to risk visiting the area denoted by poorer land. Having surveyed the potential mission territory, the joke is that Saint Patrick decided it wasn't worth risking the visit, remarking 'I bless you to the west of me!' (1985: 14).

12 This folktale variant has obviously been influenced by Irish versions of AT 461 *Three Hairs from the Devil's Beard*, where the poverty of certain tradesmen is ascribed to their opportunism in working on the Sabbath.

13 Relatively little is known about the culture of the Travelling stonemasons except that they once formed a distinct group within Irish society and had their own language, known as *Béarlagar na Saor*. They tended to lodge with the settled community in their houses or in their outhouses. Very little of their language was ever recorded (see Macalister, 1937) and it seems to have died out as a spoken language in the 1940s with the end of the nomadism on the part of the stonemasons. Although the name of this language indicates that it was the cant used by stonemasons it seems clear that it was spoken by a much wider range of Travelling people, including pedlars, knife grinders and horse trainers. This latter factor is a pointer to the existence of a more heterogeneous or amorphous travelling population in Ireland prior to the late twentieth century and the arrival of 'separate accommodation' in the form of wagons and tents etc. *Béarlagar na Saor* consists largely of innovated or modified Irish words used in an Irish grammatical framework. The question of monastic influence on 'secret' languages such as Shelta and *Béarlagar na Saor* was mooted by Celtic scholars such as Kuno Meyer and R. A. S. Macalister.

14 The travelling tailor appears as a peripheral character in many folktales where he is often depicted in the role of a trickster or a con-man. Travelling tailors appear to have formed another distinct 'group' within the Traveller population prior to the twentieth century and there are references in folklore sources to a linguistic register known as *Ceant na dTáilliúirí* (Tailors' Cant) being spoken.

15 Folklorist and amateur historian Andrew Sinclair (1908) had this description of Travelling tailors in Ireland: 'It is only since the beginning of the twentieth century or in some cases a short time before that that country tailors are making clothes for their customers in their own homes. Fifty or sixty years ago all country tailors travelled around from place to place to the homes of their customers and made their clothes there ... A master Tailor and his workmen or apprentices. – "there were generally two or three" in those far gone days may have to spend weeks in the house of a big farmer who may have to get clothes made for himself and some of his family ... They (the tailors) used to be regarded as a nuisance by some people while other and more humorous people got on very well with

them. They had their own rules and regulations. The youngest apprentice always had the carrying of the "lap-boards" – (the boards on which they pressed the seams of the clothes with the iron) and the smoothing irons' (Sinclair 1908: 9).

16  The flexible nature of Traveller work processes have been described thus: 'The essential characteristic of Travellers' economic base is self-employ-ment. Being your own boss is the important thing – being free to fit your work into the often unpredictable demands of the extended family' (McDonagh, 1994: 98).

17  Gmelch (1985) points out that Travellers even 'competed' with settled Irish by taking up what was often regarded as the 'lowest' form of subsis-tence living i.e. the *spailpín* work, those seasonal migrations to Scotland and the wealthier parts of Ireland to work in the potato fields which attracted large numbers of Irish labouring men and women in the early part of the twentieth century. Significant numbers of Travellers also worked as labourers on construction sites in England from the 1950s onwards just like their settled counterparts.

18  The fact that tinkers often undercut the local shops in providing gallons and other tinware for a lower price often left them open to the accusation that their products were inevitably inferior by virtue of how cheap they were in comparison with the sedentary competition.

19  The huge contribution of Travellers to Irish folklore is an aspect of the Irish narrative tradition that has yet to receive due cognisance or serious academic study.

20  'Beltinker' from the Irish (*béal tincéara*) – literally 'a tinker's mouth'.

21  Puck Fair is one of the oldest fairs in Ireland and a traditional gathering place for Travellers.

22  The budget was the bag/pack or box of tools which the tinker often carried on his back.

23  *Bean an tíghe* (Irish) meaning 'woman of the house'.

24  While on a state visit to Australia in 1998 the Irish President, Mary McAleese, compared the position of Australian Aborigines to that of Irish Travellers. She argued that it was necessary for Irish people to embrace the diversity in their midst, particularly in view of the increasingly multi-cultural nature of Irish society (See Opinion – *Irish Times* – 11 September 1998).

25  It is noteworthy that the narrative thrust of these stories plays a significant role in absolving the settled community from any responsibility for the amelioration of the Travellers' plight, whose suffering and marginalisation is seen simply as part of the natural order of things. This theme of indif-ference on the part of the settled community to the terrible conditions in

which many Travellers have lived is one which has been referred to in recent Traveller autobiographical writings (see Nan Joyce, 1985).

26  Kearney (2003) defines the symbolic functions of folktales concerning the 'Other' which is feared as follows: 'By telling stories about monsters we provide symbolic resolutions to enigmas – those of our origins, time, birth and death - which cannot be solved at the level of our everyday historical experience. In short, monster myths offer imaginary answers to real problems. They signal the triumph of the structural over the empirical, mind over matter' (2003: 233).

# 9 The counter-tradition and symbolic inversion

As evidenced in the Irish language archive from which these narratives have been sourced, the tradition of representation as a whole whether hostile or a favourable as regards Travellers is an element of native Irish cultural tradition. The narratives are exemplars of the hegemony of native Irish culture as set against British colonial traditions. The stories are an element of both the settled Irish narrative traditions and the Traveller community's tradition. They are simultaneously the same and 'Other'. They are both inside and outside in the same way as the guardians and tellers of these stories were, whether Traveller or 'settled'.

The intersignification of both Traveller and settled, whether in the literary or musical traditions and as encompassed in a variety of cultural impulses and languages (Irish, English, Cant/Gammon, Parlari) and as explored by both Travellers and settled community scholars, is a subject which has seen a growing body of work (Court, 1985; Walsh, 2008; Ward, 2010[1]) in recent times. In this chapter I discuss what may be termed a 'counter-tradition' to that which proposes an anti-Traveller discourse in Irish tradition. This counter-tradition manifests itself in a story entitled *Ortha an Ghreama* ('The Stitch Charm') where Jesus and Mary act as shamans or healers, 'outsiders' who morally arbitrate on the actions of the settled community.

There are many different variants of this charm/prayer, which is preserved in the form of a story.[2] The most common setting for the story is one where the Virgin Mary and the Child Jesus, in the guise of Travellers, are travelling through the countryside and seeking lodgings for night. Occasionally they are in exile in Egypt or running for their lives from King Herod. They seek lodgings for the night and find 'hospitality' refused to them, in most cases by the woman of the house. The man of the house meets them as they are about to take to the road again and he makes a bed of flax for them in the corner of the house or in an outhouse. During the night a terrible pain afflicts the man and the woman of the house asks the Travellers can they do anything to save him. Jesus or more often the Virgin Mary provides the cure while reciting the moral-laden *déilín*[3]:

> A rude wife with a gentle husband
> She put the Son of God lying in the flax,
> Mary's Mantle and the Five Fingers of Jesus
> to be placed on the site of the stitch when
> it is at its most painful. (Iml. 459: 233)

In some variants of this charm-story the backdrop for healing is the Nativity, a cataclysmic event which shapes the future history of the very world itself. The fact that the Travellers in the guise of holy people are refused hospitality when the Saviour of the world is about to be born emphasises the churlishness of their would-be hosts and is itself indicative of the importance of the virtue of charity. In other variants the context of the Travellers' plight is equally profound and urgent. They are the Holy Family in flight from King Herod and in fear of their lives, a situation which makes the refusal of their request for lodgings all the more serious. The charm-story known as *Ortha an Ghreama* can be linked to the 'Nail/Pin' stories because in each tale either Jesus or the Virgin Mary acts as a moral arbiter who assigns a negative 'recompense' or punishment (sometimes in the form of a troublesome spouse) to those who are ungenerous towards them when they seek hospitality. It can also be linked to a very old discourse in the Irish folk tradition where the Traveller/beggar is a holy personage in disguise. *Ortha an Ghreama* also directly elucidates the central role that Travelling people have for many centuries played in the healing tradition of Ireland. I located the versions of *Ortha an Ghreama* on the archival reels of the Irish Folklore Commission material in the library at the National University of Ireland, Galway. My *modus operandi* for finding these tales was to search the indexes referring to the different *Imleabhair* (Volumes) of material held on the microfiche of the IFC material. These tales are listed in the index under a range of sobriquets in including:

*'Orthaí', 'Charms', 'Ortha an Ghreama', 'Prayers', 'Leigheaseanna', 'Charity rewarded', 'Holy Family', 'Ár Slánathóir', 'An Mhaighdean Bheannaithe'* etc.

Bearing in mind the vast expanse of material covered by the IFC archive – over 250,000 pages – and the relatively difficult and time consuming methodology that is necessary to access the material, one can never say with complete certainty that one has found a complete or definitive 'picture' of a particular subject. I am satisfied however that I accessed a fairly representative selection of these tales as they appear in the archive. These tales seem to have been found throughout Ireland, or at least anywhere in Ireland where the IFC folklore collectors gathered material, and there did not seem to be any very obvious regional variations in either the frequency of the tales or the content thereof.

The following example is typical of the versions of *Ortha an Ghreama* which I came across except for the fact that the 'woman of the house' in addition to being churlish is also the recipient of the physical punishment in the form of physical sickness:

> *Prayer against the Stitch*
> It was a cold wet night in the depths of winter and heavy snow was beating down … Such a night of cold and rain had never been seen even within the memory of the oldest people. It was an exceptional night without doubt, the kind of night that you wouldn't want the worst of your animals to be out in, never mind a Christian … In the body of the tumult and the wind there was a poor Travelling woman walking slowly along the rough road, a young child by her side. 'God's help is always at hand, Mother. I see a light close to us now. Let's go towards it.' 'We must get lodging and a bed from the people of the house', said the child. There were only two people in the house … The man of the house was a quiet and honest man but that wasn't true of his wife. She was a rough, hard-hearted person. When a knock came on the door, she got up from where she was sitting and opened the door to the Traveller woman. She had no idea beforehand that it would be a Traveller woman at the door. If she had known beforehand there's no fear that she would have opened the door for her. The Traveller woman greeted her and asked her in the name of the Lord whether she and the child could come in out of the storm. 'We have no place here for Travellers', said the woman of the house sarcastically. 'We have neither a space nor a bed for you. Indeed but it's a funny time that you come looking for lodgings. Hit the road now and go somewhere else' … She was setting off again when the good-hearted man of the house called out to her. 'Maybe we can find you a place here somewhere. … Stretch back there on the flax there in the corner and it will be a sort of a bed for the two of you until morning.' She blessed him and thanked him and she came in. He put on a blazing fire and gave them a good

supper ... When he had the poor woman and her small child settled in the corner he recommenced with his work but his wife stopped suddenly and announced that she wasn't feeling very well. She said that she suddenly felt very sick ... She was feeling worse as each moment went by. The poor man was in distress. What would he do? He woke up the Travelling woman and told her the story. The child was awake also and he took great pity on the poor man.

'Mother', he says, 'would you not do something for her'.

'You do it son', says she, 'because you have the power'.

The child didn't say any more. The woman was in a very bad way now and she was screaming and in fits of pain.

'Mother, would you not do some good for her?' says he.

'You do it son', says she again, 'because you have the power'.

The child got up then and he went over to the bed where the woman was sick. He put his hand on the spot where the stitch was and he spoke as follows:

> 'A charm that was worked by Saint Brigid of the Mantle,
> A charm that was worked by Michael of the shield
> A charm that was worked by God in Heaven
> A charm that was worked by the twelve apostles
> A rude wife with a gentle husband
> That put the Body of Christ lying in the flax,
> Mary's Mantle against the stitch
> In the name of the Father, the Son and the Holy Spirit, Amen.'

No sooner had He said the words but the woman started getting better and the sickness started easing off. She knew well then who their visitors were, that it was our Saviour, a hundred praises be to Him, and his Holy Mother, and that they were in the guise of Travelling people. She was ashamed and repented then for having been so cruel to them when they asked her for lodgings. She rose and threw herself on her knees in the presence of Our Saviour and his Mother and she asked them for forgiveness. And they forgave her and Our Saviour told her to be good-hearted and free with alms from then on. He told her to always come to the help of the poor when they came calling. She promised Him that she would and she kept that promise until her dying day. (Iml. 26: 147)

Ortha *an Ghreama* garners much of its subversive narrative power from the 'ambivalent' characters who are 'holy people' in disguise. The Travellers are representative of a counter-hegemonic undercurrent in

Irish society that remains symbolically central despite constant attempts at its suppression. In *Ortha an Ghreama,* Travellers in the guise of holy people rebel against their marginalisation from the dominant discourse through their role in a countercultural healing process that incorporates both the physical and psychic healing of society as a whole. I link this counter-hegemonic discourse with the discourse of a countercultural or subversive rebellion against the exclusion of the 'Other' in the form of satirical invective and carnivalesque parody or mimicry. The discussion here explores the representative strategies, reactions and rhetorics of the 'resistant' subject within a critique of domination and in the arena that is the struggle for control of meaning. Rendering political resistance visible along the discursive surface of history, as relating to these elements of the Irish oral tradition, entails examining of sometimes fragmented and mixed texts. The author function of discourse is rendered anew as is the expertise, authenticity as attributed to the author/narrator and the constructed artefact. Foucault (1977) has theorised the intimate link that exists between the 'author function' and each individual discourse. To 'free up' text on the interpretive level an exploration of those discourses which shape the trajectory that is social power is crucial.

Oppositional discourses similar to *Ortha an Ghreama* are always fluid and in state of displacement. They are, in essence, 'new' vocabularies which usurp that which is essentialist and diminish the stability and subjectivity of that which always remains the same. The confluence between marginality and displacement is nothing new but the 'marginal' can also use displacement to his/her advantage when the opportunity arises:

> The margins, our sites of survival, become our fighting grounds and their site for pilgrimage. Thus, while we turn around and reclaim them as our exclusive territory, they happily approve, for the divisions between margin and center should be preserved, and as clearly demarcated as possible, if the two positions are to remain intact in their power relations. (Trinh, 1991: 17)

This 'in-between' space where the play of oppositional images occurs usurps stereotypes and groups employing counter-hegemonic processes attain self-consciousness often by setting themselves in opposition to other groups. Not unnaturally the self-concept which the marginal group composes or presents is interlaced with images of itself and the group or groups it is deemed oppositional to. As early as 1904,

Robert E. Park explored the similarities between the attainment of self-consciousness by both the group and the individual. Park (1904) saw marginal or disenfranchised groups who utilised counter-hegemonic processes as engaged in an identity construction that was in many ways linked reciprocally with the dominant images of their subjectivity. A dual-consciousness encompassing both self and (majority society) other is an indispensable aspect for the marginal group, given that it has to live both inside and outside the dominant culture. This nature of this dual consciousness is not fixed or immutable however. As discourses such as *Ortha an Ghreama* demonstrate, this duality is always subject to new processes of mediation through the constant transformation of the symbolic and the signifying means by which such cultural images are created and formed. Until now, many scholarly explorations deemed it 'enough' to construct marginal groups and minorities by conflating their oppositional and subaltern relations with the majority society. This is no longer the case and more critical or productive explorations need to dig deeper and examine the strategies of cultural constructedness such groups employ.

The 'in-between' or 'third' space is where the play of oppositional images and countering myths manifest themselves. Such a space permits alternative conceptions of social reality and the visibility of shared public representations and mediations which the dominant discourses have long obscured. From a historical perspective, it is here where 'counter-memory' may be discovered, that which George Lipsitz (1991) defined as follows:

> Counter-memory is a way of remembering and forgetting that starts with the local, and the immediate, and the personal … Counter-memory looks to the past for the hidden histories excluded from dominant narratives … [It] focuses on localized experiences and with oppression, using them to reframe and refocus dominant narratives purporting to represent universal experience.
>
> (Lipsitz, 1991: 213)

A powerful aspect of counter-memory and resistance occurs within the mediation that is text and lived experience and the representative strategies which are ambivalence, difference and mimicry. In *Ortha an Ghreama* ambivalence resonates in the figures of both Jesus and Mary, both of whose characters exhibit elements of both complicity and resistance, often simultaneously. In most versions of *Ortha an Ghreama* it is Jesus who confronts the Travellers' marginalisation; it is he who challenges what Sibley (1995) has termed the 'geographies of exclusion' (Sibley, 1995: 2), a fact that is all the more remarkable given that, as depicted in these stories, he is still just a child. As Bhabha suggests, resistance in the postcolonial text is essentially an interrogation of *identity*, 'a persistent questioning of the frame, the space of representation, where the image … is confronted with difference, its other' (Bhabha, 1994: 66).

In *Ortha an Ghreama* this confrontation or challenge is achieved through the power of ambivalence, an apparent compliance and resistance, a form of 'covert disobedience' if you will. The hidden or 'masked' nature of the Travellers in *Ortha an Ghreama* is indicative of their subversive and counter-hegemonic potential. They are not what they seem and the ambivalence regarding their 'true' natures is the instigation for a form of subversive resistance, a resistance that insinuates itself exactly at those 'capillary points' of social interaction where Foucault (1970) theorised resistance to take place.

The form of ambivalence which occurs here is the same as that dual existence which Bhabha explored in relation to the concept of the colonial self – the subject who 'evacuates the self as a site of identity and autonomy and … leaves a resistant trace, a stain of the subject, a sign of resistance' (Bhabha, 1994: 70). While fixed or stereotypical representations often restricted the autonomy of the Traveller, their perceived inferiority is destabilised here; it is turned on its head so that it is in fact used to achieve a form of agency. Now it is the 'outsider' or 'marginal' who achieves the position of authoritative 'Other', thereby proving that 'the authority of dominant nations and ideas is never as complete as it seems, because it is always marked by anxiety, something that enables the dominated to fight back (Huddart, 2006: 1). It is in the 'third space', Bhabha theorises, that the otherness of the 'colonised'/dominated garners its power and secures a form of authority. This space is where anxiety and ambivalence make their appearance and where once apparently impregnable cultural symbols no longer appear so fixed or primordially united as they once did. The assertion of otherness or difference on the part of the 'outsider'/Other may as often be consensual as it is confrontational. What is more important is that such affirmations of difference 'confound our definitions of tradition and modernity; realign the customary boundaries between private and public, high and low; and challenge normative expectations of development and progress' (Bhabha, 1994: 2).

This subversive ambivalence as associated with categories such as identity and tradition can also be linked with the concept of 'symbolic inversion' as theorised by critics, literary theorists and anthropologists etc. 'Symbolic inversion' as defined by Babcock (1978) includes as a central tenet the 'surprise' inversion of the 'mainstream's' 'norms' that is characteristic of the folktale *Ortha an Ghreama*: '"Symbolic inversion" may be broadly defined as any act of expressive behavior which inverts, contradicts, abrogates, or in some fashion presents an alternative to commonly held cultural codes, values, and norms be they linguistic, literary or artistic, religious, or social and political' (1978: 15).

'Symbolic inversion' both derives from and conflates a wide range of cultural analytics today. Consequently the manner in which I discuss the term here can be read as straddling a range of disciplines and incorporating both past and present uses of the term 'inversion' including concepts that are similar or analogous. 'Inversion' as defined in cultural studies today intimates a reversal of world view or the concept of the 'world upside down'. This definition appears to have remained constant since the era of the early Renaissance at least, the Oxford English Dictionary (OED) citing the meaning of 'inversion' as that which is 'a turning upside down' or 'a reversal of position, order, sequence, or relation. (OED, 1978: 1477). In literary culture this reversal of position was often associated with the negation of a particular position or argument as explained by T. Wilson in his *Logike* of 1567, 'You may confute the same by inversion, that is to saie, tournying his taile cleane contrary' (1567: 20). Inversion has from the earliest times had an intimate link with the concept of negation. Every human experience encompassing a cultural dynamic is imbued with an element of negation as indicated by historian Kenneth Burke (1968): 'The study of man as the specifically word-using animal requires special attention to this distinctive marvel, the negative' (1968: 419).

Since symbol-using is a central feature of the way in which human beings order the universe, Burke argued it was necessary for us to introduce symbolic elements into our every experience. As a consequence, human beings find that 'every experience will be imbued with negativity' (1968: 469). Discussions of symbolic inversion such as David Kunzle's essay 'World upside down' (1978), a study of 'upside down' iconography in European broadsheets, demonstrate that the concept of inversion is a very old one. It is a history which dates back to the Greek paradox as written by writers such as Homer, a history which Donaldson (1970) describes as 'an ancient and widespread one, found very extensively in popular art and literature throughout Europe from classical times (1970: 21–22).

Rosalie Colie (1966), who undertook research into the use of paradox during the Renaissance era, described symbolic inversion or the 'world upside down' as one of a range of paradoxical techniques whereby what is 'not' may be discussed, though in its strictest logical sense it cannot. Linking symbolic inversion with techniques of paradox, she saw inversion as a major convention of paradox, namely that which is actually 'impossible' or utopian. Paradox and irony as informed by inversion are seen to play on the margins of meaning, play that inhabits a free space incorporating the negative.

The philosopher Søren Kierkegaard (1968), who theorised the concept of irony, saw those techniques incorporating symbolic inversion such as paradox as operating at the limits of discourse. Like Foucault's 'capillary point', he saw the margin as the locus of a particular energy, a gap between saying and meaning wherein the ironist was negatively free. Colie's (1966) theorisation also located inversion within a position of liminality, a locale where paradoxes could play back and forth across those boundaries that are considered terminal or categorical. Inversion incorporating parody always involves the dialectic, according to her theorisation. It is by nature self critical and creative and, always 'challenging some orthodoxy, the paradox is an oblique criticism of absolute judgement or absolute convention ... at once its own subject and its own object, turning in and upon itself' (1978: 10).

Henri Bergson's *Le Rire* (1956) theorised inversion as a literary device and identified it as the ancient principle of comedy. Inversion as comedy incorporated surprise and the switching of social roles so that they became 'upside down'. It involved 'a sudden comic switching of expected roles: prisoner reprimands judge, child rebukes parent, wife rules husband, pupil instructs teacher, master obeys servant' (Donaldson, 1970: 5–6).

The comic as incorporated in the world of 'upside down' appears somewhat frivolous, the 'topsy-turvy' coalescing with the slightly anarchic. However the moral essence of the 'upside down' world incorporates a serious attack on control, on hierarchies that appear irreducible and on those systems that are closed off to the marginal elements in society.

Bergson (1956) defines this attack as an assault on 'the irreversibility of the order of phenomena, the perfect individuality of a perfectly self-contained series' (1956: 118). Bergson discussed the serious aspect to negation in his essay 'The idea of nothing' published in 1911. He pointed to the absence of negatives in nature and linked this argument to what later became known as 'negative theology'.[4] Bergson's exploration of negation was taken further by Kenneth Burke who linked symbolic inversion with negation and the negative theology he adduced in the symbolism of religious systems.

Burke (1968) identified negation as a function peculiar to religious systems. In his view God is generally defined in terms of what he is not and religions are often built in antithesis to other persuasions. As symbolic systems go, religions are amongst the most explicitly nega-tivistic of all symbolic systems.[5] Expressions of the deity or the transcendent encompass negative affirmations whose core is paradox-ical (e.g. God is infinite, God is incomprehensible etc.). As argued by Burke, the concept of a transcendent realm is an example of a 'posi-tive-seeming word for what is *really* the function of the negative' (1968: 437).

Negation as the function of symbolic systems has been theorised extensively by Burke (1961, 1968) and is analogous to the process of symbolic inversion under discussion here. Symbolic inversion as outlined in the folktales and folk-anecdotes under review here encom-passes an extension of negation because what takes place is in fact a negation of negative on the part of he/she/they who is/are marginalised. Burke (1968) refers to this type of inversion or negation as a kind of 'aesthetic negative', 'whereby any moralistic thou-shalt not provides material for our entertainment, as we pay to follow imaginary accounts of "deviants" who in all sorts of ingenious ways are represented as violating those very Don'ts' (1968: 13). Prior to Burke, Freud (1950a) had used psychoanalysis as a framework to theorise the concept of negation and come to similar conclusions as Burke as to the indispen-sable function of symbolic negation in the formation of the human psyche:

> By the help of the symbol of negation, the thinking process frees itself from the limitations of repression and enriches itself with the subject-matter without which it could not work efficiently ... the achievement of the function of judgement only becomes feasible ... after the symbol of negation has endowed thought with a first degree of independence from the results of repression and at the same time from the sway of the pleasure principle. (1950a: 182–185)

The ambivalent and sometimes dangerous aura that encircles the concept of negation has meant that studies of symbolic processes, whether undertaken by philosophers, social scientists or literary critics, have tended to ignore the importance of the concept of negation within cultural systems and the importance of questions such as that posed by Derrida (1974): 'What is the relation between the self-eliminating generation of metaphor and concepts of negative form?' (1974: 9).

A reluctance to engage with negation is understandable to a certain degree. Any focus on the negative inevitably runs counter to the psychological habits and cultural conditioning we experience in conjunction with the strongly positivist emphases of today's social sciences. An engagement with the negative or that which is considered counteractive is necessary however if we wish to come to a full understanding of the subversive undercurrent within cultural patterns or what Geertz (1966) calls those 'elements of a culture's own negation which in ordinary, quite un-Hegelian fashion are included within it' (1966: 65). Theorists of the 'Other' have identified the process of inversion as linked with those binary divisions which characterise symbolic ordering between 'self' and Other and between differing peoples and places in a range of political contexts.

The 'low-Other' that is the catalyst of symbolic inversion is always a site of contradiction, the site for mutually incompatible representation and conflicting desires. Representations of the 'low' Other or those lower strata (whether of the body, of literature, of society or of place) are a loci of ambivalence, an ambivalence which gives the Other its particular subversive energy. The negated 'Other' is both desired and reviled, and the subject of debasement and longing. This recurrent pattern whereby the 'top' or 'self' tries to reject or eliminate the 'bottom' or 'Other' was constitutive of the evolution of Western society as delineated by Said (1978). The mythical Orient as 'constructed' by a Europe intent on the legitimisation of colonialism was the locus of a profound ambivalence. The Orientalist strategy depended on '[a] flexible positional superiority, which puts the Westerner in a whole series of possible relationships with the Orient without ever losing him the upper hand' (1979: 2). Said also made the observation however that 'European culture gained in strength and identity by setting itself off against the Orient as a sort of … underground self' (1979: 3).

The theoretical pretexts for the discourses of Orientalism and colonialism have increasingly come to be reviewed in more recent scholarship however, a review which questions the 'tidy' nature of their classification, separation and dichotomisation. Where modern knowledge attempted to impose order, the result has generally been an increased sense of ambivalence. Counter-hegemonic and subversive processes on the part of the 'low-Other' are now often perceived to have been of a more profound, vibrant and ambivalent nature than had been previously assumed. This recent 'discovery' of power on the part of the repressed or the counter-hegemonic is in part because it is only recently that the repressed or the subaltern has had the courage and the means to assert itself through the discourses and technologies of modern communication. Said (1989) saw in this 'return of the repressed' a significant reason for why the grand narratives of modernity are beginning to lose their legitimacy. He attributed the West's epistemological crisis to the 'disturbing appearance' of various others, including those 'others' from former colonies. It was only when the subaltern in the guise of 'women, Orientals, blacks and other "natives"' actively resisted their subordination and 'made enough noise' that they came to be listened to. Prior to this 'they were more or less ignored, like the servants of the 19th century novel' (1989: 210).

Said identified this development whereby the 'repressed' has returned with a vengeance as fundamental to the historical problem of modernism in the West. As a consequence the grand claims made for modernity and the Enlightenment now seem increasingly irrelevant or in Said's words little more than 'windy hypocrisy' (1989: 210). The disruption occasioned by the appearance of the 'repressed' has had the effect of shocking modernity from its complacency according to Said:

> Europe and the West were being asked to take the Other seriously. This, I think, is the fundamental historical problem of modernism. The subaltern and the constitutively different suddenly achieved disruptive articulation exactly where in European culture silence and compliance could previously have been depended on to quiet them down. (1989: 222)

While Said spoke of the return of the 'repressed' his theorisation did not develop in its entirety, according to a number of critics who identified fundamental gaps in his definitions of colonial culture's constituent elements.

The biggest criticism of Said was that his theorisation of Orientalism was too fixed or static in nature (see Bhabha, 1994; Mudimbe, 1988; Porter, 1983; Thomas, 1994; Young, 1995 etc.). Porter (1983) criticised the over-reliance of Said on the discursive approach to colonial discourse, a discourse that was 'attractive' because of its unitary nature – 'a unity derived from a common and continuing fascination with and threat from the East, of its irreducible otherness' (1983: 151). A somewhat essentialist or unitary view of the nature of Orientalism left no room for transcending Orientalist discourse of identifying the ambivalences within it. African postcolonialist critic V. Y. Mudimbe (1988, 1994) used Foucauldian 'archaeology' to theorise 'African gnosis' or that range of discourses or knowledge prevalent in the West regarding Africa and attempted to theorise the tendency towards unitary discourses evident in Occidentalist-rooted analyses of the 'Other' such as Orientalism. He found the Occidentalist/Orientalist discourse concerning Africa to be skewed from its inception because of its failure to acknowledge an African epistemological locus.

> The fact of the matter is that, until now, Western interpreters as well as African analysts have been using categories and conceptual systems which depend on a Western epistemological order. Even in the most explicitly 'Afrocentric' descriptions, models of analysis explicitly or implicitly, knowingly or unknowingly, refer to the same order. (1988: x)

Porter (1983) attributed the unitary or essentialist traits evident in Said's Orientalist theorisation to the monologic nature inherent in discourse theory and the importance of theorising hegemony as process:

> his use of discourse theory prevents him from seeing any evidence of such alternatives in the past. In fact because he does not reflect on the significance of hegemony as process, he ignores in both Western scholarly and creative writing all manifestations of counter-hegemonic thought … The consequence is *serious.* The failure to take account of such efforts and contributions not only opens Said to charges of promoting Occidentalism, it also contributes to the perpetuation of that Orientalist thought he sets out to demystify in the first place. (1983: 151–152).

For Porter, any analyses of the Self-Other duality must include the acknowledgement that hegemonic and counter-hegemonic discourses exist simultaneously. Thomas (1994) develops this critique of a colonial discourse that is perceived as unitary or monologic by pointing to the ambivalence, insecurity and flexibility that is characteristic of certain colonialist discourses. He considers it misleading to assume that all colonial enterprises entailed the imagining of, or a will to, total dominance. He finds Said's imputation that discourses of cultural difference in the spheres of autobiography, travel writing, anthropology etc. were always party to aggression and hostility to be a somewhat generalising and unproductive mode of theorisation. In his view there are too many forms of colonial representation which are, 'at least at one level, sympathetic, idealizing, relativistic and critical of the producers' home societies' (1994: 26).

Ambivalence as a cornerstone of colonial discourse provides for similar re-assessment of Said's Orientalist paradigm by Bhabha. Like Thomas, he sees Orientalism as overly totalising based as it is on the assumption 'that an unequivocal intention on the part of the West was always realised through its discursive productions' (Bhabha cited in Young, 1995: 161). Any understanding of colonial discourse that views its manifestation as an instrumental construction of knowledge is too essentialist in his view. It is also problematic because it lays undue emphasis on the fetishisation of the 'Other' which it attempts to undermine. Bhabha advocates instead a conceptualisation which accepts the ambivalence at the centre of colonial discourse, those protocols of fear, fantasy and desire that have the potential to engage with and dismantle hegemonic processes.

Porter (1983) posits three practical ways whereby cultural analytics can allow for the recognition of counter-hegemonic discourses. The first involves those representations which may contain certain aspects of ideological distantiation. The second avenue involves the manifestation of an alternative canon in public culture, one which involves more direct representations of the counter-hegemonic. The third approach is that which is most applicable to the concerns of this thesis. It is an approach whereby a dialogue between the coloniser and the colonised ensues, 'a dialogue that would cause subject/object relations to alternate, so that we might read ourselves as the others of our others and replace the notion of a place of truth' (Porter, 1983: 153).

Mudimbe's work on Africanism probably holds the clue to future mappings of the postcolonialist and the counter-hegemonic as encompassed in postmodern episteme. He calls for an increasingly deconstructive approach to analyses of discourses such as Africanism, an approach which would give due justice to the heterogeneous character of colonial culture. To get a more complete picture of the influences which have shaped Africanism it is necessary to embrace the diverse nature of those discourses which have shaped representations of Africa and its people. Africanism is not a homogeneous entity, but is constructed rather by a range of discursive formations or 'speeches', all of which contribute to a diversity of encounter between self and other. These discursive formations, as theorised by Mudimbe, are never static.

They are constantly evolving and represent the articulations of an ongoing process, characterised by the interaction and battle of the hegemonic and counter-hegemonic perspective[6], a perspective which is nevertheless an exemplar of the same episteme.

The clear irony of this debate is that colonial power has always been the site of ambivalence or ambiguity. Colonial attempts to impose order premised on 'modern knowledge' encompassing classificatory and dichotomist practices have always had ambivalent results precisely because the relationship of colonist and 'Other' has been hybrid rather than separatist in nature. Fanon (1967) has probably provided the most incisive insights into the ambivalence that characterised colonial subjugations of the 'Other'. Using the perspectives provided by psychoanalysis Fanon demonstrated the nature of the colonised as incorporating the duality of other and self or what he alluded to as black skin and white mask. Describing perceptions of his own race, Fanon (1967) negated the function of the negro as an emblem of 'difference' and pointed instead to the role of the negro as both 'other and self':

> In Europe the Negro has one function: that of symbolising the lower emotions, the baser inclinations, the dark side of the soul. In the collective unconscious of homo occidentalis, the Negro – or, if one prefers, the color black – symbolises evil, sin, wretchedness, death, war, famine. All birds of prey are black ... Without thinking, the Negro selects himself as an object capable of carrying the burden of original sin. The white man chooses the black man for his function, and the black man who is white also chooses the black man ... After having been the slave of the white man, he enslaves himself.
>
> (1967: 191–192)

Far from being the locus of certainty, colonial culture as defined by Fanon is instead a site of ambivalence and uncertainty, an uncertainty which can only be kept at bay by the violence of rigid categorisation and 'othering'. Traditional approaches to the colonial 'Other' have insisted on its distantiation and categorisation in an attempt to override the problems of ambivalence. These have proven fruitless however and have culminated in the self-destruction of the coloniser according to postcolonial theorists such as Bauman (1991):

> Ambivalence may be fought only with a naming that is yet more exact, and classes that are yet more precisely defined: that is, such

operations as will set still tougher (counter-factual) demands on the discreteness and transparency of the world and thus give yet more occasion for ambiguity. The struggle against ambivalence is therefore both self-destructive and self-propelling. (1991: 2)

Bauman, along with Fanon, sees emancipation in a postcolonial situation as lying in the appearance of the stranger, the 'Other', that hybrid subject who is at home in both spheres. Postmodernism and postcolonialism are characterised by this hybridity, an interdependence that sees the 'return of the repressed' set the impetus for the definition of new 'truths' and new 'realities'. The phenomenon of positional superiority and repression in the Self-Other paradigm is not only confined to the phenomenon of colonial or neo-colonial representation. The same ambivalence whereby 'top' endeavours to eliminate the 'bottom'/'Other' for reasons of status or prestige only to find that it is in some way dependent on this 'Other' recurs within different symbolic domains of (especially) bourgeois society, particularly from the period of the Renaissance onwards. Stallybrass and White (1986) outline the development of this dynamic of the 'low-Other' as follows: 'We find the same constitutive ambivalence around the slum and the domestic servant in the nineteenth century; around the disposal of 'waste' products in the city (though not in pre-Renaissance rural culture); around the carnival festivity of popular culture; around the symbolically base and abject animals like the pig and the rat' (1986: 5).

Not alone does the 'top' in the symbolic domain attempt to eliminate or reject the 'low-Other'. The 'top' also actually seeks to centrally include what is symbolically low as a constituent within its own (often eroticised) fantasy life. This psychological dependence on those 'Others' who are opposed and excluded at the social level has as its end result the construction of a subjectivity that is ambivalent, one where power, fear and desire are fused in a conflictual and elusive fashion. What appears peripheral socially often comes to assume a central dynamic in the symbolic sphere as outlined by Hegel in *The Phenomenology of the Mind* (1964) where he discussed the dialectic of the master and the servant. His classic inversion of the master-servant relationship was the catalyst for a process of self-enfranchisement and the genesis of that form of negation which he termed the 'unhappy consciousness'. The concept of inversion and the symbolic centrality of the 'excluded' Other has assumed a role of some prominence in recent anthropological studies, particularly those studies which have analysed so-called 'primitive' or 'traditional' societies. The earliest of these studies have linked inversion with the classificatory nature of humankind's systems of symbolic ordering: 'For the classificatory body of a culture is always double, always structured in relation to its negation, its inverse. "All symbolic inversions define a culture's lineaments at the same time as they question the usefulness and absoluteness of its ordering"' (Babcock 1978: 29).

The *Anneé sociologique* school of writing encompassing scholars such as Durkheim, Van Gennep and Mauss and Hertz all located inversion within a classificatory framework that incorporated ritualised behaviour or 'rites of passage'. Leach (1953), who developed some of Van Gennep's ideas on symbolic representation, associates symbolic inversion with 'liminal' events that signal 'rites of passage' or 'rites of rebellion' such as seasonal or end of year festivities, funerals and other occasions that include rituals or events incorporating symbolic 'reversals' (see Gluckman 1962, 1965; Norbeck, 1963, 1970).

Another well-known anthropologist, John Middleton (1960), who researched the symbolic systems of the African tribe the Lugbara, saw inversion as an aspect of history that was present in the presocial period. His research located Lugbara symbolic inversion in the form of mythical or 'inverted' beings who existed prior to the formation of Lugbara society. These mythical personages behaved in ways which are the opposite of the ways expected of normal socialised persons in Lugbara society today. He identified 'inversion' as representative of the presocial period 'before there was an ordered society, when there was instead a world of social disorder or chaos' (Middleton in Needham, 1973: 372). Inversion as a function of those classificatory systems wherein people universally turn their classifications 'upside down or disintegrate them entirely' was Needham's (1963) analysis of the role of symbolic inversion in cultural systems. Anthropologists have differed regarding the subversive power or otherwise of these symbolic inversions. Some of the earliest studies of 'primitive' societies in Africa defined inversion in terms of a 'steam-valve' process (see Schurtz, 1902), whereby periodic social tensions were alleviated before they could threaten the social order in any significant manner. Max Gluckman (1963, 1965) who undertook anthropological study in East Africa, described inversion or rites of reversal as a constrained form of 'ritual protest' which actually served to strengthen the *status quo* rather than having any lasting subversive effect: 'Rites of reversal obviously include a protest against the established order ... they are intended to preserve and strengthen the established order (1965: 109).

For Gluckman periodic or ritual 'rebellion' was actually indicative of a settled and firmly established social order because this form of protest was only 'effective so long as there is no querying of the order within which the ritual process is set' (1965: 130). A similarly pessimistic view of the effectiveness of symbolic inversion has been put forward by many intellectuals in the Marxist tradition who examined inversion for any potential it might have as a source for revolutionary consciousness-raising. In Trotsky's view the seasonal folk rebellions which were symptomatic of life in rural Russia were a hindrance to the emergence of a revolutionary consciousness and worked simply to bolster further the established order. Bakhtin has been the primary advocate of the 'carnivalesque' concept as a mobile set of symbolic practices and discourses which underpinned social revolt and conflict before the nineteenth century. While Bakhtin championed the 'carnivalesque' as a utopian model for social change, some social theorists have remained unconvinced as to its power to impose societal change.[7] Eagleton (1981) saw the symbolic inversion that was symptomatic of 'carnival' as a relatively[8] ineffective attempt at the counter-hegemonic:

> carnival is so vivaciously celebrated that the necessary political criticism is almost too obvious to make. Carnival, after all, is a licensed affair in every sense, a permissible rupture of hegemony, a contained popular blow-off as disturbing and relatively ineffectual as a revolutionary work of art. As Shakespeare's Olivia remarks, there is no slander in an allowed fool. (1981: 148)

Marx, however, identifies ritual rebellion as a positive and significant step towards the development of a revolutionary class consciousness. The argument as to whether the symbolic inversion of the 'carnivalesque' is intrinsically radical or conservative will continue amid a necessity for increased historical research into those structural explanations that have been put forward for ritual and/or symbolic rebellion. It is an unnecessary argument in a sense since attempting to classify the carnivalesque along these lines falls into the trap of essentialising the process that is carnivalesque transgression. Stallybrass and White (1986) provide a *via media* between both points of view which eschews the modern tendency to essentialise the carnivalesque and politics: 'The most that can be said in the abstract is that for long periods carnival may be a stable and cyclical ritual with no noticeably transformative effects but that, given the presence of sharpened political antagonism, it may often act as catalyst and site of actual[9] and symbolic struggle' (1986: 14).

Irrespective of these various arguments, it is the altering potential of symbolic inversion as incorporating elements of the grotesque and the carnivalesque which I wish to focus attention on here. Symbolic inversion as outlined in *Ortha an Ghreama* can be seen as a form of 'negative feedback' (Bateson, 1958: 288), as one of the means by which the cultural system corrects itself. Symbolic inversion as instanced in *Ortha an Ghreama* challenges the classificatory world view[10] and defines a culture's lineaments at the same time as it questions[11] the usefulness and the rigidity[12] of the way the world is ordered. It can be seen as a creative form of negation, an important reminder of the potentiality of the *mundus inversus*. It reminds us 'of the need to reinvest the clean with the filthy, the rational with the animalistic, the ceremonial with the carnivalesque in order to maintain cultural vitality … the *mundus inversus* does more than simply mock our desire to live according to our usual orders and norms; it reinvests life with a vigor and a *Spielraum* attainable (it would seem) in no other way' (Babcock 1978: 32).

> *The Holy Person in Disguise*
> In Irish culture the folktale *Ortha an Ghreama* has at its core a symbolic inversion which carries a profound meaning. The powerful nature of this inversion includes a robust attack on closed systems of control and categorisation, what Bergson (1956) referred to as 'the irreversibility of the order of phenomena' (1956: 118). The 'marginal' Travelling person is actually a holy personage in disguise. He or she who is denigrated or perceived to live in a 'liminal' state is actually central to the symbolic reconstitution of societal structure and meaning. 'The low-Other is despised and denied at the level of political organization and social being whilst it is instrumentally constitutive of the shared imaginary repertoires of the dominant culture' (Stallybrass and White, 1986: 5–6).

*Ortha an Ghreama* witnesses a clever re-ordering of the situation, whereby the figures of Jesus and Mary usurp their marginal status. Harnessing the power that is ambivalence, they use a combination of strategies, mimicry and difference included to resist imposed representations of their identity and 'exceed … the frame of the image' (Bhabha cited in Huddart, 2006: 88) thereby transforming their 'inferior' position into that of authoritative 'Other'. An important reference point here as relating to literature generated in postcolonial societies is Homi Bhabha's 'Of mimicry and man'. Here Bhabha develops a number of concepts exemplifying how subjugated, colonised groups resist dominant power structures by entering a 'new' relationship with the societal forces they confront. Mimicry of the dominant discourse is one such strategy of resistance, a method whereby the 'marginal' appears to lose his/her independence while simultaneously posing a threat to the 'disciplinary' powers. Such an approach permits those whose voice may be 'muted' or ignored to work within 'the rules' (Bhabha, 1994: 128) and yet engage with cultural practices in such a way as to reveal their own agency. The irony here is that through the processes of mimicry and difference the marginal paradoxically becomes an 'inferior' only to resist that inferiority and undermine the dominant mode of representation. Rather than restrict the autonomy of the marginalised, Bhabha (1994) demonstrates how the actual performance of mimicry serves as a practice of resistance in large part due to its capability for generating the metonymic or 'partial presence', a figure whom people can recognise, yet is 'almost the same, but not quite' (Bhabha 1994: 123). In order to resist signification they engage in a form of 'repetition [that is] ... resemblance in part' (Bhabha 1994: 129). They are familiar and yet there is something strange and discomfiting about them. They have altered the relations through a new negotiation on their part, one which encompasses difference and serves to 'rearticulate the sum of knowledge from the perspective of the signifying position of the minority that resists totalization – the repetition that will not return as the same ... producing other spaces of subaltern significance' (Bhabha, 1994: 233).

The symbolic inversion or re-ordering of societal and symbolic relations evident in *Ortha an Ghreama* can be linked with a wider and very wide-ranging discourse in Irish popular tradition where the liminal figure of the Travelling tradesman, poet, shaman, jester or fool acts to 'transgress' the normal 'categories' of social life and thereby criticise and subvert official hierarchies. This symbolic discourse as evidenced in Irish tradition has strong affinities with the concept of the carnivalesque as outlined by Bakhtin and encompasses imagery and social satire that is often topsy-turvy, grotesque and excessive. The topsy-turvy discourse of the carnivalesque also has much in common with the elusive figure known as the fool, poet-shaman or trickster as defined by Alan Harrison in his study *The Irish Trickster* (1989):

> He [the fool]...is sometimes nearly divine, sometimes positively subhuman. He can be the one who emphasizes wrongs through his satire of the social order and he can be the scapegoat who is sacrificed on behalf of that same social order ... he exists in human

society but also in the unknown world outside and by his passage
between the two he can help to establish the boundaries between
them and increase the area of human knowledge and behaviour.
(1989: 21)

This discussion has acted as a prelude to a more detailed analysis of the
folktale *Ortha an Ghreama*. It has served to highlight the ambivalence
that circumvents the figure of the Traveller as representative of a
counter-hegemonic undercurrent that has its roots in the 'philosophical' and subversive laughter of the Renaissance. The 'low-Other' in the
figure of the Traveller poet-shaman instigates a rupture of the hierarchical and the hegemonic in Irish society, a rupture which serves to
regenerate and renew the cosmic and the social into an indivisible
whole. This regenerative function takes the form of a subversive rebellion against the exclusion of the 'Other' by means of symbolic inversion
and an irreverent laughter that dismantles hierarchies, a grotesque and
carnivalesque laughter that manages disorder through the comic. In
*Ortha an Ghreama* the figure of Jesus plays a number of roles, a fact
which links his character with the archetype of the shaman: 'The
shaman becomes the child, whether playfully or seriously, and is able to
address people with whom he would normally have avoidance relationships' (Jennings, 1995: 109).

His role-taking involves a duality and thereby 'represents a dialectic
between the person and the event or object, whereby each is synthe-
sised within a single expressive form' (Peacock, 1968: 172). This new
and temporary dramatisation of the 'betwixt and between' show role
inversion as the key to a new process of definition. Bakhtin's concept of
the 'carnivalesque' directs attention to the marginal as a locus for transformation, counter-production and the interrogation of established
'truths': 'In the world of the carnival the awareness of people's immor-
tality is combined with the realisation that established authority and
truth are relative' (Bakhtin, 1968: 10).

Bakhtin's (1981) theorisation of the carnivalesque incorporated the
central concepts of 'dialogism' and 'heteroglossia' whereby multiple
perspectives are presented through a range of contrasting voices,
thereby resisting the regularising and totalising tendencies of monologic forces, whether they be literary or linguistic. Bakhtin's definition
of the term 'heteroglossia' is particularly appropriate to what happens
in the role inversion of *Ortha an Ghreama*, an inversion that reinforces
the importance of the polysemous and the necessity for dialogue
between world views that appear diametrically opposed to one another.

Heteroglossia is described as another's speech in another's language. Its function is the expression of two diverse viewpoints simultaneously i.e. the direct intention of the character who is speaking and the refracted intention of the author or narrator. Bakhtin (1981) links his concept of 'heteroglossia' to the dialogic nature of a Dostoevsky novel in a manner which is analogous to the dual and dramatic nature of the Traveller/Jesus described in *Ortha an Ghreama*: '[The novel] ... is constructed not as a whole of a single consciousness, absorbing other consciousness as objects into itself, but as a whole formed by the inter-action of several consciousnesses, none of which entirely becomes an object for the other' (1984: 18).

The dramatic and reinterpretative power of the heteroglossic is due to its enactment of a multiplicity of voices. The paradoxical nature of the dialogic as incorporated in *Ortha an Ghreama* evidences the poly-semous nature of symbolic inversion and the potential for a range of dialogues. The ambivalence that accompanies the perversion of order or values is a generic feature of the 'marginal' character who disturbs symbolic hierarchies as described by anthropologists who have studied the roles of trickster/clown figures in 'primitive' societies. Arden-King (1979), who studied the role of ritual clowns in South American *pueb-los*, describes the fear generated by this symbolic ambivalence:

> Clowns make us aware through purposeful action that the most dangerous condition of being human is one in which there is no order. Clowns flirt with that most dangerous condition, that which has no precedent or predictable issue. The ultimate immanence is non-order, not disorder or chaos. For all human groups the ultimate taboo is non-order, and the clown plays his proper role when he stands outside of order. (1979: 56)

It is through embracing this ambivalence that a greater understanding ensues between the self and the 'other'. Norbeck (1979) theorised the dialogic nature of the relationship between self and others and the dialectic that is framed within the process of symbolic inversion. Role inversions as incorporated in the dramatisation of cultural and social values are considered aberrations of everyday behaviour. Norbeck suggests that the opposite ought to be true and periodic role inversions should instead be accommodated within the norms of behaviour. The inversion of normally accepted behaviour through dramatisation or the use of narrative makes such events more memo-rable by 'framing them off' from an everyday context (Norbeck, 1979:

51). The inversions or ritual clowns, trickster and other marginals embody the central paradox of individual role-play and the collective drama. These 'rites of reversal' make clear that nothing is as it appears and the society is not as it seems. The *pueblo* ritual clown works to define the human condition by presenting opposite yet complementary possibilities for human action as outlined by Arden-King (1979): 'It is not that humour and outrageous behaviour as entertainment are unimportant, but the constant potential for the elicitation of non-order – the creation of another way of human being – appears to be unique to their role' (1979: 57).

The symbolic archetype that is the 'marginal' works to re-create meaning through role-taking or enactment which is the central defining activity of drama itself. The archetype is a 'bricoleur' or myth-maker who takes and develops the things at hand by imaginatively recombining them, thereby constituting 'the return of the subject, as the interrogative agency' (Bhabha, 1994: 265). He generates 'structure' through creating or re-creating the dramatic metaphor and thereby endowing it with personal meaning. His role can, in itself, be seen as a dramatic metaphor since it is a mediating device that connects the unconnected. Louis Hieb (1972) succinctly describes the function of the archetype as incorporated in the figure of the ritual clown as follows: 'The figure of the ritual clown mediates the oppositions of time and space versus liminality, social structure versus communitas, and reality and seriousness versus inversion and humour' (1972: 165–166).

The power of narratives such as *Ortha an Ghreama* lies in the fact that the symbolic action instituted by the archetype/shaman uses the same features as everyday life but transforms and inverts them. Socially inverted behaviour as evidenced in the dramatic action is understood within the context of sympathetic (or homeopathic) medicine and magic where balance is the 'cure' or the state which is desired. The archetype works towards this balance by reproducing those features which are causing imbalance. In the case of ritual clowns the everyday vices of greed and selfishness are symbolically and vicariously treated by the gluttony and selfishness of the ritual clowns as evidenced in their dramatic roles. In *Ortha an Ghreama* Jesus and Mary in the guise of Travellers are refused lodgings by the hard-hearted 'woman of the house'. Although he is often depicted as an 'innocent' newborn, Jesus is often reluctant to perform the healing as a consequence of their inhospitable treatment by the 'settled' community:

> She woke up the child and she said to Jesus,
> 'Wouldn't it be a pity not to heal him.
> 'Oh Mother', says he 'if we can let us not to cure him'.
> Herself and Saint Joseph carried the child over so that he was above the
>     sick man. She held the right hand of the child and said the words:
> 'A rude woman with a courteous woman,
> Mary's Mantle and her Son (the healer of sickness),
> The Body of Christ lying in the flax',
> And then with the sign of the Cross saying:
> 'In the name of the Father, the Son and the Holy Spirit. Amen'.
>     (Iml. 46: 162)

The ambivalent[13] attitude exhibited by Jesus embodies the paradoxical nature of his role as a liminal figure with power who acts not only as a catalyst for symbolic inversion but also questions the nature of humanity and its shared values and norms.

Jesus as shaman/trickster is seen to define the human condition by presenting opposite yet complementary possibilities for human action. His reluctance to perform the healing smacks of ambivalence, an ambivalence that emphasises the reflexive aspect of his actions. Norbeck and Farrer (1979) suggest that the human mind functions best when it is operating in a dialectic mode as it is this mode which gives rise to the creative and the spontaneous. Rubenstein (1975) sees play incorporating an ambivalence between 'subjective' and 'objective' reality as that which is emotionally analogous to aesthetic expression and the formation of a new level of understanding. Turner sees play as a major aspect of liminality. It incorporates the quality of recombining behaviour which occurs in non-ritual situations, strange or bizarre patterns. What was known now becomes the unknown and the ordinary becomes exotic. The rules of so-called normal and acceptable behaviour are shattered, as outlined by Victor Turner (1982):

> When elements are withdrawn from their usual settings and recombined in totally unique configurations … those exposed to them are startled into thinking anew about persons, objects, relationships, social roles and features of their environment hitherto taken for granted. Previous habits of thought, feeling and action are disrupted. They are thus forced and encouraged to think about their society, their cosmos and the powers that generated and sustain these.
>
>     (1982: 205)

Rites of reversal incorporating symbolic inversion and role transformation such as that which takes place in *Ortha an Ghreama* present a mediation taking place between two realities, a mediation that is likely to result in a form of humour, a humour that is both ambivalent and frightening. Kealiinohomoku (1980), who studied the social function of ritual clowns amongst the Zuni people, described the humour of the clowns as an essential feature in their creation of a form of 'communitas'. Communitas was a consequence of the creation of fresh and new relationships between people who might previously have had little contact. The creativity necessary for the development of this communitas was one which was inextricably linked with humour. Both Kealiinohomoku (1980) and Koestler (1964) saw humour as a necessary consequence of the tension generated by the juxtaposition of two previously unrelated experiences. This tension is resolved through the emotional response of humour which establishes balance and resolves any dissonance. The reflexive humour of inversion or topsy-turvydom is a consequence of a number of situations incorporating the inversion or expectations. These include the most basic individual role transformation (i.e. someone taking on a role and becoming someone else) and the collective inversion of cultural norms generated by shamans and ritual clowns. Douglas defines this humour as a form of drama: 'The joke merely affords opportunity for realising that an accepted pattern has no necessity. Through drama, licence is given to "play with" accepted modes of behaviour and action, changing them slightly, inverting them totally or even perverting their purpose' (Douglas in Hieb, 1972: 19).

In *Ortha an Ghreama* the humour lies in the fact that the audience listening to the story can see/imagine the mistake the churlish settled community is making by refusing hospitality to the travelling holy people. This humour is a form of playfulness that contributes to the establishment of meaning and has strong analogies with Neelands and Goode's (1995) categorisation of the notion of playfulness as it occurs in the realm of the symbolic:

> We use the term playfulness to describe the basic human instinct to play with the relationships between symbols and their orthodox meanings in order to express or create new possibilities of meaning. Playing with symbol systems, loosening ties between sign and signified, transforming meanings by creating new and fresh symbolic relationships ... helps us to consider the meaning of our lived experience. (1995: 16)

The response of Jesus to their rejection is sometimes ambivalent[14], an ambivalent and grotesque form playfulness which is designed to drive the moral message of the story home to the audience. Turner (1978) sees ambivalence within ritual as crucial to the power of ritual as a function within symbolic systems. In his view, 'when ritual loses the capacity to play with ideas, symbols and meanings, and thus loses its "cultural resilience", it ceases to be a shared agency for collective reflexivity' (1978: 72). Its playful and grotesque aspects are bolstered by the fact that it is the 'man of the house' who suffers despite the fact that he has exhibited more kindness towards the Travellers than his wife:

> 'Do something for him', the Virgin Mother said to Our Saviour,
>     praise be to her always.
> 'I won't', says he. 'The man is alright', says he.
> She asked him again to do something for him.
> 'I won't', says he. 'The man is alright and his wife doesn't deserve it.
>     You do it', says he to the mother, great praise be to her forever.
>
> (Iml. 1150: 24)

Jesus and Mary as depicted in *Ortha an Ghreama* use both inversion and a form of ritual healing to mediate between their own reality as Travellers and the reality of the world from which they have been excluded. Their role has a dramatic potential analogous to that of a range of other archetypes incorporating the figure of the shaman/trickster/clown who function in an environment incorporating the use of ritual. Their use of a ritual process has a unitary function since it involves not only a 'physical' healing but also a psychic healing, i.e. a cultural transformation of the dramatic structure of knowledge. The healing depicted in *Ortha an Ghreama* situates the moral commentary/balance provided by the outsiders/Travellers process within an intersubjective and communal context. Its aim is analogous to that of ritual drama as outlined by Charlotte Frisbe (1980): 'Ritual drama, in dealing with life itself, is a process which serves to unite humans with other humans, as well as humans with other-than-humans, the revealed with the unrevealed worlds, the visible with the invisible' (1980, 24–25).

Diggle and Hieb (2004) identifies ritual behaviour as evidenced in the role of the ritual clown as the prerequisite for a sense of 'communitas' or a dialogue between the 'acceptable and unacceptable, that which is familiar and that which is considered strange' (2004: 185–186). Ritual behaviour imbues many aspects of the healing tradition in

Ireland including the healing traditions of those who are considered 'marginal' or 'outside the norms' of the community, such as Travellers. In *Ortha an Ghreama* the duality that fuses the temporal and the divine is emphasised through the role of Travellers in 'religious' healing and the spiritual iconography that imbues these healing rituals. In many variants on this narrative the Holy Family do more than just function as the 'Other' who act as a moral arbiter on the actions of their hosts in the 'settled' community. They are also the enforcer of certain Christian tenets including that of punishment for evil that is committed. The Child Jesus is depicted as the enforcer of a moral 'retribution' that is both harsh and immediate – i.e. the terrible pain which afflicts the 'man of the house'. This ties in with the popular belief that it is not only in the afterlife that our behaviour will be 'balanced'. Whatever measure which the giver gives to others in this life is that which they in turn receive either in the afterlife or more immediately in this life. The 'recompense' or *guí* (prayer/wish) of the holy personage in *Ortha an Ghreama* is one that is designed to make the audience think very carefully about the consequences of their actions towards those who seek hospitality.

> *Ortha an Ghreama*
> Our Saviour and His mother were going around and they went in to a house and the house was full of flax and the bed they got to lie on was the bales of flax and when they were leaving in the morning Our Saviour put a pain on the father. 'Oh', says His mother to him, 'why did you put a pain on him, wasn't he very good to us.' 'Oh, it will hurt her too,' says Our Saviour, 'when she sees him and you can cure him' and He said: 'Fear séimh ag bean bhorb'.
>
> (Iml. 809: 403)

That it is the 'kinder'[15] of the 'settled people' who suffers the physical punishment is part of the 'ambiguous' power of the narrative:

> 'Oh indeed', said the Son of God. 'I'll give her a fright before daylight comes.' 'What will you do with her?' said the Mother.
> 'I'll put a pain in the side of the man of the house', he said.
> 'Wouldn't that be a big pity to do that to such a nice courteous man who gave us lodgings?', said the Mother.
> 'You'll see him jumping all over the house in a minute', said He.
>
> (Iml. 48: 275)

or

> The bed the woman of the house gave them was on the tow that
> they extract from the flax. The Mother and child didn't like this as a
> bed. He [the child] put a searing pain on the man of the house and
> the man was very sick. (Iml. 1038: 141)

The inversion evident in Jesus's 'strange' behaviour also has strong
affinities with the 'ordering' function of other shaman types such as
ritual clowns whose inversions are initially indicative of institutionalised
chaos. The 'inverted' behaviour of Jesus in his apparently 'selfish' allo-
cation of punishment echoes the selfish manner in which the Travellers
have been treated. Fyfe (1998) describes the strong association
between socially inverted behaviour (on the part of the ritual clown)
and the context and use of sympathetic or homeopathic medicine and
magic: 'Balance is the desired state; and imbalance is treated by reproducing those features which are causing imbalance. For example, greed
and selfishness within everyday life will be symbolically and vicariously
treated by the gluttony and selfishness of the ritual clowns' (1998: 220).

In some variants of *Ortha an Ghreama* Jesus goes further than
simply 'applying' the punishment and explains the moral reasoning
behind his actions:

> *The Stitch Prayer*
>> 'A prayer worked by Mary and her Son,
>> A prayer worked by Brigid of the mantle
>> A prayer worked by Michael of the shield,
>> A prayer that God worked with power,
>> A rude woman with a kind gentle husband,
>> That put the Body of Christ lying on the flax last night,
>> Mary's Mantle to the stitch.
>> In the name of the Father, the Son and the Holy Spirit.'
>
> When the Virgin and her Son went looking for lodgings they didn't
> get it. That is the story. The man said to let her in and the woman of
> the house said she wouldn't unless they were prepared to sleep on
> the flax, and that is what they did to the Virgin in the end. Our Lord
> inflicted the pain on the man and the Virgin Mary said to Our Lord
> that they should go back and heal the man, that the man was a good
> man and why had he inflicted a sickness on him. Our Lord said he
> had done it to make the woman think carefully about things.
>
> (Iml. 148: 427)

The use of symbolic inversion in order to impart a more profound message also operated as a form of protection for a wide range of Travellers including tinkers, healers, 'poor scholars' and other nomadic craftsmen when attempts were made to marginalise them. The inversion of 'official' hierarchies which culminates in an ironic dependence on the 'excluded' Other has parallels in a much wider and subversive 'top down' discourse in Irish folklore as indicated by the following anecdote:

> *The Priest and the Travelling Man*
>> There was a Travelling man and one day he was walking along the road and he was passing a church and the parish priest and three men were lifting a big heavy rock near the church. The Travelling man said to them.
>> 'I will give you a hand',
>> He did not have a good suit of clothes on him and the priest said to him,
>> 'Off with you, you're not going to join any company of men'.
>> 'O', said the Travelling man walking on, and he looked back at the priest, and he said to him, 'The One who composed is better than the one who criticised'.
>> That was to say that it was the Son of God who composed it.
>> That was when the priest understood what he meant and he said,
>> 'O, that is true'. The priest thanked him (for his words) and asked him for forgiveness and admitted that what he said was wrong.
>> (Iml. 1862: 70)

Some versions of *Ortha an Ghreama* serve as a brief 'sermon'.[16] In addition to defending those who are considered outside the 'norms' of society they often function to impart a specific moral message directly to the story's audience. At times this moral 'tenet' as contained in the narrative is a simple observation on the nature of human existence such as the following:

>> A rude husband with a gentle wife, but the Son of God left lying on the flax,
>> A gentle man with a rude wife, but the Son of God left lying on the flax.'
>> You never saw a couple – you never saw any pair – that could 'get on' with one another and never have the slightest disagreement.
>> (*Ar Aghaidh*, 28 Nollag, 1938: 6)

On other occasions the moral precept extols the benefits of those stati in life which appear on first glance to be unattractive, unwanted or 'topsy-turvy'. The clear implication of the charm-story is that Traveller people are holy personages or that saintly people like Jesus and Mary can be found travelling in the guise of those who may appear poor or downtrodden. While many variants on the charm-story simply end with the punishment of inhospitality there are others where the 'settled' community are seen to realise the consequences of their misbehaviour and react with humility and a firm purpose of amendment:

> Do bhíos aici go maith ansin cé bhí aici gur bé Ár Slanuighthóir é féin, céad moladh go deó leis agus a Mháthair Naomhtha do bhí ann éide locht siúbhal. Do tháinig náire agus aithreachas uirri i dtaobh bheith có cruaidh leó nuair d'iarradar lóistín uirr.
> (Iml. 26: 147 – respondent from County Kerry)

> (She knew then exactly who they were – that it was Our Saviour himself, a thousand praises forever to him, and his Holy Mother who were there – and that they were in the guise of Travellers. She was ashamed and repentant then because of her cruelty to them when they came seeking lodgings).

> Do chuaidh an tinneas ar gcúl agus sin é an am nuair a ainithnuig-headar cé bhí aca. As sin amach do bhí grásta Dé ar bhean an tighe agus a rath ortha. (Iml. 1533: 161)

> (The pain went away and it was then that they recognised who was there. From then on the grace of God was in the woman of the house and she benefited from its gifts).

> D'éirigh sí aniar as a leabaidh is do chaith sí féin ar a glúinibh i bhfi-adhnis a' t-Slánuightheora agus a Mháthair agus d'iarr párdún air na go h-aithrígheadh orrtha agus chomh maith do fuair agus dubhairt a' t-Slánuightheoir léi go brách arís an fhaid mhairfeadh sí gan aoinne d'éiteach fé óstaideacht na h-oidhche ná fé deire a loir-geochadh é ar son Dé is bheith go maith i gcómhnuidhe dá bochtaibh féin is bheith is fóirithint ortha nuair a casfaí chuici iad. Gheall sí dó go ndéanfadh agus do coingibh sí an geallamhaint sin go dtí lá a báis. (Iml. 27: 280)

(She got up out of the bed and she threw herself on her knees in the presence of the Saviour and his Mother and she asked them for forgiveness and they forgave her and the Saviour said to her never to refuse anybody ever again who would seek lodgings for the night or anyone who would seek lodgings in the name of the Lord – and that they should always be generous to the poor in their midst and to look after them when they came across them. She promised him that she would do as he asked and she kept that promise until the day of her death).

Some variants even build on this moral imperative and explain the Christian necessity to exhibit kindness and hospitality towards those considered to be poorer or who are without lodgings of their own. The following example recorded from the well-known County Kerry storyteller Peig Sayers indicates that the medieval idea whereby poverty was equated with holiness survived in Ireland well into the modern era:

*The Stitch-Prayer*
We should never be disheartened or ashamed of poverty. It is a very good thing to be poor, especially for the person who can carry the burden of poverty in a dignified manner. Our holy master was poor and his poor saintly mother, and they are merciful and glorious, and they will help us from the place that they are in now because they were themselves on this earth once.
(My translation from – R. Flower, 1957; 71 – recorded from an IFC respondent in Dunquin, County Kerry)

That the moral imperative of hospitality should be applied to all Travellers and not just those who reveal themselves to be saints or members of the Holy Family is indicated by the following:

A gentle woman with a rude husband,
A prayer for the burning stomach
  that the Son of God left lying on the flax.'
A man who came looking for lodgings on the night that Our Saviour
  was born in the stable. The man of the house put him out, even
  though the woman of the house didn't want that. The
  (travelling) man was only gone when the man got a terrible pain
  in his stomach. His wife went after the poor man and this is the
  cure he gave her. (Iml. 355: 377)

In *Ortha an Ghreama* Travellers, in the guise of holy people, are seen as agents of subversion who provide a temporary challenge to the 'normal' social order. The Travellers are seen to assume a role which mediates between the story's narrator/audience and their world since the role is based on the dual process of imaginatively projecting into, and creating a representation of, the world. As a shaman figure the Traveller takes on an intermediary role incorporating two realities – the Traveller world and the settled world – at once. This role-play on the part of the figure of the Traveller is indicative of a commonality of experience which is real or imagined, a commonality which mediates between people. The ritual drama that is *Ortha an Ghreama* serves to emphasise the commonality of human experience and endeavour, within a framework of differentiated behaviour. It is what Erikson (1959) refers to as 'separateness transcended and ... distinctiveness confirmed' (1979: 141). Courtney (1982) echoes Erikson's description of communal drama, a drama which is based on acknowledgement and respect. Courtney argues that ritual drama can function as a meaningful metaphor for the notion of community, rather than of society. While society is predicated on power and status, ritual behaviour as a reflection of community is based on acknowledgement and reciprocity. The topsy-turvy and paradoxical nature of the Traveller-shaman generates an attitude of mind which is reflexive, interpretative and self-conscious. The story's audience is forced to think hard on the symbolic dilemma inherent in the tale and the moral choices which the story's protagonists decide upon. The Traveller-shaman thus echoes Bakhtin's fundamental questioning of the assumption that there is a distinction between the social and the individual. In Bakhtin's (1981) view the very nature of reality is dialogic and polysemous. It is not possible to separate the 'self' from the 'other'. From birth to death, who we are, how we think, what we understand and how we act are all dependent on our present or past relationships with people. Since the human consciousness is social as opposed to individual, it is always imbued with ambivalence. This ambivalence, inherent in the dialogic, generates a tension which strives towards a deeper understanding between 'self' and 'other'. This tension strives for resolution through the symbolic incorporation of both viewpoints, that is the spiritual and the profane. By symbolically dramatising the societal conflict that takes place between the Traveller and the settled person's world view the shaman goes some way towards resolving this conflict.

The symbolic action which occurs is 'the microcosm which irreducibly implies, recalls and reflects upon the social macrocosm'

(Geertz, 1986: 13). The Travellers are depicted as ritual figures whose role is seen to incorporate a new reality, one which stresses unity and harmony and mediation between opposites. The symbolic duality inhabited by the Travellers allows society's values to be transformed and endowed with a new meaning, a meaning the imposition of which Geertz (1972) defines as 'the primary condition of human existence' (1972: 509). The dual role of the Traveller figures in *Ortha an Ghreama* has strong analogies with an anthropological definition of role-taking in the rituals of non-Western societies as defined by Courtney (1982) where the self is identified with the 'other': 'It ... [the role-play] allows the individual to embody the experience of the 'other' within the form of the role; thus the role mediates the subjectively felt experience and the objectively perceived "other"' (1982: 52).

In *Ortha an Ghreama* the Irish travelling and settled communities are depicted in an oppositional framework, an opposition which is reconciled through the ritual figure of the shaman. The depiction of the Travellers is analogous with that of other shaman or ritual-clown figures who 'dissolve' their environment and represent a powerful statement of 'process'. This statement is predicated on a kind of ritual of rebellion whereby strongly countercultural feelings and ideas are expressed, albeit within a frame of reference which is ritualised and culturally permitted. The liminal phase encompassed in the ritual of the *Ortha* allows the figure of the Traveller, a figure who is permeated with cultural ambiguity, to move from one social position to another. The dramatic metaphor that is the Traveller becomes a shared agent for cultural reflexivity. It incorporates the participants' (storyteller/audience) felt experience and serves to re-create the categories through which they perceive reality – what Turner (1968) refers to as those 'axioms underlying the structure of society and the laws of the natural and moral orders' (1968: 7). The ambiguous and reflexive nature of the boundary that the Travellers inhabit is central to the paradoxical role they are seen to play in *Ortha an Ghreama* and is analogous with other similar shaman-type figures. This reflexivity demands that the audience reflect upon both the contrary and complementary sides of the cultural interaction between 'settled' and Traveller, a reflexivity which needs unearthing from what appears to be ordinary or commonplace. Handelman (1981) discussing the ritual/boundary role of the ritual-clown in 'primitive' society, describes this reflexivity which culminates in revelation as follows:

Such boundaries or frames are compatible only with ritual phases which evoke a sense of the sacred that is buried ordinarily within the routine and the commonplace. Such frames, by evoking both the sacred and its contrary, heighten the consciousness of participants to sentiments of holiness. Such frames may be termed 'boundaries of transition', for their concern is less with belief than it is with preparing participants to believe ... they erase distinctions between the sacred and the secular, and they prepare the way for the advent of the deity. (1981: 338).

When the Travellers of *Ortha an Ghreama* are 'unmasked' as the holy people they really are, they, like the ritual clowns known as the *capakobam*, bring the boundary to the sacred centre thereby erasing societal distinctions. They open the way to the reaffirmation of the world as a unity of interdependent parts by introducing a meta-message[17] which overrides paradox. Leach (1976) links this metacommunicative function with the regenerative power that resides in the limen or those ambiguous interfaces that he sometimes refers to as 'dirt'. Handelman (1981) defines such power as 'the changing of the shape and meaning of the cosmos: if boundaries are altered, then so is the relationship between those parts which these borders order' (1981: 342). Turner (1974) sees the dissolving of boundaries as a primary attribute of liminality. In his view liminality is a medium which functions to shape archetypes or root metaphors into 'radically simplified' and 'generic' models of the ordinary social order (1974: 202). The interaction between generalised cultural meaning and individual consciousness serves to 'validate a conceptual world view by conforming and re-creating extant myths' (Schechner, 1980: 103). This re-creation is a function of the anti-structural within the liminal.

> The anti-structural model of the social order not only arises within the medium of liminality – it is also an 'essential' version of social structure. In other words, its premises are composed of essential values, beliefs, and precepts, about how the world should be constituted ... Within liminal boundaries, the ordinary social order is taken-apart and put-together in an essential version of social structure, viz., anti-structure. (Handelman 1981: 252)

While anti-structure includes certain strong sentiments (e.g. those of 'communitas') which critique the social structure, Turner (1974) argues that it is the re-amalgamation of anti-structure with social structure that re-invigorates the latter and ensures the regeneration of cosmic (and hence social) order.[18] The ritualised[19] nature of this renewal validates certain working paradigms for action as outlined by Turner (1968):

> In ritual … primitive society reappraises its ideology and structural form, and finds them good. Refractory behaviour and the expression of conflict are allowed, even in some instances prescribed, to release energies by which social cohesion is recognised to be the outcome of the struggle … [it is] often a struggle to overcome the cleavages caused by contradictions in the structural principles of the society itself. A struggle may also arise from the resistances of human nature to social conditioning. Or both kinds of struggle may provoke and exacerbate one another. In any case the structure of each kind of ritual betrays marks of the struggle in its symbolisms and enjoined behaviour. (1968: 237–238)

The narrative power of *Ortha an Ghreama* lies in its reflexivity, a reflexivity which is particularly pertinent in a society as traditionally 'homogeneous' as Ireland. The ritual drama[20] that is the *Ortha* is generative of new meaning thereby contributing to the reinvention of culture for the narrator/audience and the healer practitioners who used the *Ortha*. The Travellers in *Ortha an Ghreama* embody the role of cosmic messengers who attempt to instigate changes of perception and attitude, changes which can transform by means of their collective[21] or universal significance.

In this chapter the existence and functioning of a counter-tradition to anti-Traveller prejudice as it exists in the Irish folktale tradition has been explored. Folktales like *Ortha an Ghreama* form a discourse where Travellers are seen to subvert their assignation of 'outcast' or 'negative Other' as incorporated in 'anti-Traveller' folktales like the 'Nail' and 'Pin' legends. At its most basic, the moral imperative of a narrative-charm such as *Ortha an Ghreama* and associated folktales like the 'Wishes' tale is the necessity to exhibit 'hospitality' towards all Travellers or those regarded as less well off or without lodgings of their own. That the *lucht siúil* (Travellers) are often travelling in the guise of holy personages and are in a sense God's representatives on earth is the sub-text of the narrative. The idea that it is dangerous or unlucky to refuse hospitality to those who request it amalgamates both 'medieval' Christian and traditional Gaelic ideas regarding the necessity for charity.

Given the narrative and moral thrust of these tales and the central role played by Travellers in the Irish healing and storytelling traditions it is very likely that Travellers themselves had a large role in the promulgation and preservation of this counter-tradition as encompassed in *Ortha an Ghreama*. The extent to which this 'subversive tradition', countervailing the 'negative Other' depiction of Travellers, suffused the iconography of both the religious/prayer and traditional healing traditions in Ireland is testament to the strength of these narratives and the importance this 'counter-tradition' once held. *Ortha an Ghreama* as promulgated by storytellers in both the Travelling and 'settled' communities can be seen as a direct inversion of Traveller ostracisation as incorporated in narratives like the 'Nail' and 'Pin' legends.

In *Ortha an Ghreama* the Traveller is portrayed as a shaman-type figure who incorporates a duality fusing the temporal and the divine. The liminal position inhabited by the Traveller is transformed so that his marginal societal position dissolves. This transformation of the liminal position is indicative of an erosion of the societal distinctions that exist between different groups within Irish society. The Travellers of *Ortha an Ghreama* represent an otherworldly form of order that transforms the temporal and erases distinctions between the sacred and the secular so that the fullness of a new 'truth' can be revealed. The transformative dualism evident in *Ortha an Ghreama* is also indicative of one of the folktale's major functions in the twentieth century, as outlined by Marina Warner (1995):

> in conditions of radical change on the one hand, and stagnation on the other, with ever increasing fragmentation and widening polarities, with national borders disappearing in some places and returning with a bloody vengeance in others … the need to belong grows ever more rampant as it becomes more frustrated, there has been a strongly marked shift towards fantasy as a mode of understanding, as an ingredient in survival, as a lever against the worst aspects of the status quo and the direction it is taking. (1985: 415)

Instead of being perceived as sinners/outcasts whose marginalisation is a deserved form of punishment, the Travellers in *Ortha an Ghreama* are indicative of a profound symbolic reversal. They are agents of subversion in the guise of holy people who provide a temporary challenge to the 'normal' social order. The Travellers assume a role which mediates between the story's narrator/audience and their world, a role encompassing the dual process of imaginatively projecting into, and creating a representation of, the world. As a shaman figure the Traveller takes on an intermediary role incorporating two realities – the Traveller world and the 'settled' world – at once. The Traveller emphasises the dialogic essence that is the self, as theorised by Bakhtin: 'To live means to participate in dialogue: to ask questions, to heed, to respond, to agree and so forth. In this dialogue a person participates wholly and thoroughly throughout his life. He invests his entire self in discourse, and this discourse enters into the dialogic fabric of human life, into the world symposium' (1984: 293).

The Traveller as depicted in *Ortha an Ghreama* is a figure indicative of an attitude of creative disrespect, a figure engaged in a re-ordering of long-established discourses and imaginaries. The Traveller figure is suggestive of 'new forms of identification that may confuse the continuity of historical temporalities, confound the ordering of cultural symbols and, traumatize tradition' (Bhabha, 1994: 257). The symbolic inversion which the Traveller invokes is representative of a subtle yet radical opposition to the hegemonic, the monologic and that which is illegitimately powerful. It is indicative of the fact that the classificatory body of a culture is always double, always structured in relation to its inverse, its negation. It reminds us that culture's most powerful symbolic repertoires are often located at its borders or margins. It echoes Babcock's (1978) comments on the centrality of symbolic process in the regeneration of culture: 'Far from being a residual category of experience, it is its very opposite. What is socially peripheral is often symbolically central, and if we ignore or minimize inversion and other forms of cultural negation we often fail to understand the dynamics of symbolic processes generally' (Babcock, 1978: 32).

## NOTES

1   Some of the most recent studies have used recently available (online) records to trace intercultural linkages in terms of marriage between both communities (see Ward, 2010).

2   *Ortha an Ghreama* is one of the most common charms/prayers in the popular traditions of both Ireland and Scotland.

3   *Déilín* – Irish: literally 'rigmarole', 'sing-song' or 'litany'. The *déilíní* uttered in narrative-charms.

4   The concept of 'negative theology' was once confined to the traditions of mysticism and hermeticism. It is today a fairly common subject of discussion in what is commonly referred to as radical (or the new) theology.

Negation as creative symbolic has been discussed by Cox (1970) who has criticised the tendency of radical theologians to ignore the playful and festive aspects of negation. Cox's discussion of negation proposed a 'theology of juxtaposition', a discourse which has much in common with Burke's theorisation of symbolic inversion and its relation to the notion of 'aesthetic negation'.

5    Burke (1968) follows Hegel and Nietzsche in arguing a negativistic nature of religion as a symbolic system. One of the core definitions of man as a moral being encompasses the negativistic according to Burke, citing the prescription 'thou shalt not' (1968: 12–13).

6    As examples of the counter-hegemonic in present day Africa, Mudimbe has in mind those discourses incorporating otherness, alterity and ideologies which seek to place negritude, black culture and African philosophy at their centre, those discourses which he says 'might be considered to be the best established in the present-day intellectual history of Africa' (Mudimbe, 1988: xi).

7    Sales (1983) cites two reasons as to why he considers carnivalesque subversion to be a controlled form of social transgression: 'First of all, it was licensed or sanctioned by the authorities themselves. They removed the stopper to stop the bottle being smashed altogether. The release of emotions and grievances made them easier to police in the long term. Second, although the world might appear to be turned upside down during the carnival season, the fact that Kings and Queens were chosen and crowned actually reaffirmed the status quo. Carnival was, however, Janus-faced. Falstaff is both the merry old mimic of Eastcheap and the old corruptible who tries to undermine the authority, or rule, of the Lord Chief Justice. The carnival spirit in early-nineteenth century England as well as in sixteenth century, could therefore be a vehicle for social protest and the method for disciplining that protest' (1983: 169).

8    Eagleton (1981) is ambivalent about the liberating potential of the 'carnivalesque', describing it in the as follows: 'Carnival laughter is incorporating as well as liberating, its lifting of inhibitions politically enervating as well as disruptive. Indeed from one viewpoint carnival may figure as a prime example of the mutual complicity of law and liberation, power and desire, that has become the dominant theme of contemporary post-marxist pessimism' (1981: 149).

9    It is striking how carnival and carnivalesque transgression coincided with violent social classes (see Burke, 1978; Davis, 1975; Thompson, 1972).

10   Hamnett (1967) points out the dangers that accompany the classificatory world view: 'Classification is a pre-requisite of the intelligible ordering of experience, but if conceptual categories are reified, they become obstacles

rather than means to the understanding and control of both physical and social reality' (1967: 387).

11   The Travellers as depicted in *Ortha an Ghreama* are not seen to reject totally the order of the socio-cultural world. Instead, they work to remind the story's audience of the arbitrary condition that is the imposition of order on the audience's environment and experience. In doing this, they enable the audience to view certain aspects of that order more clearly by virtue of the fact that they have turned this order upside down or inside out. In doing so, they echo Nietzsche's (1966) statement: 'Objections, digressions, gay mistrust, the delight in mockery are signs of health: everything unconditional belongs in pathology' (1966: 90).

12   Marcel Détienne (1979) links his questioning of the classificatory with the cultural vitality of our philosophical systems of thought: 'A system of thought … is founded on a series of acts of partition whose ambiguity, here as elsewhere, is to open up the terrain of their possible transgression at the very moment when they mark off a limit. To discover the complete horizon of a society's symbolic values, it is also necessary to map out its transgressions, its deviants' (Détienne 1979: ix).

13   Although some variants of *Ortha an Ghreama* suggest that Jesus' reluctance to utilise his healing powers is a direct consequence of his shabby treatment by his would-be hosts, in others we are told that this is not always the central reason for his reluctant attitude. His reluctance is sometimes tied to the role of the spiritual in his healing. He says that he is in fact not yet ready to perform miracles in the public sphere thereby echoing the Wedding Feast of Cana story in the Gospel – 'My time has not come yet' (John 2:5) 'Out in the night the husband got a colic and at length and at last the mother said to the Son to do some good for the man that left them inside for the night. / 'My hour didn't come yet,' says He, 'Let you do it.' / 'Ah, no' says she, 'I'll not take the rod out of your hand.' / So 'tis then He started His prayer' (Iml. 1371: 245 – IFC respondent from Kilrush, County Clare).

14   In a very occasional variant of the narrative-charm *Ortha an Ghreama*, it is actually stated in the narrative that Jesus has deliberately inflicted the pain on the 'man of the house' so as to teach his wife a lesson.

15   In most variants of *Ortha an Ghreama* it is the 'man of the house' who suffers the pain although he has been kinder to the Travellers.

16   That the 'shabby' treatment given to the Holy Family in *Ortha an Ghreama* was incorporated into the discourse of Travellers and used as a form of symbolic inversion with a certain satirical intent is indicated by the following 'reminder' issued by the blind west of Ireland Traveller-poet Anthony Raftery which survived in Irish popular tradition: 'When Raftery

was going around and looking for lodgings wherever he could find it he called one night into a certain man. And he was the type of man who didn't have much room in his house. There was a fistful of ferns in the corner of the house – probably for burning – for using in the fire. This man had three young sons. They went to bed and Raftery came in seeking lodgings. Well I don't have any good place to put you but I don't want to put you out. You can stay until morning. Raftery said that he didn't mind so long as he could stay in the shelter of the house. When the three boys were gone to sleep the old man arranged a bed for him on the pile of the ferns. He arranged the bed of ferns so that it was as neat as possible. And when he was getting ready for bed himself, one of his sons spoke in the back of the room. He spoke in a low voice so that Raftery would not hear him. 'Well', he says. 'You'll hear talk about this bed of ferns yet', says the son. Raftery overheard him. When the man of the house was asleep Raftery says: 'I am fairly well-travelled, / I am always going, walking the country, / I am going through the country and meeting the poor and the naked, / Many's the place that I have bedded down, / Throughout the breadth of this country and me miserably poor, / And although I've walked the whole country / I was never a fern-hen until tonight!' (Iml. 368: 375–377).

17  Willeford (1969), who studied the role of the fool in 'primitive' society, identifies a similarly reflexive function in the 'fluid' social role of the fool – 'the fool as a borderline figure holds the social world open to values that transcend it' (1969: 137).

18  The rejuvenation of the cosmic order in *Ortha an Ghreama* is a consequence of the Travellers' critique of social structure, a critique that incorporates ritual healing. Handelman (1981) has pointed to the central role of this renewal in the positing of anti-structural sentiment as applied to 'primitive' or tribal societies: 'The rejoining of anti-structure to social structure … renews the latter. This emphasis on the renewal, the rejuvenation, or the regeneration, of cosmic (and hence social) order, often is striking in the calendrical rites of tribal societies, particularly those associated with the solstices and the equinoxes. Anti-structure, in such rites (and in others as well), calls forth the imagery of enduring and valid truths, of a unity of interdependent parts that is monumental in what it subsumes, and of the *punctum indifferens*, the point(s) of rest which stabilizes and anchors sacred structures in space and out-of-time' (1981: 352).

19  It is worth noting the evidence for the resurgence of ritual behaviour in modern times, a resurgence which is often representative of oppositional social and political stances. The women's movement, movements incorporating various forms of civil protest and the 'New Age' movement,

including different groups of New Age Travellers have all deliberately created formalised ritual behaviour as a response to dominant cultural ideologies. A good example of the latter grouping is the Dongas 'tribe' of New Age Travellers in Britain which led the opposition to road-building schemes in various areas of Britain during the 1990s. John Fox, a ceremonial artist and founder of the Welfare State Theatre Company in Britain expresses this new cultural dynamic whereby people in the West wish to emulate the ritual behaviour of many in non-Western societies, rituals which invert and transform the ordinary into the extraordinary: 'We are looking for a culture which may well be less materially based but where people will actively participate and gain power to celebrate moments that are wonderful and significant in their lives. Be this building their own houses, naming their children, burying their dead, announcing new partnerships, marking anniversaries, creating new sacred spaces and producing whatever drama, stories, songs, rituals, ceremonies, pageants and jokes that are relevant to the new values and new iconography' (Fox in Fyfe, 1998: 149).

20   It is generally acknowledged that the Western European tradition has separated drama from other activities in life. The power of involvement whereby personal concerns and social ones are linked with dramatic involvement has tended to diminish or disappear entirely within the cultures of the West. The opposite remains the case in many non-Western or so-called primitive societies. In these societies art (culture), religion and daily life fuse together in drama so that cultural meanings are renewed and recreated 'on a stage as wide as society itself' (Diamond, n.d.: 31).

21   Walens (1982) describes the ceremonial rituals of Northwest Coast Native Americans as an attempt to achieve a new and collective awareness that has significance far beyond the confines of the social group: 'Through the display of crests Northwest Coast ceremonies provided for the expansion of the self and the group beyond the social boundaries and in doing so linked human beings with each other and to the vital forces of the cosmos. Rituals make opposites equivalent: a local house becomes the entire universe, a human being becomes a cosmic being, the past of myth becomes manifest in the rituals of the present. The expansion of the self and the group to equivalence with the cosmos is achieved by the close identification of individuals with the spirit-beings whom they portray in dance and embody in this world' (1982: 23).

# 10 The dichotomy of Self and Other: Some considerations

This volume has traced the development of the Traveller image as 'Other' through mythical and binary discourses of alterity. Until the recent arrival of a more overtly multicultural society in Ireland Travellers have constituted the 'Other' for mainstream Irish society. As 'Other' they have often acted as objects on whom power is exercised. Their representation and the roles constructed for them have been determined primarily by the settled community and have been influenced by the need to define national, social and class identity. This project of representation has used the tools of mythology and history. These two related aspects of the Irish popular tradition reinforce the fact that myth and history can never be seen as entirely separate entities.

The construction of history is itself a process of mythologising and the various guises in which the Traveller image manifests itself in Irish tradition indicate that contemporary myth has deep roots in popular perceptions of history. The myth or construction that is the Traveller image is created by what is spoken or written to form a part of history and is perpetuated through contemporary notions of history and tradition. The discourses of modernity, whether formed at the individual level or (perhaps more commonly today) at the level of the mass media, work to sanction, reiterate and consolidate the myths of a people. The perpetuation of myth and stereotype is interwoven through history, as outlined by Roland Barthes (1972): 'It is human history which converts reality into speech, and it alone rules the life and death of mythical language ... Ancient or not, mythology can only have a historical foundation, for myth is a type of speech chosen by history' (1972: 23).

Central to this thesis has been an investigation of the manner by which Irish people have defined themselves in terms of Otherness, using the Traveller image as a projective mechanism. My analysis has shown that anti-Traveller Othering, like the anti-Irish Othering of the colonial era, is a complex and interwoven network of images which serves to unsettle the authority and homogeneity of totalising metanarratives. This unsettling effect claims to undermine that 'ontological imperialism' which Levinas (1961) said was resonant of the history of Western philosophy, a process where the relation with the other was accomplished through its assimilation with the self.

The dichotomy between self and Other represented in this volume has been central to a modernity crippled by crises of identity, representation and legitimisation. It can be argued that the most radical aspect of the cultural discourse known as postmodernism[1] has been this politics of identity, difference and the margins. The essential opposition or struggle between self and other is the core of this politics of difference and is a fundamental aspect of human existence, as outlined by de Beauvoir (1972): 'The category of the Other is as primordial as consciousness itself. In the most primitive of societies, in the most ancient mythologies, one finds the expression of a duality – that of the Self and the Other ... Otherness is a fundamental category of human thought' (1972: 21).

As a conclusion to this examination of Traveller alterity I wish to briefly discuss the philosophical possibilities that exist for a movement beyond the 'politics of difference' as it currently stands and the potential for a new theoretic dualism of Self/Other. Poststructuralist thinkers such as Jacques Derrida have been to the fore in this theoretical evolution and I discuss his notion of *différance* as a roadmap for future theoretical engagement with the concept of the 'Other'. Postmodernism involves a radical critique of universal reason and truth. From the perspectives of a politics of difference, postmodernism sets out to show that certain narratives have been marginalised as a function of power. This marginalisation has been foregrounded through the materiality of language and the politics of representation. The postmodern condition has marked a shift in the priority of the Self over the Other. It involves a reinvention of the Self under the conditions of difference. Delanty (2000) sums up this shift in perspective in the following manner:

> Modernity reached its limits with the recognition that its most cherished discourses were founded on an act of violence against the Other ... Postmodernity, I would suggest, involves a deepening of this problematic ... If the Holocaust marked the culmination of the modern quest for mastery and the determination of the Other by the Self, postmodernity as a post-colonial and post-Holocaust discourse forces us to see the Self through eyes of the Other ...

Underlying these shifts in the constitution of subjectivity is a certain scepticism in the durability of any narrative of the identity of the Self for the question of non-identity must always be posed. In the context of vague pluralism and multiculturalism and the collapses of the self-confidence of the Eurocentric worldview, the prospect of any universal discourse of identity is in question. (2000: 3)

The ambivalence concerning identity which Delanty describes can be linked to the postmodernist critique of traditional philosophy. The postmodern critique has focused on the attempts of traditional philosophy to know essential truths which can provide objective criteria by which we may judge our representations 'accurately' and the subsequent moral positions which arise from this. As an inherent feature of the Western philosophic condition the notion of transcendentalism is criticised either directly or indirectly. Postmodern philosophical critiques imply that objects, truths and concepts of reality lie somehow outside of and prior to any contingent or spatio-temporal factors, including our description of them. The viewpoint from which these objects, truths and concepts are described is also perceived as outside of and prior to any contingent factors which could affect this description of them. For postmodernists there is no transcendental viewpoint from which these truths and realities can be known.

Derrida criticises the Western philosophical tradition for the way it has downgraded the notion of the sign and its never-ending search for what lies beneath it – the signified. Derrida's deconstruction encompassed in his concept of *différance* represents an effort to explore an otherness that appears on the margins or outside traditional philosophical reason. His deconstructive project can be viewed primarily as an attempt to examine the assumptions of Western philosophy. His aim has been to illustrate the falsity of humankind's desire for unmediated truth.[2] This falsity has been inherent in Western rationality since the time of Plato, and has produced hierarchically-ordered concepts based upon binary oppositions. Attempts at the totalisation of text in accordance with these binaries can be seen to depend upon a generalised form of the differences it proposes to subsume.

Derrida's greatest achievement, in my view, is his exposition, through *différance*, of the manner in which language and meaning have been constructed and constituted in such a way as to perpetuate this exclusion. Derrida's deconstruction overturns hierarchies so as to give a new precedence to the 'Other' and to liberate all concepts from what Derrida sees as the dominance of the logos or the logocentric hierarchy. He sees logocentrism as a homogenising power that attempts to impose centres, borderlines and limits where none can hold except by the repression of the trace. Logocentric ontotheology seeks out the comfort of a central presence, aiming always to subordinate writing to 'a full presence which is beyond play' (Derrida, 1978: 279). The logocentrism which Derrida rebels against Spivak (1996) describes as 'Humankind's common desire ... for a stable centre, and for the assurance of mastery through knowing or possessing' (1976: xi). The logocentric is the nature of human discourse. It aspires to mastery of the object of knowledge and it does this through a combination of repression, hierarchisation and assimilation: 'Any discourse is constituted as an attempt to dominate the field of discursivity, to arrest the flow of differences, to construct a centre' (Laclau and Mouffe 1985: 112).

Logocentrism desires a situation where alternative meanings can exclude one another so that textual order can be maintained and meaning can be fully realised. Since binary oppositions are conventionally held to constitute language's building blocks, Derrida says they are normally regarded in terms which signify an original or derivative meaning – that is, a hierarchy of positive and negative terms. These derivative oppositions are the product of logocentrism as outlined by Spivak (1976): 'It is the longing for the centre – that spawns hierarchical oppositions. The superior term belongs to presence and the logos; the inferior serves to define its status and mark a fall' (1976: lxix).

This volume has examined the mediation on the part of the Irish people of the question of the centre – in this case, self-definition – and the projection of essentialist definitions onto the 'Other' (Travellers) in a binary, hierarchical framework using the same essentialist, 'natural' and self-interested representations as the coloniser. Derrida argues the necessity to exclude any notion of 'natural' hierarchies among signifiers or discourses since all hierarchies are constructed. His notion of *différance* problematises fixed borders and subverts the rigid conceptual oppositions that are indicative of logocentrism. Logocentrism relies on conceptual oppositions which are mutually dependent on one another. Each term in an opposition differs/defers (and infers) its other. The subordinate term operates to supplement the original but Derrida reminds us that this supplement is necessary at the outset because of a lack in the original. Derrida sees the oppositional dynamic between inside/outside, origin/supplement, self/other as open and dynamic as opposed to balanced, closed and static. This metaphysical opposition is by nature undecidable as any given opposition of terms depends on the force (*différance*) that precedes them – they are its effects – and this force works constantly to unsettle their relationship. Oppositions are engendered with meaning only 'after the possibility of trace' (Derrida, 1976: 47).[3] This deconstructive logic leaves oppositional meaning with the potential to act as a subversive force: 'At the point at which the concept of *différance* intervenes, all the conceptual oppositions of metaphysics (signifier/signified; sensible/intelligible; writing/speech; passivity/activity) – to the extent that they refer to the presence of something present – become non-pertinent' (Derrida, 1982: 29).

Rather than merely collapse differences into one another Derrida's concept of *différance* creates an imploded homogeneity. Its logic is centrifugal, deconstructing from within while simultaneously affirming and generating difference.[4] Postmodern theorists such as Derrida and Foucault have worked to critique logocentrism, the essentialisation of identity and the exclusionary logic that accompanies the metanarratives of the West. The analysis of the 'othering' discourse that imbues the image of the Traveller in Irish tradition is analogous with this fundamental problem as evidenced in the Western imaginary. How can knowledge – and therefore, theory and history – be constituted through the comprehension and incorporation of the 'Other'? Modernity in the Western world, encompassing Enlightenment episteme, has framed, legitimated and disseminated its knowledge of itself through what Lyotard referred to as the Grand Narrative, where the hegemonic Self/Same spoke for all. Since it disavowed any source of identity that emanated from outside itself, modernity elevated its own putative universality to the status of a new transcendent. Postmodernists, however, have waged a war against these totalising metanarratives in an effort to disrupt logocentrism and reach those marginal *loci* of being that survive where there is alterity, absence, aporia and the Other.

Derrida's notion of *différance* is one method whereby the exclusionary logic of metanarrative can be undermined. The concept of *différance* is the tool which Derrida uses to deconstruct the Western 'metaphysics of presence'. It is a force disseminating a heterogeneous power, one which is replete with radically subversive potential. It interrupts texts so as to problematise the structuring of borderlines and oppositions, thereby undermining the logocentric fixed meaning. It is analogous with Foucault's politics of strategic resistances[5] because the political implications of *différance* for the Self/Other power dialectic are equally radical. *Différance* as theorised by Derrida has a positive and disseminating dynamic because it resists the order and stability that the logos requires and rebels against all those forces of homogenisation that try to impose or uphold a centred authority.

Since meaning itself 'originates' in *différance*, neither the signified nor the referent is present beyond the signifier. The suppression of the trace and a longing for presence have been central attributes of the history of logocentric metaphysics. In Derrida's view reality is never experienced as presence since textuality has already moulded our perception of the world. He argues that there is no such thing as a 'pure' or 'true' presence. Instead we have chains of differential marks which resist attempts to impose closure by an eternal process of differing and differing again, this constant deferral serving to neutralise any limit that power attempts to impose. He describes this textual deferral in the following way: 'Reading … cannot legitimately transgress the text towards something other than it … There is nothing outside the text' (Derrida, 1976: 158).

Derrida's deconstructive notion of *différance* suggests a new conceptualisation of reality. It advocates a reading of reality and presence which incorporates openness, plurality and opacity. Words and texts acquire their meaning in sequences of differences and differential relations. A fixed meaning incorporating a totalisation of language does not exist. Instead language consists of a conflictual and unbalanced hierarchy of discourses where there is no totality but only the causal chains and movements of forces instead. The play of this ever-shifting trace has always been in tension with both history and presence. History itself has been a struggle to constitute presence (order) through the repression of the trace (*différance*). Identity and its representation are consequences of the interdependency between same and other, a play of inferences.[6] To assert one's own differential identity according to a postmodernist viewpoint, therefore, involves 'the inclusion in that identity of the other, as that from whom one delimits oneself' (Laclau 1977: 3). For theorists such as Derrida every identity is relational[7], incorporating Self and Other and the affirmation of difference is a precondition for the existence of any identity. As Paul Ricoeur has argued in *Oneself as Another* (1992) a postmodernist concept of identity should not be formed as it has been previously i.e. through a simple rejection of the 'Other'. What is needed in place of a binary logic of opposition and negation is a complex process of interaction whereby identity can be negotiated based on mutual respect and dialogue. Postmodernist philosophy is increasingly seeking ways in which to build on the theories of Derrida and Foucault so as to connect with that polysemous alterity that is somewhere within the unstoppable play of representation, that postmodern alterity of the indefinable 'middle' which Samuel Beckett (1979) termed the 'Unnameable':

> perhaps that's what I feel, an outside and an inside and me in the middle, perhaps that's what I am, the thing that divides the world in two, on the one side the outside, on the other the inside, that can be as thin as foil, I'm neither one side not the other, I'm in the middle, I'm the partition, I've two surfaces and no thickness, perhaps that's what I feel, myself vibrating, I'm the tympanum, on the one hand the mind, on the other the world, I don't belong to either. (1979: 352)

The spirit of this postmodernist quest has been eloquently summarised by Alan Wolfe (1992) who notes that:

> the essence of the approach is to question the presumed boundaries between groups: of signifiers, peoples, species or texts. What appears at first glance to be a difference is reinterpreted, discovered to be little more than a distinction rooted in power or a move in a rhetorical game. Differences, in other words, never have a fixed status in and out of themselves; there are no either/ors nor are there no not either/ors. (1992: 310)

Modern thinkers including Levinas, Kristeva, Kearney and Volf have all attempted to theorise an interlacing mechanism that can bridge the gap between an otherness that is absolute and an otherness which is relative. Miroslav Volf (1996), who theorises the Self/Other dualism from a theological perspective, envisages the self and other working together in a negotiation of identity that involves dialogue and interaction. He refers to the seminal myth of Creation to suggest a new form of Self/Other dynamic. He cites the work of Platinga (1995), who drew attention to the way Genesis portrayed God's creative activity as a pattern of 'separating' and 'binding together':

> So God begins to do some creative separating: he separates light from darkness, day from night, water from land, the sea creatures from the land cruiser ... At the same time God binds together: he binds humans to the rest of creation as stewards and caretakers of it, to himself as bearers of his image, to each other as perfect complements. (1995: 29)

Creation as described in Genesis exists as an intricate pattern of 'separate-and-bound-together' entities.[8] More precisely it means what German theologian Michael Welker (1995) describes as the 'formation and maintenance of a network of the relations of interdependence' (1995: 24). Volf (1996) sees this definition of Creation as a template for a new form of identity:

> The account of creation as 'separating-and-binding' rather than simply 'separating' suggests that 'identity' includes connection, difference, heterogeneity. The human self is formed not through a simple rejection of the other – through a binary logic of opposition and negation – but through a complex process of 'taking in' and 'keeping out'. We are who we are not because we are separate from the others who are next to us, but because we *are* both *separate* and *connected,* both *distinct* and *related;* the boundaries that mark our identities are both barriers and bridges. (1996: 66)

A similarly polysemous process of 'intersignification' is proposed by Kearney (2003), who sees the challenge of mediating between the Self/Other dialectic as an aspect of the project of the Enlightenment that will remain 'unenlightened until it comes to terms with strangers, gods or monsters that it has all too often ostracised or ignored' (2003: 7). He advocates a diacritical hermeneutics that can make 'the foreign more familiar and the familiar more foreign' (2003: 11). He is hopeful that human estrangement in the postmodern era can be overcome by means of 'a hermeneutic retrieval of selfhood through the odyssey of otherness' (2003: 19). Perhaps the most useful mapping of the Self/Other dialectic has been provided by Emmanuel Levinas who based much of his philosophy on the Jewish mystical and Kabbalistic traditions. He posits a relationship of sociality whereby the self instead of assimilating the other opens itself to it through a dialogic relation with it, a relationship which like Derrida's is fused in the realm of language. Levinas recommends a new form of language, a language of dialogue, as highlighted by Robert Young (1990):

> whereas language's function in conceptualizing thought is to suppress the other and bring it within the aegis of the same, in dialogue language maintains the distance between the two, 'their commerce', as Levinas puts it, 'is ethical'. Dialogism allows for 'radical separation, the strangeness of the interlocutors, the revelation of the other to me'. The structure of dialogue, moreover, disallows the

taking up of any position beyond the interlocutors from which they can be integrated into a larger totality. The relationship between them, therefore, is not oppositional, nor limitrophe, but one of alterity. (1990: 14–15)

Levinas, like Derrida, objects to the implicit violence in the historical process of knowledge which endeavours to appropriate and sublate the essence of the other into itself – 'Western philosophy coincides with the disclosure of the other where the other, in manifesting itself as a being, loses its alterity. From its infancy philosophy has been struck with a horror of the other that remains other' (Levinas, 1996: 25). He links epistemological violence against the 'Other' with warfare. The frequency of warfare in the modern era is a consequence of an ambivalent morality which overlooks the extent to which 'war constitutes the philosophical concept of being itself' (Young, 1990: 13). Warfare involves not just the injury or annihilation of persons, but also:

> interrupting their continuity, making them play roles in which they no longer recognize themselves, making them betray not only commitments but their own substance … Not only modern war but every war employs arms that turn against those who wield them. It establishes an order from which no one can keep his distance; nothing henceforth is exterior. (Levinas in Young, 1990: 13)

The political history of the Other is linked to an ontology which, though outwardly directed, remains always centred in an incorporating self – the 'imperialism of the same' (Levinas, 1969: 53) European philosophy has duplicated much of Western foreign policy where democracy at home is maintained through the suppression of colonial or neocolonial oppression abroad or minority and ethnic groups at home. Levinas opposes this 'Western' 'freedom' based on self-interest and calls for a new form of justice which respects the alterity of the other through dialogue. Both Levinas and Derrida recommend dialogism through the medium of language as the way to a future ethical relationship between Self and Other. Dialogism allows for 'radical separation, the strangeness of the interlocutors, the revelation of the other to me' (Levinas, 1961: 73).

Through language it is possible for an ethical dialogue between Self and Other, a hermeneutic retrieval of the Self through the odyssey of Otherness. It is through such an odyssey along those borderlands that separate Us from the Others that 'we may become more ready to acknowledge strangers in ourselves and ourselves in strangers' (Kearney 2003: 20).

A new interrogation with the identity 'constructs' that are 'Irish' and 'Traveller' is long overdue and it is to be hoped that this book will prove some small contribution to this ongoing process. Such a development can only be beneficial in unearthing those rich and varied layers that have contributed to the fashioning of Irish identity in the postcolonial era.

A particular focus of any such interrogation should be directed towards those 'liminal' zones of culture – a number of which have been considered in this book – those contested spaces at the interstices of Irish identity where Irish Otherness has been formulated. The Irish Other is a conception which should be celebrated and engaged with on a reciprocal level. A respectful dialogue with the Irish Other is all the more important given that the Irishnesss that is Irish Traveller identity – the Traveller Other –is, in reality, an 'alterity within identity'. It is an alterity that has intersignified with the construct of Irish identity itself. It is a unique identity and one which is analogous with Kristeva's (1991) description of the 'stranger' in our midst: 'The stranger is neither a race nor a nation ... we are our own strangers – we are divided selves' (1991: 268).

## NOTES

1   The privileged status given to the question of Otherness or difference in postmodernism has led some writers to construe it as the defining feature of postmodern politics. Hence, for example: 'Modernism ... Postmodernism. What is the difference? The difference might involve the question of difference itself' (Taylor, 1990: 13). The notion of undecidability as linked to the politics of difference has been echoed in similar fashion by Hutchens (2005): 'The awareness of difference and contradiction, of being inside and outside is never lost ... in the postmodern' (1989: 14).

2   Foucault (1984) also echoes this questioning of the concept of transcendental truth. In his view, truth is relative to an archive or 'episteme' within which validity can be discussed, but outside of which it has no absolute or universal relevance.

3   *Différance* unceasingly dislocates or undermines meaning, but it is also the source of any meaning. As Derrida puts it, it is 'the play which makes possible nominal effects' (Derrida, 1982: 26). It constitutes incessant

self-displacement and equivocal movement from one mark to another, and consequently it is (the source of) undecidability. *Différance* signifies a contextualised play, a systematic and regulated play of forces over time. The context for the movement of *différance* is a field of differential political forces.

4    The term '*différance*' is itself imbued with ambiguity and undecidability. It veers towards sameness (against the concept of absolute oppositions) but it also simultaneously works towards a radical alterity (against the pressures of homogenisation), with no final stabilisation of meaning.

5    Foucault (1972) challenged the repression of the marginal through an 'archaeology of silence', that is, the archaeology of all those whose 'words deprived of language, forgotten words on whose omission the Western world was founded' (1972: 170). By means of this archaeology, Foucault attempted to unearth those ideas that had been silenced through fixed and limited patterns of knowledge. The cultural significance of his archaeology is that it seeks to 'untie all those knots that historians have patiently tied; it increases differences, blurs the lines of communication, and tries to make it more difficult to pass from one thing to another'.

6    Derrida's theorisation of *différance* implies a displacement or dispersal of the self-identity that is the sign. Instead of the self-identity of the sign there exists a plurality of clashing discourses and diffracted traces. Through the 'play' of the trace, the (non)originary concept that is *différance* deconstructs 'fixed' metaphysical oppositions that refer to alternative forms of presence, as explained by Derrida (1978): 'Play is the disruption of presence. The presence of an element is always a signifying and substitutive reference inscribed in a system of differences and the movement of a chain. Play is always play of absence and presence, but if it is to be thought of radically, play must be conceived of before the alternative of presence and absence. Being must be conceived as presence or absence on the basis of the possibility of play and not the other way around' (1978: 292).

7    Derrida's concept of *différance* resists the logocentric impulse by its incessant movement of difference. *Différance* differs from a traditional dialectical approach in that it always exceeds the totality of the conceivable. It is playing movement that produces the effects of difference through the resurrection of the 'middle voice'.

8    A number of theologians have also highlighted the patterns of 'intersignification' between Self/Other that run through the story of Jesus Christ's life. Christ transgressed the boundaries of Self/Other as delineated within Jewish society by socialising with social outcasts, peoples who practised despised trades, Gentiles, Samaritans and those others who failed to keep

the religious Law. His final moments were spent hanging on a Cross between two criminals. Volf (1996) cites the Apostle Paul's comment – 'It is Christ who lives in me' – after giving the report of his own crucifixion as an example of the de-centring and 're-centring' that is at the heart of the Judaeo-Christian tradition: 'The self is both 'de-centered' and 're-centred' by one and the same process, by participating in the death and resurrection of Christ through faith and baptism ... the center of the self – a center that is both inside and outside – is the story of Jesus Christ, which has become the story of the self. More precisely, the center is Jesus Christ crucified and resurrected who has become part and parcel of the very structure of the self' (1996: 70).

# Bibliography

Acton, T. (1974) *Gypsy Politics and Social Change*. London: Routledge and Kegan Paul

Acton, T. (1994) 'Categorising Irish Travellers' in S. Ó Síocháin, M. McCann and J. Ruane (eds.) *Irish Travellers: Culture and Ethnicity*. Belfast: Institute of Irish Studies, Queen's University of Belfast

Acton, T. (ed.) (1997) *Gypsy Politics and Traveller Identity*. Hatfield: University of Hertfordshire Press

Adorno, T. and Horkheimer, M. (eds.) (1973) *Dialectic of Enlightenment*. London: Allen Lane

Alexander, J. (1988) *Durkheimian Sociology: Cultural Studies*. Cambridge: Cambridge University Press

Althusser, L. (1971) *Lenin and Philosophy, and Other Essays*. London: Monthly Review Press

Arden-King. A. B. (1974) *Coban and the Verapaz: History and Cultural Process in Northern Guatemala*. New Orleans: Middle American Research Institute

Arensberg, C. and Kimball, S. (eds.) (1937) *The Irish Countryman: An Anthropological Study*. London: Macmillan

Arnold, H. (1958) *Vaganten, Komodianten, Fieranten und Briganten*. Stuttgart: Verlag Georg Thieme

Arnold, H. (1965) *Die Zigeuner. Herkunft und Leben der Stämme im deutschen Sprachgebiet*. Freiburg: Walter-Verlag

Ashcroft, B., Griffiths, G. and Tiffin, H. (eds.) (1995) *The Post-Colonial Studies Reader*. London: Routledge

Atkinson, P. and Hammersley, M. (eds.) (1992) *Ethnography: Principles in Practice*. London: Routledge

Babcock, B. (1978) *The Reversible World: Symbolic Inversion in Art and Society*. London: Ithaca

Bakhtin, M. (1968) *Rabelais and his World*. Massachusetts: MIT Press

Bakhtin, M. (1981) *The Dialogic Imagination: Four essays*. Texas: University of Texas Press

Barnes, B. (1975) 'Irish Travelling people' in E. F. Rehfisch (ed.) *Gypsies, Tinkers and other Travellers.* London: Academic Press

Barth, F. (1969) *Ethnic Groups and Boundaries.* London: Allen and Unwin

Barth, F. (1975) 'The social organisation of a pariah group in Norway' in E. F. Rehfisch (ed.) *Gypsies, Tinkers and other Travellers.* London: Academic Press

Barthes, R. *et al.* (1972) *Analyse Structurale et Exegese Biblique: Essais d'Interpretation; [De] Roland) Barthes, Francois Bovon, Franz J. Leenhardt, Robert Martin-Achard et Jean Starobinski.* Neuchatel: Delachaux et Niestle

Barthes, R. (1977) *Poetique du Recit.* Paris: Editions du Seuil.

Barthes, R. (1993) *Mythologies.* London: Vintage

Bartlett, T. (1992) *The Fall and Rise of the Irish Nation.* Dublin: Gill and Macmillan

Bateson, G. (1958) *Naven: A survey of the problems suggested by a composite picture of the culture of a New Guinea tribe drawn from three points of view.* Stanford: Stanford University Press

Battaglia, D. (1995) *Rhetorics of Self-making.* Berkeley: University of California Press

Bauman, Z. (1991) *Modernity and Ambivalence.* New York: Cornell University Press

Beckett, S. (1979) *Molloy; Malone Dies; The Unnameable.* London: John Calder

Beier, A. (1985) *Masterless Men: The Vagrancy Problem in England 1560–1640.* London: Methuen

Belton, B. (2005) *Gypsy and Traveller Ethnicity: The Social Generation of an Ethnic Phenomenon.* New York: Routledge

Bergson, H. (1911) *The Idea of Nothing. Creative Evolution.* New York: Rinehart and Winston

Bergson, H. (1956) 'Le rire' in W. Sypher (ed.) *Comedy.* New York: Doubleday

Bewley, V. (1974) *Travelling People.* Dublin: Veritas

Bhabha, H. E. (1990) *Nation and Narration.* London: Routledge

Bhabha, H. (1994) *The Location of Culture.* London: Routledge

Bhabha, H. (1996) 'The other question' in P. Mongia (ed.) *Contemporary Postcolonial Theory: A Reader.* London: Routledge

Bhreathnach, A. (1998) 'Travellers and the print media: words and Irish identity.' *Irish Studies Review* 6 (3): 285–290

Bhreathnach, A. (2006) *Becoming Conspicuous: Irish Travellers, Society and the State.* Dublin: UCD Press

Binchy, A. (1993) *The Status and Functions of Shelta* (Unpublished PhD thesis) Oxford University

Binchy, A. (1994) 'Travellers' language: A sociolinguistic perspective' in S. Ò. Síocháin, M. McCann and J. Ruane (eds.) *Irish Travellers: Culture and Ethnicity*. Belfast: Institute of Irish Studies, Queen's University

Binchy, A. (2002) 'Travellers' use of Shelta' in J. M. Kirk and D. P. Ó Baoill (eds.) *Travellers and their language*. Belfast: Cló Ollscoil na Banríona

Bobcock, R. and Thompson, K. (eds.) (1985) *Religion and Ideology*. Manchester: Manchester University Press

Breathnach, R. B. (1947) *The Irish of Ring, Co. Waterford*. Dublin: Dublin Institute for Advanced Studies

Burke, K. (1961) *The Rhetoric of Religion: Studies in Logology*. Boston: Beacon Press

Burke, K. (1964) *Permanency and Change: An Anatomy of Purpose*. California: Hermes

Burke, K. (1968) 'A dramatistic view of the origins of language and postscripts on the negative' in *Language as Symbolic Action: Essays on Life, Literature and Method*. Berkeley: University of California Press

Burke, P. (1978) *Popular Culture in Early Modern Europe*. London: Temple Smith

Cahoone, L. (ed.) (1996) *From Modernism to Postmodernism: An Anthology*. Cambridge, Mass.: Blackwell Publishers

Campbell, D. (1910) *Reminiscences and Reflections of an Octogenarian Highlander*. Inverness: The Northern Counties Newspaper and Printing and Publishing Company

Campion, E. (1963) *Two Bokes of the Histories of Ireland*. Assen: Van Gorcum

Canny, N. (1973) 'The ideology of English colonisation from Ireland to America.' *William and Mary Quarterly* 30: 581–596

Cardoso, C. (1971). 'Die Flucht nach Agypten in der mundlichen portugiesis-chen Uberlieferung.' *Fabula* 12

Carney, J. (1967) *The Irish Bardic Poet*. Dublin: Dolmen Press

Cauley, W. and Ó hAodha, M. (eds.) (*In Press*) (2004). *The Candlelight Painter – The Life and Work of Willy Cauley, Traveller, Painter and Poet*. Dublin: A. and A. Farmar Publishing

Charny, I. (ed.) (1999) *Encyclopaedia of Genocide*. Santa Barbara, California: ABC-CLIO

Chatard, M. and Bernard, M. (eds.) (1959) *Zanko, Chef Tribal*. Paris: Le Vieux Colombier

Chatwin, B. (1987) *The Songlines*. London: The Picador Press

Cheng, V. (1995) *Joyce, Race, and Empire*. Cambridge: Cambridge University Press

Chowers, E. (2000) 'Narrating the modern's subjection: Freud's theory of the Oedipal complex.' *History of the Human Sciences* 13 (3): 23–45

Cixous, H. (1975) *La jeune née*. Paris: U.G.É

Clancy, P., Drudy, S., Lynch, K. and O'Dowd, L. (eds.) (1986*) Ireland, A Sociological Profile*. Dublin: Institute of Public Administration

Clark, C. and Greenfields, M. (2006) *Here to Stay: The Gypsies and Travellers of Britain*. Hatfield: University of Hertfordshire Press

Clébert, J-P. (1963) *The Gypsies*. London: Penguin

Clébert, J-P. (1967) *The Gypsies*. Harmondsworth: Penguin

Cohn, W. (1973) *The Gypsies*. London: Addison-Wesley

Colie, R. (1966) *Paradoxia Epidemica: The Renaissance Tradition of Paradox*. New Jersey: Princeton University Press

Collins, M. (1994) 'The sub-culture of poverty – A response to McCarthy' in S. Ó Síocháin, M. McCann and J. Ruane (eds.) *Irish Travellers: Culture and Ethnicity*. Belfast: The Institute of Irish Studies, The Queens University of Belfast

Conners, G. (2000) 'Gerry Conners' in J. Hines and D. Keenan (eds.) *In Our Own Way: Tales from Belfast Travellers*. Belfast: Belfast Traveller Support Group

Corner, J. and Hawthorn, J. (eds.) (1994) *Communication Studies*. London: Edward Arnold

Cottaar, A., Lucassen, L. and Willems, W. (eds.) (1998) *Gypsies and Other Itinerant Groups: A Socio-Historical Approach*. London: Macmillan Press

Court, A. (1985) *Puck of the Droms: The Lives and Literature of the Irish Tinkers*. California: University of California Press

Courtney, R. (1982) *Outline History of British Drama*. N.J.: Littlefield, Adams

Cox, H. (1970) *The Feast of Fools: A Theological Essay on Festivity and Fantasy*. New York: Harper and Row

Crawford, M. (1976) 'Genetic affinities and origin of Irish tinkers' in G. Lasker *Biosocial Interrelations in Population Adaptation*. The Hague: Mouton

Crawford, M. and Gmelch, G. (1974) 'The human biology of Irish tinkers: Demography, ethnohistory and genetics.' *Social Biology* 21: 321–331

Cronin, M. (1996) *Translating Ireland*. Cork: Cork University Press

Culler, J. D. (1983) *On Deconstruction: Theory and Criticism after Structuralism*. London: Routledge & Kegan Paul

Curtin, C. and Wilson, T. (eds.) (1990) *Ireland from Below: Social Change and Local Communities*. Galway: Galway University Press

Curtis, L. (1984) *Nothing but the Same Old Story: The Roots of Anti-Irish Racism*. London: Information on Ireland

Curtis, L. P. (1968) *Anglo-Saxons and Celts. A Study of Anti-Irish Prejudice in Victorian England*. Connecticut: University of Bridgeport

Curtis, L. P. (1997) *Apes and Angels. The Irishman in Victorian Caricature*. Washington: Smithsonian Institute Press

Dahnhardt, V. (1909) *Natursagen II: Eine Sammlung Naturdeutender Sagen, Marchen, Fabeln und Legenden*. Leipzig: B. G. Teubner

Davis, K. (1975) *Administrative Law and Government*. St. Paul, MN: West Publishing

Davis, N. Z. (1975) *Society and Culture in Early Modern France*. Stanford: Stanford University Press

de Beauvoir, S. (1972) *The Second Sex*. London: Penguin Books

de Bhaldraíthe, T. (1959) *English-Irish Dictionary*. Baile Átha Cliath: Oifig an tSoláthair

de Saussure, F. (1972) *Cours de Linguistique Générale*. Paris: Payot

Degh, L. (1965) *Folktales of Hungary*. London: Routledge and Kegan Paul

Delaney, P. (2000) 'Migrancy and cultural disappearance' in P. J. Matthews (ed.) *New Voices in Irish Criticism*. Dublin: Four Courts Press

Delaney, P. (2003) 'Representations of the Travellers in the 1880s and 1900s'. *Irish Studies Review*, 11 (2): 155–164

Delaney, P. (2004) 'Stories from below: Sean Maher and Nan Joyce' in *Studies: An Irish Quarterly Review*, 93 (372) (Winter): 461–472

Delanty, G. (2000) *Modernity and Postmodernity: Knowledge, Power and the Self*. London: SAGE Publications

Delargy, J. (1942) 'The study of Irish folklore.' *Dublin Magazine*. XVII (3): 19–26

Derrida, J. (1974) 'White mythology: Metaphor in the text of philosophy.' *New Literary History* (6): 5–74

Derrida, J. (1976) *Of Grammatology*. London: Johns Hopkins University Press

Derrida, J. (1978) *Writing and Difference*. London: Routledge and Kegan Paul

Derrida, J. (1982) *Margins of Philosophy*. Chicago: University of Chicago Press

Detienne, M. (1979) *Dionysos Slain* [translated from the French] by M. Muellner and L. Muellner]. Baltimore: Johns Hopkins University Press

Detienne, M. (1989) *Dionysos Slain*. Michigan: U-M-I Out-of-Print Books on Demand

de Vaux de Foletier, F. (1961) *Les Tsiganes dans l'ancienne France*. Paris: Connaissance du Monde

Diamond, S. (n.d.) 'The primitive and the civilised.' *Tract* 18: 3–44

Diggle, S. and Hieb, L. (2004) 'From La Tijera to San Luis: Farm and Faith on the Rio Puerco.' *Agricultural History*, 78 (2) (Spring) 166–190

Dillman, A. (1905) *Zigeuner-Buch: Herausgegeben zum amtlichen Gebrauche im Auftrage des K.B. Staatsministeriums des Innern vom Sicherheitsbureau der K. Polizeidirektion München*. München: Dr. Wild'sche Buchdruckerei

Donahue, N. and Gmelch, S. (eds.) (1986) *Nan: the Life of an Irish Travelling Woman*. London: Souvenir

Donaldson, I. (1970) *The World Upside Down: Comedy from Jonson to Fielding*. London: Oxford University Press

Douglas, M. (1966) *Purity and Danger: An Analysis of Concepts of Pollution and Taboo*. London: Routledge & Kegan Paul

du Gay, P., Hall, S., Janes, L., Mackay, H. and Negus, K. (eds.) (1997) *Doing Cultural Studies: The Story of the Sony Walkman*. London: Sage in association with the Open University

Duilearga, S. Ó. (1977) *Leabhar Sheáin Í Chonaill – Sgéalta agus Seanchas ó Íbh Ráthach*. Baile Átha Cliath: Comhairle Bhéaloideas Éireann

Dunne, P. and Ó hAodha, M. (eds.) (2004) *Parley-Poet and Chanter – A Life of Pecker Dunne*. Dublin: A. and A. Farmar Publishing

Durkheim, É. (1938) *The Rules of Sociological Method*. Chicago: Chicago University Press

Durkheim, É. (1954) *The Elementary Forms of the Religious Life*. London: Allen and Unwin

Durkheim, É. (1964) *Essays on Sociology and Philosophy*. London: Harper & Row

Dyer, R. (1993) *The Matter of Images*. London: Routledge

Dymmok, J. (1842) *A treatice of Ireland*. Dublin: Irish Archaeological Society

Eagleton, T. (1981) *Walter Benjamin, or, Towards a Revolutionary Criticism*. London: Verso

Eagleton, T. (1988) *Nationalism, Colonialism and Literature – Nationalism, Irony and Commitment*. Derry: Field Day Pamphlets

Eagleton, T. (1991) *Ideology*. London: Verso

Eagleton, T. (1995) *Heathcliff and the Great Hunger: Studies in Irish Culture*. London: Verso

Ennis, M. (1984) *The Victims*. Dublin: Committee for the Rights of Travellers

Erikson, E. (1959) *Identity and the Life Cycle*. New York: International Universities Press

Fanon, F. (1986) *Black Skin, White* Mask. London: Pluto

Fanon, F. (1967) *Black Skin, White Masks*. New York: Grove Weidenfeld

Finlay, T. (1893) 'The Jew in Ireland.' *The Lyceum* VI (70): 215–218

Fisher, S. (ed.) (1958) *Body Image and Personality*. Princeton: Van Nostrand

Fitzgerald, G. (1992) *Repulsing Racism – Reflections on Racism and the Irish*. Dublin: Attic Press

Flower, R. (1957) 'Measgra ón Oileán Tiar.' *Béaloideas* Iml. XXV: 71

Forgacs, D. (ed.) (1985) *Antonio Gramsci – Selections from Cultural Writings*. London: Lawrence and Wishart

Foster, R. (1988) *Modern Ireland 1600–1972*. London: Allen Lane

Foucault, M. (1970) 'Theatrum Philosopicum.' *Critique* 282: 885–908

Foucault, M. (1972) *The Archaeology of Knowledge* [Translated by A. M. Sheridan Smith]. London: Tavistock Publications

Foucault, M. (1977) 'What is an author?' in D. F. Bouchard (ed.) *Language, Counter-Memory, Practice*. New York: Cornell University Press

Foucault, M. (1981) 'The order of discourse' in R. Yang (ed.) *Untying the Text*. London: Routledge

Foucault, M. (1984) *The Archaeology of Knowledge*. London: Tavistock Press

Foucault, M. (1985) *The Use of Pleasure: The History of Sexuality, Volume 2*. London: Penguin

Foucault, M. (1985) *The History of Sexuality, Volume 1: An Introduction*. London: Allen Lane

Foucault, M. (1990) *Archaeology of Knowledge*. London: Routledge

Fowler, H. W. (ed.) (1978) *The Concise Oxford Dictionary of Current English* (6th ed.). Oxford: Oxford University Press

Fraser, A. (1995) *The Gypsies*. Oxford: Blackwell

Freire, P. (1970) *Cultural Action for Freedom*. Massachusetts: MIT Press

Freud, S. (1938) *The Basic Writings of Sigmund Freud*. New York: The Modern Library

Freud, S. (1950a) 'Negation' in J. Strachey (ed.) *Collected Papers*. London: Hogarth Press, 5: 181–185

Freud, S. (1950b) *Totem and Taboo*. London: Routledge

Freud, S. (1957) *Collected Papers*. London: Hogarth Press

Frisbe, C. (1980). *Southwestern Indian Ritual Drama*. Albuquerque: University of New Mexico Press

Fyfe, H. (1998) *Drama as Structure and Sign*. PhD. University of Limerick

Gaster, M. (1923) 'Rumanian popular legends of the Virgin Mary.' *Folklore* 34: 45–85

Geertz, C. (1966) *Person, Time, and Conduct in Bali: An Essay in Cultural Analysis*. New Haven: Yale University Press

Geertz. C. (1972) *Myth, Symbol and Culture*. New York: Norton

Geertz, C. (1986) *The Uses of Diversity*. Massachusetts: Tanner

Geremek, B. (1992) *The Idea of a Civil Society*. New York: National Humanities Center

Gibbons, L. (1996) *Transformations in Irish Culture*. Cork: Cork University Press in association with Field Day

Gluckman, M. (1962) *Essays on the Ritual of Social Relations*. Manchester: Manchester University Press

Gluckman, M. (1965) *Politics, Law and Ritual Tribal Society*. Oxford: Basil Blackwell

Gmelch, G. (1977) *Tinkers and Travellers: The Urbanisation of an Itinerant People*. California: Cummings

Gmelch, G. (1985) *The Irish Tinkers: The Urbanization of an Itinerant People*. California: Waveland Press

Gmelch, G. and Gmelch S. (eds.) (1976) 'The emergence of an ethnic group: The Irish tinkers.' *Anthropological Quarterly* 6 (3): 225–238

Gmelch, G. and Kroup, B. (eds.) (1978) *To Shorten the Road: Travellers' Folktales from Ireland*. Dublin: O'Brien Press

Gmelch, S. B. (1974) *The Emergence and Persistence of an Ethnic Group: The Irish 'Travellers'*. PhD. Santa Barbara: University of California

Gmelch, S. B. (1975) *Tinkers and Travellers: Ireland's Nomads*. Dublin: O'Brien Press

Gmelch, S. B. (1990) 'From poverty subculture to political lobby: The Traveller rights movement in Ireland' in C. Curtin and T. Wilson (eds.) *Ireland from Below: Social Change and Local Communities*. Galway: Galway University Press

Gorman, B. (2002) *King of the Gypsies*. UK: Milo

Graham, C. (1994) '"Liminal spaces": Post-colonial theories and Irish culture.' *The Irish Review* (Autumn–Winter) 16: 29–43

Graham, C. and Kirkland, R. (1999) *Ireland and Cultural Theory*. London: Macmillan

Gramsci, A. (1971) *Selections from Prison Notebooks*. London: Lawrence and Wishart

Grant, A. (1994) 'Shelta: The secret language of Irish Travellers viewed as a mixed language' in M. Mous (ed.) *Mixed Languages: 15 Case Studies in Language Intertwining*. Amsterdam: Uitgave IFOTT: 123–150

Greenblatt, S. (1980) *The Improvisation of Power*. Chicago: University of Chicago Press

Greenblatt, S. (1984) *Renaissance Self-fashioning*. Chicago: University of Chicago Press

Greene, D. (1954) 'Early Irish society' in M. Dillon (ed.) *Early Irish Society*. Dublin: Published for the Cultural Relations Committee of Ireland at the Sign of the Three Candles

Grellmann, H. (1783) *Historischer Versuch uber die Zigeuner*. Gottingen: J. Dieterich

Grellmann, H. (1787) *Dissertation on the Gipsies: Being an Historical Enquiry, concerning the manner of life, family economy, customs and conditions of these people in Europe, and their origin*. London: G. Bigg

Gronemeyer, R. (1987) *Zigeuner im Spiegel früher Chroniken und Abhandlungen: Quellen vom 15. bis zum 18. Jahrhundert*. Giessen: Focus

Groome, F. H. (1880) *In Gipsy Tents*. Edinburgh: William P. Nimmo

Halifax, J. (1982) *Shaman, The Wounded Healer*. London: Thames and Hudson

Hall, S. (1997) *Representation: Cultural Representations and Signifying Practices*. London: Sage in association with the Open University

Halliday, M. (1976) in G. Kress (ed.) *Halliday, System and Function in Language*. London: Oxford University Press

Hamnett, I. (1967) 'Ambiguity, classification, and change: The function of riddles.' *Man* 2: 279–292

Hancock, I. (1987) *The Pariah Syndrome: An Account of Gypsy Slavery and Persecution*. Michigan: Karoma Publishers

Hancock, I. (1989) 'Gypsy history in Germany and neighboring lands: A chronology leading to the Holocaust and beyond' in D. Crowe and J. Kolsti (eds.) *The Gypsies of Eastern Europe*. Armonk, NY: E. C. Sharpe

Hancock, I. (1992) 'The roots of inequity: Romani cultural rights in their historical and cultural context.' *Immigrants and Minorities* 11 (1)

Hancock, I. (1999) 'The Roma: Myth and reality.' *Patrin Web-Journal*: 1–13. www.geocities.com/paris/512/mythandreality.htm (accessed 2 February 2011).

Handelman, D. (1981) 'The ritual clown: Attributes and affinities.' *Anthropos*. 76: 321–370

Harper, J. (1977) *The Irish Travellers of Georgia*. M.A. University of Georgia

Harrison, A. (1989) *The Irish Trickster*. Sheffield: Sheffield Academic Press for the Folklore Society

Hawthorn, G. (1994) *Enlightenment and Despair: A History of Social Theory*. Cambridge: Cambridge University Press

Healy, T. (1992) *New Latitudes: Theory and English Renaissance Literature*. London: Edward Arnold

Hegel, G. (1964) *Hegel's Political Writings*. Oxford: Clarendon Press

Helleiner, J. (1998) *The Travelling People: Cultural Identity in Ireland*. PhD. University of Toronto

Helleiner, J. (2000) *Irish Travellers: Racism and the Politics of Culture*. Toronto: University of Toronto Press

Henderson, W. (1879) *Notes on the folk-lore of the Northern Counties of England and the Borders*. London: W. Satchell, Peyton and Co. for the Folk-Lore Society

Henry, G. (1992) *The Irish Military Community in Spanish Flanders 1586–1621*. Dublin: Irish Academic Press

Heymowski, A. (1969) *Swedish 'Travellers' and their Ancestry. A social isolate or an ethnic minority?* Uppsala: Almqvist and Wiksell

Hieb, L. (1972) 'Meaning and mismeaning: Towards an understanding of the ritual clown' in A. Ortiz (ed.) *New Perspectives on the Pueblos*. Albuquerque: University of New Mexico Press

Hill, C. (1970) *God's Englishman: Oliver Cromwell and the English Revolution*. London: Wiedenfeld and Nicholson

Hooper, G. and Graham, C. (eds.) (2002) *Irish and Postcolonial Writing: History, Theory, Practice*. Basingstoke: Palgrave Macmillan

Huddart, D. (2006) *Homi K. Bhabha*. London: Routledge

Hughes, K. (1967) 'The golden age of early Christian Ireland' in T. Moody (ed.) *The Course of Irish History*. Cork: Mercier Press

Husband, C. (1982) *'Race' in Britain: Continuity and Change*. London: Hutchinson

Hutchens, B. C. (2005) *Jean-Luc Nancy and the Future of Philosophy*. Chesham: Acumen

Hyland, J. (ed.) (1993) *Do you Know Us at All?* Dublin: Parish of the Travelling People

*Irish Folklore Commission 'Tinker Questionnaire'* (1952) (unpublished archival records) accessed at NUIG (National University of Ireland, Galway).

Jameson, F. (1981) *The Political Unconscious: Narrative as a Socially Symbolic Act*. London: Methuen

Jennings, S. (1995) *Theatre, Ritual and Transformation*. London: Routledge

Johnson, P. (1980) *Ireland: A History from the Twelfth Century to the Present Day*. London: Eyre Methuen

Joyce, N. (1985) *Traveller: An Autobiography*. Dublin: Gill and Macmillan

Jusserand, J. J. (1889) *English Wayfaring Life in the Middle Ages*. London: Ernest Benn

Kamen, H. (1986) *European Society 1500–1700*. London: Hutchinson

Kayser, W. (1963) *The Grotesque in Art and Literature*. Bloomington, Indiana: Indiana University Press

Kealiinohomoku, J. (1980) 'The drama of the Hopi ogres' in C. Frisbe (ed.) *Southern Indian Ritual Drama*. Albuquerque: University of New Mexico Press

Keenan, M. (2000) 'Molly Keenan' in J. Hines and D. Keenan (eds.) *In Our Own Way: Tales from Belfast* Travellers. Belfast: Belfast Traveller Support Group

Kenny, M. (1996) *The Routes of Resistance – Travellers and Second-level Schooling*. PhD. Trinity College Dublin

Kenrick, D. and Clark, C. (1999) *Moving On: The Gypsies and Travellers of Britain*. Hertfordshire: University of Hertfordshire Press

Kenrick, D. and Puxon, G. (eds.) (1972) *The Destiny of Europe's Gypsies*. London: Sussex University Press in association with Heinemann

Keogh, D. (1998) *Jews in Twentieth-century Ireland: Refugees, Anti-semitism and the Holocaust*. Cork: Cork University Press

Kephart, W. (1982) *Extraordinary Groups*. New York: St. Martin's Press

Khazanov, A. (1995) *After the USSR: Ethnicity, Nationalism and Politics in the Commonwealth of Independent States*. Wisconsin: The University of Wisconsin Press

Kiberd, D. (1995) *Inventing Ireland*. London: Jonathan Cape

Kierkegaard, S. (1968) *The Concept of Irony*. Bloomington, Indiana: Indiana University of Press

Klaar, M. (ed.) (1963) *Christos und das verschenkte Brot. Neugriechische Volkslegenden und Legendenmarchen*. Germany: Kassel

Klein, M. (1957) *Envy and Gratitude: A Study of Unconscious Sources*. London: Tavistock Publications

Klein, M. (1960) *Our Adult World and its Roots in Infancy*. London: Tavistock

Klein, M. (1997) *Envy and Gratitude and Other Works 1946–1963*. London: Vintage

Koestler, A. (1964) *The Act of Creation*. London: Hutchinson

Kohler-Zulch, I. (1993) 'Die Geshichte der Kreutznagel: Version und Gegenversion? Uberlegungen zur Roma-Varianten' in *Telling Reality. Folklore Studies in Memory of Bengt Holbeck*. Copenhagen: M. Chestnutt

Kristeva, J. (1974) *Des Chinoises*. Paris: Éditions des Femmes

Kristeva, J. (1982) *Powers of Horror*. New York: Columbia University Press

Kristeva, J. (1991) *Strangers to Ourselves*. New York: Columbia University Press

Kunzle, D. (1978) 'World upside down: The iconography of a European broadsheet type' in B. Babcock (ed.) *The Reversible World: Symbolic Inversion in Art and Society*. London: Ithaca

Lacan, J. (1966) *Ecrits 1*. Paris: Editions du Seuil

Lacan, J. (1971) *Ecrits 2*. Paris: Editions du Seuil

Lacan, J. (1977) *The Four Fundamental Concepts of Psycho-analysis*. London: Hogarth Press

Laclau, E. (1977) *Politics and Ideology in Marxist Theory: Capitalism, Fascism, Populism*. London: Verso Editions

Laclau, E. and Mouffe, C. (eds.) (1985) *Hegemony and Socialist Strategy: Towards a Radical Democratic Politics*. London: Verso

Lanters, J. (2008) *The 'Tinkers' in Irish Literature*. Dublin: Irish Academic Press

Lash, S. and Urry, J. (eds.) (1994) *The Polity Reader in Cultural Theory*. Cambridge: Polity Press in association with Blackwell Publishers

Leach, E. R. (1953) *Political Systems of Highland Burma: A Study of Kachin Social Structure*. UK: Berg

Leach, E. (1968) *A Runaway World?* London: Oxford University Press

Leach, E. (1969) *Genesis As Myth And Other Essays*. London, Jonathan Cape

Lebow, N. (1973) 'British Historians and Irish History.' *Èire-Ireland* VIII (4)

Lee, J. (1989) *Politics and Society in Ireland 1912–1985*. Cambridge: Cambridge University Press

Leerssen, J. (1996) *Mere Irish and Fíor-Ghael: Studies in the Idea of Irish Nationality, its Development and Literary Expression prior to the Nineteenth Century*. Cork: Cork University Press

Leland, C. (1882) *The Gypsies*. Boston: Houghton, Mifflin and Company

Leland, C. (1891) 'Shelta.' *Journal of the Gypsy Lore Society* 2 (4): 321–323

Levinas, E. (1961) *Totalité et infini: Essai sur l'extériorité*. The Hague: M. Nijhoff

Levinas, E. (1969) *Totality and Infinity: An Essay on Exteriority*. Pittsburgh: Duquesne University Press

Levinas, E. (1996) *Basic Philosophical Writings – Emmanuel Levinas*. Bloomington, Indiana: Indiana University Press

Lévi-Strauss, C. (1964) *Mythologiques*. Paris: Plon

Lévi-Strauss, C. (1971) *L'homme nu*. Paris: Plon

Lewis, O. (1963) *Life in a Mexican Village: Tepoztlán Re-studied*. Urbana: University of Illinois Press

Liégeois, J-P. (1987) *Gypsies and Travellers: Socio-cultural Data, Socio-political Data*. Council for Cultural Cooperation, Council of Europe

Liégeois, J-P. (1994) *Roma, Gypsies, Travellers*. Strasbourg: Council of Europe

Lipsitz, E. (1991) *World Jewish Directory. Vol.1*. Ontario: J.E.S.L. Educational Products

Lis, C. and Hugo, S. (1979) *Poverty and Capitalism in Pre-industrial Europe*. London: Humanities Press

Lofgren, O. (1993) 'The cultural grammar of nation-building' in P. J. Anttonen and R. Kvideland *Nordic Frontiers*. Turku: Nordic Institute of Folklore

Lombroso, C. (1918) *Crime: Its Causes and Remedies*. Boston: Little Brown and Co.

Longley, E. (1994) *The Living Stream: Literature and Revisionism in Ireland*. Newcastle-upon-Tyne: Bloodaxe Books

Lucassen, J. (1987). *Migrant Labour in Europe between 1600 and 1900. The Drift to the North Sea*. Beckenham: Croom Helm

Lyotard, J-F. (1984) *The Postmodern Condition: A Report on Knowledge*. Manchester: Manchester University Press

Macalister, R. A. S. (1937) *The Secret Languages of Ireland, with special reference to the origin and nature of the Shelta language: Partly based upon collections and manuscripts of the late John Sampson*. Cambridge: Cambridge University Press

Mac Aoidh, C. (1994) *Between the Jigs and Reels*. Leitrim, Ireland: Drumlin Publications

Mac Cana, P. (1970) *Celtic Mythology*. London: Chancellor

Mac Greil, M. (1996) *Prejudice in Ireland Revisited: Based on a National Survey of Intergroup Attitudes in the Republic of Ireland*. Dublin: Survey and Research Unit, St Patrick's College, Maynooth.

MacGréine, P. (1931) 'Irish tinkers or "Travellers", some notes on their manners and customs, and their secret language or "cant"'. *Béaloideas: the Journal of the Folklore of Ireland Society* 3: 170–181

MacGréine, P. (1932a) 'Irish tinkers or "Travellers".' *Béaloideas: the Journal of the Folklore of Ireland Society* 3 (2): 170–186

MacGréine, P. (1932b) 'Further notes on tinkers' "cant".' *Béaloideas: the Journal of the Folklore of Ireland Society* 3 (3): 290–303

MacGréine, P. (1934) 'Some notes on tinkers and their "cant".' *Béaloideas: the Journal of the Folklore of Ireland Society* 4 (3): 259–263

MacLaughlin, J. (1995) *Travellers and Ireland: Whose Country, Whose History?* Cork: Cork University Press

MacLaughlin, J. (1996) 'Travellers are still victims of a Victorian image of society.' *Sunday Tribune*, 12 September

MacLean, E. and Landry, D. (1995) *Selected works of Gayatri Chakravorty Spivak*. London: Routledge

MacMahon, B. (1971) 'A Portrait of Tinkers.' *Natural History* 80 (10)

MacNeill, E. (1919) *Phases in Irish History*. Dublin: M. H. Gill

MacRitchie, D. (1889) 'Irish Tinkers and their Language.' *Journal of the Gypsy Lore Society* 1 (6): 350–357

Maffesoli, M. (1993) *The Shadow of Dionysus: A Contribution to the Study of the Orgy*. Albany: State University of New York Press

Maffesoli, M. (1993) 'Introduction.' *Current Sociology* 41 (2): 1–6

Maher, S. (1972) *The Road to God Knows Where*. Dublin: Talbot Press

Mahr, A. (1943) 'The Gypsy at the Crucifixion of Christ.' *Ohio Journal of Science* 43: 17–21

Mariani, P. and Kruger, B. (1989) *Remaking History*. Seattle: Bay Press

Marx, K. (1965) *Pre-Capitalist Economic Formations*. New York: International Publishers

Mayall, D. (1982) *Itinerant minorities in England and Wales in the nineteenth and early twentieth centuries: A study of Gypsies, Tinkers, Hawkers and Other Travellers* PhD. University of Sheffield

Mayall, D. (1987) *Gypsy-Travellers in Nineteenth-Century Society*. Cambridge: Cambridge University Press

Mayall, D. (1988) *Gypsy-Travellers in Nineteenth-Century Society*. Cambridge: Cambridge University Press

Mayall, D. (2004) *Gypsy Identities 1500–2000. From Egipcyans and Moon-men to the Ethnic Romany*. London: Routledge

McCarthy, P. (1971) *Itinerancy and Poverty: A study in the sub-culture of poverty*. M.A. University College Dublin

McCarthy, P. (1994) 'The sub-culture of poverty reconsidered.' in S. Ò Síocháin, M. McCann and J. Ruane (eds.) *Irish Travellers: Culture and Ethnicity*. Belfast: Institute of Irish Studies, Queen's University

McCormick, A. (1907) *The Tinkler-Gypsies*. Dumfries, Scotland: Maxwell

McDonagh, M. (1994) 'Nomadism in Irish Travellers' identity' in S. Ò Síocháin, M. McCann and J. Ruane (eds.) *Irish Travellers: Culture and Ethnicity*. Belfast: Institute of Irish Studies, Queen's University

McDonagh, M. (2000a) 'Origins of the Travelling people' in E. Sheehan (ed.) *Travellers – Citizens of Ireland*. Dublin: Parish of the Travelling People

McDonagh, M. (2000b) 'Ethnicity and culture' in E. Sheehan (ed.) *Travellers – Citizens of Ireland*. Dublin: Parish of the Travelling People

McDonagh, M. (2000c) 'Nomadism' in E. Sheehan (ed.) *Travellers – Citizens of Ireland*. Dublin: Parish of the Travelling People

McDonagh, M. and McDonagh, W. (1993) 'Nomadism' in J. Hyland (ed.) *Do you know us at all?* Dublin: Parish of the Travelling People

McDonagh, M. and McVeigh, R. (eds.) (1992) *Minceir Neeja in the Thome Munkra: Irish Travellers in the USA*. Belfast: Belfast Travellers Education and Development Group

McHoul, A. W. and Grace, W. A. (1997) *Foucault Primer: Discourse, Power, and the Subject*. Victoria, Australia: Melbourne University Press

McGrath, S. (1955) *Miscellaneous Information on Tinkers, Particularly in County Clare*. Irish Folklore Commission

McKerrow, R. (ed.) (1982) *Explorations in Rhetoric: Studies in honor of Douglas Ehninger*. Illinois: Scott Foresman

McLoughlin, D. (1994) 'Ethnicity and Irish Travellers: Reflections on Ni Shúinéar' in S. Ó Síocháin, M. McCann and J. Ruane (eds.) *Irish Travellers: Culture and Ethnicity*. Belfast: Institute of Irish Studies, Queen's University

McVeigh, R. (1992a) 'The Specificity of Irish Racism.' *Race and Class*. 33 (4): 31–45

McVeigh, R. (1992b) *Racism and Travelling People in Northern Ireland*. 17th Report of the Standing Advisory Commission on Human Rights

McVeigh, R. (1994) 'Theorising sedentarism: The roots of anti-nomadism.' [Paper for ESRC Romani Studies Seminar] University of Greenwich. Belfast: Campaign for Research and Documentation

McVeigh, R. (1996) *The Racialisation of Irishness: Racism and Anti-Racism in Ireland*. Belfast: Campaign for Research and Documentation

McVeigh, R. (1997) 'Theorising sedentarism: The roots of anti-nomadism' in T. Acton (ed.) *Gypsy Politics and Traveller Identity*. Hatfield: University of Hertfordshire Press

Mercer, K. (1994) *Welcome to the Jungle: New Positions in Black Cultural Studies*. London: Routledge

Meyer, K. (1891) 'On the Irish origin and age of Shelta.' *Journal of the Gypsy Lore Society* 2: 257–266

Meyer, K. (1909) 'The secret languages of Ireland.' *Journal of the Gypsy Lore Society* New Series, 2 (3): 241–246

Meyer, M. (1921) *Les Contes Populaires de le Flandre*. Helsinki: Suomalainen tiedeakatemia

Middleton, J. (1960) *Lugbara Religion*. Oxford: Oxford University Press

Miege, G. (1715) *The Present State of Great Britain and Ireland*. London: J. Nicholson

Miles, R. (1989) *Racism*. London: Routledge

Mitchell, S. and Black, A. (eds.) (1995) *Freud and Beyond: A History of Modern Psychoanalytic Thought*. New York: Basic Books

Mitchell, T. (1994) *Flamenco Deep Song*. New Haven: Yale University Press

Mongan, B. (2000) 'Bernie Mongan' in J. Hines and D. Keenan (eds.) *In Our Own Way: Tales from Belfast Travellers*. Belfast: Belfast Traveller Support Group

Mongia, P. (1996) *Contemporary Postcolonial Theory: A Reader*. London: Arnold

Montagu, A. (1972) *Statement on Race*. Oxford: Oxford University Press

Moore, R. I. (1987) *The Formation of a Persecuting Society: Power and Deviance in Western Europe, 950–1250*. Oxford: Basil Blackwell

Moore-Gilbert, B. (1997) *Postcolonial Theory: Context, Practices, Politics*. London: Verso

Moore-Gilbert, B. (ed.) (1983) Literature and Imperialism: A conference organised by the English Department of the Roehampton Institute in February 1983. London: English Department of the Roehampton Institute of Higher Education

Moore-Gilbert, B. and Colwell, D. (eds.) (1998) *Empire and Literature*. London: University of London

Moryson, F. (1617) *An Itinerary Written by Fynes Moryson Gent*. Glasgow: James MacLehose

Mudimbe, V. (1988) *The Invention of Africa: Gnosis, Philosophy and the Order of Things*. Indianapolis: Indiana University Press

Mudimbe, V. (1994) *The Idea of Africa*. Indianapolis: Indiana University Press

Myerhoff, B. (1982) 'Rites of passage: Process and paradox' in V. Turner (ed.) *Celebration: Studies in Festivity and Ritual*. Washington: Smithsonian Institution Press

Nandy, A. (1983) *The Intimate Enemy*. Delhi: Oxford University Press

Neat, T. (1996) *The Summer Walkers – Travelling People and Pearl-Fishers in the Highlands of Scotland*. Edinburgh: Canongate Books

Needham, R. (1963) 'Introduction' in E. Durkheim and M. Mauss (eds.) *Primitive Classification*. London: Cohen and West

Needham, R. (ed.) (1973) *Right and Left: Essays on Dual Symbolic Classification*. Chicago: University of Chicago Press

Neelands, J. and Goode, J. (1995) 'Playing on the Margins of Meaning: the Ritual Aesthetic in Community Performance.' *Nadie Journal* 19 (1)

Ní Shúinéar, S. (1994) 'Irish Travellers, ethnicity and the origins question' in S. Ó Síocháin, M. McCann and J. Ruane (eds.) *Irish Travellers: Culture and Ethnicity*. Belfast: Institute of Irish Studies, Queen's University

Nietzsche, F. (1966) *Beyond Good and Evil: Prelude to a Philosophy of the Future* [translated, with commentary, by Walter Kaufmann]. New York: Vintage Books

Norbeck, E. (1963) 'African rituals of conflict.' *American Anthropologist* 65: 1254–1279

Norbeck, E. (1970) *Religion and Society in Modern Japan: Continuity and Change*. Texas: Tourmaline Press

Norbeck, E. and Farrer, C. R. (eds.) (1977) *Forms of Play of Native North Americans*. St. Paul: West Publishing Co.

Nord, D. E. (2006) *Gypsies and the British Imagination, 1807-1930*. New York: Columbia University Press

Ó Baoill, D. P. (1994) 'Travellers' cant – Language or register' in S. Ó Síocháin, M. McCann and J. Ruane (eds.) *Irish Travellers: Culture and Ethnicity*. Belfast: Institute of Irish Studies, Queen's University

O'Boyle, M. B. (1990) *The Alienation of Travellers from the Education System: A Study in Value Orientations*. M. Ed Thesis (Unpublished) National University of Ireland, Maynooth

Ó Ciosáin, N. (1998) 'Boccoughs and God's poor: Deserving and undeserving poor in Irish popular culture' in Foley, T. and Ryder, S. (eds.) *Ideology and Ireland in the Nineteenth Century*. Dublin: Four Courts Press: 93–99

O'Connell, J. (1992a) 'Working with Irish Travellers' in *DTEG File*. Dublin: Pavee Point Publications

O'Connell, J. (1992b) 'The need for imagination in work with Irish Travellers' in *DTEDG File*. Dublin: Pavee Point Publications

O'Connell, J. (1994a) *Reach Out: Report on the 'Poverty 3' Programme 1990–94'*. Dublin: Pavee Point Publications

O'Connell, J. (1994b) 'Ethnicity and Irish Travellers' in S. Ó Síocháin, M. McCann and J. Ruane (eds.) *Irish Travellers: Culture and Ethnicity*. Belfast: Institute of Irish Studies, Queen's University

O'Connell, J. (1995) 'Travellers and history' in N. Ní Laodhóg (ed.) *A Heritage Ahead: Cultural Action and Travellers*. Dublin: Pavee Point Publications

Ó Dónaill, N. (ed.) (1977) *Foclóir Gaeilge-Béarla*. Baile Átha Cliath: Oifig an tSoláthair

O'Dowd, A. (1987) *Migratory Agricultural Workers*. PhD. University College Dublin

Ó Fearadhaigh, M. and Wiedel, J. (eds.) (1976) *Irish Tinkers*. London: Latimer New Dimensions Ltd

Ó Floinn, B. (1995) 'Travellers and the oral tradition' in N. Ní Laodhóg (ed.) *A Heritage Ahead: Cultural Action and Travellers*. Dublin: Pavee Point Publications

Ó Giolláin, D. (2000) *Locating Irish Folklore: Tradition, Modernity, Identity*. Cork: Cork University Press

Ó hAodha, M. (2001) 'Caint nó Cant: Teanga an Lucht Siúil' in Ó hUigínn, R. agus MacCóil, L. (eds.) *Bliainiris*. Meath: Carbad

Ó hAodha, M. (2002a) 'Travellers' language: Some Irish language perspectives' in J. M. Kirk and D. P. Ó Baoill (eds.) *Travellers and their Language*. Belfast: Cló Ollscoil na Banríona

Ó hAodha, M. (2002b) 'Exoticising the Gypsies: The case of Scott Macfie and the Gypsylorists' in J. M. Kirk and D. P. Ó Baoill (eds.) *Travellers and their Language*. Belfast: Cló Ollscoil na Banríona

Ó hAodha, M. (2002c) 'Tionchar na Gaeilge ar Shelta Lucht Taistil' in Ó hUigínn, R. agus MacCóil, L. (eds.) *Bliainiris*. Meath: Carbad

O hAodha, M. and Tuohy, D. (2008) *Postcolonial Artist: Johnny Doran and Irish Traveller Tradition*. Newcastle, UK: Cambridge Scholars

Ò Héalaí, P. (1977) 'Moral values in Irish religious tales.' *Bèaloideas – The Journal of the Folklore of Ireland Society* 42–44: 176–212

Ò Héalaí, P. (1985) 'Tuirse na nGaibhne ar na Buachaillí Bó – Scéal Apacrafúil Dúchasach.' *Béaloideas* 53: 87–129

Ó Hógáin, D. (1982) *An File – Staidéar ar Ósnádúrthacht na Filíochta sa Traidisiún Gaelach*. Baile Àtha Cliath: Oifig an tSolàthair

Ó Hógáin, D. (1985) *The Hero in Irish Folk History*. Dublin: Gill and Macmillan

Okely, J. (1975) 'Gypsies Travelling in Southern England' in E. F. Rehfisch (ed.) *Gypsies, Tinkers and other Travellers*. London: Academic Press

Okely, J. (1983) *The Traveller-Gypsies*. Cambridge: Cambridge University Press

Okely, J. (1984) 'Ethnic identity and place of origin: The Traveller Gypsies in Great Britain' in J. Vermeulen (ed.) *Ethnic Challenge – The Politics and Ethnicity of Europe*. Gottingen: Edition Herodot

Okely, J. (1994) 'An Anthropological Perspective on Irish Travellers' in S. Ó. Síocháin, M. McCann and J. Ruane (eds.) *Irish Travellers: Culture and Ethnicity*. Belfast: Institute of Irish Studies, Queen's University

O'Meara, J. J. (1982) *The History and Topography of Ireland/Gerald of Wales*. Harmondsworth: Penguin

Ó Muirithe, D. and Nuttall, D. (eds.) (1999) *Folklore of County Wexford*. Dublin: Four Courts Press

O'Reilly, M. and Kenny, M. (eds.) (1994) *Black Stones around Green Shamrock*. Dublin: Blackrock Teachers Centre

Ò Síocháin, S., McCann. M. and Ruane, J. (eds.) *Irish Travellers: Culture and Ethnicity*. Belfast: Institute of Irish Studies, Queen's University

Ó Súilleabháin, S. (1942) *A Handbook of Irish Folklore*. Dublin: Folklore of Ireland Society

Ó Súilleabháin, S. (1970) *A Handbook of Irish Folklore*. Detroit: Singing Tree Press

Ó Súilleabháin, S. (1977) *Legends from Ireland*. London: Batsford

O'Toole, E. B. (1972) *An Analysis of the Life Style of the Travelling People of Ireland*. M. Phil. New York University

Park, C. (1904) *The King of the Beasts*. London: Blackie and Son

Partridge, A. (1983) *Caoineadh na dTrí Muire – Téama na Páise i bhfilíocht bhéil na Gaeilge*. Baile Átha Cliath: An Clóchomhar Tta

Peacock, J. (1968) 'Society as narrative' in R. F. Spencer (ed.) *Forms of Symbolic Action*. Washington: Washington University Press

Peart, S. A. (2001) *English Images of the Irish 1570–1620*. PhD. University of Limerick

Peart, S. A. (2002) *English Images of the Irish 1570–1620*. Wales: The Edwin Mellen Press

Phelan, J. and Rabinowitz, P. (eds.) (2005) *A Companion to Narrative* Theory. Oxford: Blackwell

Platinga, C. (1995) *Not the Way It's Supposed to Be: A Breviary of Sin*. Michigan: Eerdmans

Plumb, J. H. (1969) *England in the Eighteenth Century (1714–1815)*. London: Penguin

Point, P. (1994) *Nomadism, Now and Then*. Dublin: Pavee Point

Porter, B. (1983) *Britain, Europe and the World 1850–1982: Delusions of Grandeur*. London: Allen & Unwin

Pound, J. (ed.) (1971) *The Norwich Census of the Poor, 1570*. Norfolk: Norfolk Record Society

Power, C. (2004) *Room to Roam: England's Irish Travellers*. London: Action Group for Irish Youth

Puxon, G. (1967) *The Victims (Itinerants in Ireland)*. Dublin: ITM

Quinn, D. B. (1966) *The Elizabethans and the Irish*. New York: Ithaca

Quintana, B. and Floyd, L. (eds.) (1972*) Qué Gitano: Gypsies of Southern Spain*. New York: Rinehart and Winston

Rakow, L. and Wackwitz, L. (eds.) (2004) *Feminist Communication Theory: Selections in Context*. London: Sage

Ranelagh, J. (1981) *Ireland: An Illustrated History*. London: Collins

Richards, D. and Cairns, S. (eds.) (1990) *Writing Ireland: Colonialism, Nationalism and Culture*. Manchester: Manchester University Press

Ricoeur, P. (1992) *Oneself as Another*. Chicago: University of Chicago Press

Ritter, R. (1937) *Ein Menschenschlag*. Leipzig: Georg Thieme

Ritter, R. (1938) 'Zur Frage der Rassenbiologie und Rassenpsychologie der Zigeuner in Deutschland.' *Reichgesundheitsblatt,* 22: 425–426

Ritter, R. (1941) 'Die Asozialen, ihre Vorfahren und ihre Nachkommen.' *Fortschritte der Erbpathologie, Rassenhygiene und ihrer Grenzgebiete*, V (4): 137–155

Roberts, S. (1836) *The Gypsies*. London: Longmans

Rokala, K. (1973) *A Catalogue of Religious Legends in the Folklore Archive of the Finnish Literature Society*. Turku: Finnish Literature Society

Rubenstein, J. (1975) *Structual Ambivalence in Ritual Drama*. PhD. New School of Social Research. New York

Said, E. (1978) *Orientalism*. London: Penguin

Said, E. (1986) *Literature and Society*. Baltimore: Johns Hopkins University Press

Said, E. (1989) 'Yeats and decolonization' in P. Kruger (ed.) *Remaking History*. Seattle: Bay Press

Said, E. (1993) *Culture and Imperialism*. London: Chatto and Windus

Sales, R. (1983) *English Literature in History 1780–1830: Pastoral and Politics*. London: Hutchinson

Salgado, G. (ed.) (1972) *Cony-Catchers and Bawdy Baskets: An Anthology of Elizabethan low life*. Harmondsworth: Penguin

Sampson, J. (1891) 'Tinkers and their Talk.' *Journal of the Gypsy Lore Society* 2: 204–221

Schechner, R. and Appel, W. (eds.) (1990) *By Means of Performance: Intercultural Studies of Theatre and Ritual*. Cambridge: Cambridge University Press

Schroeder, J. (1983) 'Gypsy crime in America.' *Centurion: a police lifestyle magazine* 1 (6)

Schubert, U and Schubert, K. (1983) *Judische Buchkunst Schubert*. Graz, Austria: Akademische Druck- u. Verlagsanstalt

Schurtz, H. (1902) *Altersklassen und Mannerbunde: Eine Darstellung der grundformen der Gesellschaft*. Berlin: G. Reimer

Segal, H. (1997) *Reason and Passion: A Celebration of the Work of Hanna Segal*. New York: Routledge

Sibley, D. (1981) *Outsiders in Urban Society*. Oxford: Basil Blackwell

Sibley, S. (1995) *Geographies of Exclusion: Society and Difference in the West*. New York: Routledge

Sinclair, A. (1908) 'Irish stonemasons in America.' *Journal of American Folklore* 16 (2): 12–17

Smyth, G. (1998) *Decolonization and Criticism: The Construction of Irish Literature*. London: Pluto

Spivak, G. C. (1995) *The Spivak Reader*. New York: Routledge

Spivak, G. C. (1996) 'Can the subaltern speak?' in *The Spivak Reader*. London, Routledge

Spivak, G. C. (1996) 'Deconstructing historiography.' in D. Landry and G. MacLean (eds.) *The Spivak Reader*. London: Routledge

Spivak, G. C. (1997) 'More on power/knowledge – Outside in the teaching machine' in B. Moore-Gilbert (ed.) *Postcolonial Theory: Contexts, Practices, Politics*. London: Verso

Stallybrass, P. and White A. (ed.) (1986) *The Politics and Poetics of Transgression*. London: Methuen

Staples, R. (1982) *Black Masculinity: The Black Male's Role in American Society*. San Francisco: Black Scholar Press

Sutherland, A. (1975). 'The American Rom: a case of economic adaptation' in E. F. Rehfisch (ed.) *Gypsies, Tinkers and other Travellers*. London: Academic Press

Sutherland, A. (1975) *Gypsies: The Hidden Americans*. London: Tavistock Publications

Synge, J. M. (1980) *In Wicklow, West Kerry and Connemara*. Dublin: O'Brien Press

Takaki, R. (1979) *Iron Cages: Race and Culture in Nineteenth-century America*. New York: Knopf

Task Force of the Travelling Community (1995) *Report of the Task Force on the Travelling Community*. Dublin: Stationery Office

Taylor, L. (1989) *Time to Listen: the Human Aspect in Development*. London: Intermediate Technology Publications

Thomas, Z. (1994) *Healing Touch: The Church's Forgotten Language*. Kentucky: Westminster/John Knox Press

Thompson, D. (1978) *The Voice of the Past: Oral History*. Oxford: Oxford University Press

Thompson, S. (1955) *Motif-index of Folk-literature: A Classification of Narrative Elements in Folktales*. Bloomington: Indiana University Press

Thomson, P. (1972) *The Grotesque*. London: Methuen

Toelken, B. (1979) *The Dynamics of Folklore*. Boston: Houghton Mifflin

Tolson, A. (1996) *Mediations*. London: Edward Arnold

Tong, D. (1989) *Gypsy Folk Tales*. New York: Harcourt Brace and Co.

Trumpener, K. (1992) 'The time of the Gypsies: A "People without History" in the Narratives of the West'. *Critical Inquiry*, 18 (4): 860–861

Turner, V. (1968) *The Drums of Affliction: A Study of Religious Processes among the Ndembu of Zambia*. Oxford: Oxford University Press

Turner, V. (1974) *The Ritual Structure: Structure and Anti-structure*. Hardmondsworth: Penguin

Turner, V. (1982) *Celebration: Studies in Festivity and Ritual*. Washington, DC: Smithsonian Institution Press

Turner, V. (1986) *The Anthropology of Performance*. New York: PAJ Publications

Turner, V. (1992) *From Ritual to Theatre: The Human Seriousness of Play*. New York: New York City Performing Arts Journal Publications

Ua Duinnín, P. (1901) *Amhráin Eoghain Ruaidh Uí Shúilleabháin*; Baile Átha Cliath: Oifig Dìolta Foilseacháin Rialtais

Van Dijk, T. (1993) *Elite Discourse and Racism*. London: Sage

Van Gennep, A. (1960) *The Rites of Passage*. London: Routledge and Paul

Vansina, J. (1961) *Oral Tradition: A Study in Historical Methodology*. Chicago: Aldine Publishing Company

Vansina, J. (1985) *Oral Tradition as History*. London: Heinemann

Vesey-Fitzgerald, B. (1973) *Gypsies of Britain: An Introduction to their History*. Newton Abbot: David and Charles

Volf, M. (1996) *Exclusion and Embrace*. Nashville: Abingdon Press

Walens, S. (1982) 'The weight of my name is a mountain of blankets: potlatch ceremonies' in V. Turner (ed.) *Celebration Studies in Festivity and Ritual*. Washington: Smithsonian Institution Press

Walsh, C. (2008) *Postcolonial Borderlands: Orality and Irish Traveller Writing*. Newcastle, UK: Cambridge Scholars Publishing

Ward, C. (1992). 'Chrissie Ward' in *Traveller Ways, Traveller Words*. Dublin: Pavee Point

Warde, M. (2009) *'The Turn of the Hand': A Memoir from the Irish Margins*. UK: Cambridge Scholars Publishing

Warde, M. (2010) *'The Turn of the Hand': A Memoir from the Irish Margins*. UK: Cambridge Scholars Publishing

Warner, M. (1995) *From the Beast to the Blonde: On Fairy Tales and their Tellers*. London: Vintage

Waugh, P. (1989) *Feminine Fictions: Revisiting the Postmodern*. London: Routledge

Wehler, H. U. (1987) *Deutsche Gesellschaftsgeschichte. Vom Feudalismus des Alten Reiches bis zur defensiven Modernisierung der Reformara 1700–1815*. Munich: Beck

Welch, R. (1993) *Changing States: Transformations in Modern Irish Writing*. London: Routledge

Welker, M. (1995) *Kirche im Pluralismus*. Gutersloh, Germany: Kaiser Taschenbuch

White, H. (1973) *Metahistory*. Baltimore: Johns Hopkins University Press

Willeford, W. (1969) *The Fool and his Sceptre*. London: Edward Arnold

Willems, W. (1997) *In Search of the True Gypsy. From Enlightenment to Final Solution*. London: Frank Cassells

Wilson, T. (1567) *The Rule of Reason: Conteinying the Arte of Logike*. London: Ihon Kingston

Wolfe, A. (1992) 'Democracy versus sociology: Boundaries and their political consequences' in H. J. Gans, M. Lamont, M. Fournier *et al.* (eds.)

*Cultivating Differences: Symbolic Boundaries and the Making of Inequality*. Chicago: University of Chicago Press

Yeats, W. B. (1969) *The Second Coming*. London: Macmillan

Yinger, J. M. (1982) *Countercultures – The Promise and Peril of a World Turned Upside Down*. New York: The Free Press

Yoors, J. (1967) *The Gypsies*. New York: Simon and Schuster

Young, R. (1990) *White Mythologies – Writing History and the* West. New York: Routledge

Young, R. (1995) *Colonial Desire: Hybridity in Theory, Culture, and Race*. London: Routledge, 1995

Zawadzki, B.(1948) 'Limitations of the scapegoat theory of prejudice' in *The Journal of Abnormal and Social Psychology*, 43, 127–141

Ziff, T. (1995) *Distant Relations: Cercanias Distantes: Clann i gCéin*. Santa Monica: Smart Art Press

Zimmermann. G. (2001) *The Irish Storyteller*. Dublin: Four Courts Press

# Index